Next-Gen Managed File Transfer

Securing and Streamlining Data Flows with AI

by **Raghava Chellu**

Copyright Page

Title: *Next-Gen Managed File Transfer: Securing and Streamlining Data Flows with AI*
Author: Raghava Chellu
© 2025 Raghava Chellu
All rights reserved.

For permissions, inquiries, or speaking engagements, please contact:
raghava.mftsolutions@gmail.com

Table of Contents

Preface

In every modern enterprise, data movement is the silent engine powering collaboration, compliance, customer experience, and critical operations. While the world obsesses over applications, APIs, and analytics, a quieter, foundational technology continues to ensure that data moves securely, reliably, and efficiently from system to system, business to business, and region to region: Managed File Transfer (MFT).

I began this journey over **15 years ago**, working with some of the world's most complex IT ecosystems. Over time, I witnessed firsthand how traditional MFT solutions, once revolutionary, have struggled to keep pace with cloud adoption, edge computing, regulatory complexity, and the sheer scale of data growth. File transfer has moved beyond batch jobs and protocol support; it now demands intelligence, adaptability, and real-time enforcement. It was this realization that led me to write this book.

Next-Gen Managed File Transfer: Securing and Streamlining Data Flows with AI is my attempt to reframe how we think about MFT in the modern enterprise. This book is not just about securing transfers or replacing legacy tools; it's about evolving MFT into a core digital trust layer. One that's intelligent, automated, policy-aware, and deeply embedded into cloud-native, AI-augmented, and zero-trust ecosystems.

In the chapters that follow, I aim to bridge the gap between foundational MFT principles and forward-looking innovation. We'll explore architectural patterns, real-world use cases, and emerging technologies from AI-powered classification and anomaly detection to blockchain-based audit trails and decentralized edge transfers. Whether you're a system architect, security engineer, compliance officer, or IT strategist, this book offers insights you can apply in both operational environments and strategic transformation initiatives.

I hope this work serves not just as a guide, but as a catalyst for reimagining how your organization moves and secures its most valuable digital assets in an increasingly complex, connected, and intelligent world.

Thank you for being part of this journey.

Raghava Chellu
Author

PART 1: Foundations of Managed File Transfer (MFT)

1 Introduction to MFT

In the modern digital enterprise, data is a vital asset that must be moved, processed, and delivered reliably and securely. Organizations constantly exchange sensitive information such as financial records, customer data, healthcare documents, and proprietary business files across internal departments, external partners, and cloud platforms. To manage these growing data exchange requirements, businesses have turned to Managed File Transfer (MFT) solutions.

Managed File Transfer (MFT) refers to a class of software tools and technologies designed to provide secure, automated, and auditable file transfers. Unlike traditional methods such as FTP, SFTP, FTPS, HTTPS, or Email attachments, MFT solutions offer enterprise-grade features that address the security, compliance, and operational needs of businesses handling high volumes of sensitive data. At its core, MFT simplifies and strengthens the way files are transferred, reducing manual intervention while ensuring that data is protected at every stage of its journey.

MFT solutions provide centralized control over file movement, allowing organizations to define, monitor, and manage file transfers through a single interface. Core capabilities include end-to-end encryption, access control, authentication, automated workflows, and real-time visibility into transfer statuses. These features are essential for industries subject to strict regulatory compliance, such as healthcare (HIPAA), finance (PCI-DSS, SOX), and government (FISMA, GDPR).

Traditional file transfer tools often lack visibility and reliability. Failed transfers, missing files, or data breaches can occur without detection. MFT overcomes these challenges by offering detailed audit logs, alerting mechanisms, and failover capabilities to ensure high availability and transparency. This not only reduces the risk of data loss or corruption but also supports better incident response and governance.

Modern MFT platforms are also built to integrate with a wide variety of enterprise systems, including ERP, CRM, cloud storage, and APIs. This enables seamless data flows between business-critical applications, streamlining processes like order fulfillment, billing, customer onboarding, and regulatory reporting. Some advanced MFT solutions are now adopting *Artificial Intelligence* (AI) and *Machine Learning* (ML) to predict potential transfer failures, optimize routing, and automatically adapt to changing network conditions ushering in a new era of intelligent data movement.

In essence, Managed File Transfer has become a strategic enabler for secure and efficient digital operations. It ensures that organizations can move data with confidence-reliably, compliantly, and at scale while laying the foundation for more automated, AI-enhanced data ecosystems.

1.1. About Managed File Transfer

Managed File Transfer (MFT) is a secure, reliable, and automated technology designed to facilitate the exchange of data particularly files between systems, users, applications, and organizations. Unlike basic file transfer protocols such as FTP or email, MFT solutions provide centralized control, visibility, compliance, and security over all file transfer activities.

At its core, MFT addresses the challenges of traditional file transfer methods by delivering an enterprise-grade solution capable of handling complex data exchange workflows. It ensures that files are delivered on time, to the right destinations, and in compliance with data protection and privacy regulations.

1.2. Key Characteristics of MFT

1.2.1 Security

In an era of increasing cyber threats, strict compliance regulations, and growing data exchange volumes, security is one of the most critical pillars of Managed File Transfer solutions. MFT platforms are designed to protect sensitive data throughout its lifecycle at rest, in transit, and during processing while also providing governance and control mechanisms to prevent unauthorized access and ensure accountability.

MFT is a significant upgrade from traditional file transfer methods (e.g., FTP, email, USB drives), which lack the built-in security features required by modern enterprises.

MFT provides robust encryption for files in transit and at rest, using File Transfer protocols such as FTP with PGP Encryption/Decryption, SFTP, FTPS, HTTPS, AS2, Pel, PeSIT-HS, and Pel-S. It also supports secure authentication methods (e.g., Key-Based Authentication, Multi-Factor Authentication) and integrates with *Identity and Access Management* (IAM) systems.

1.2.2 Automation

MFT allows organizations to automate file transfer processes through workflows or job scheduling in both Cloud and On-Premise. For example, a company might configure an MFT solution to automatically send sales data to a partner every evening at the specified time window or to retrieve files from a remote server at scheduled intervals.

1.2.3 Visibility and Monitoring

In any modern digital infrastructure, data transparency and real-time oversight are critical. In the context of Managed File Transfer (MFT) applications, visibility and monitoring refer to the ability to track, observe, and manage file transfer operations end-to-end from initiation to delivery across the entire data flow.

Without proper visibility, organizations face challenges such as failed transfers going unnoticed, compliance risks, security vulnerabilities, and increased time spent troubleshooting. MFT solutions are designed to eliminate these blind spots by offering centralized dashboards, live monitoring tools, audit trails, and alert systems.

1.2.4 Governance and Compliance

In today's regulatory landscape, businesses can't afford to treat data movement as a background task. Whether transferring payroll records, healthcare data, customer financials, or intellectual property, organizations must ensure that every file transfer complies with industry standards, government regulations, and internal policies. This is where Governance and Compliance become crucial pillars of a Managed File Transfer (MFT) solution.

Governance in MFT refers to the policies, controls, and oversight mechanisms that ensure file transfers are managed securely, responsibly, and in alignment with business and regulatory requirements. It involves:

- Defining who can access what and when

- Establishing rules and workflows for how files are handled

- Monitoring activities and enforcing accountability

- Documenting and auditing data movement

Governance ensures that data movement aligns with business objectives, risk management strategies, and legal obligations.

Compliance is about meeting the specific data protection standards and regulatory requirements enforced by governments, industry bodies, or customers. MFT helps organizations comply with regulations such as:

- GDPR (General Data Protection Regulation – EU)

- HIPAA (Health Insurance Portability and Accountability Act – US)
- PCI-DSS (Payment Card Industry Data Security Standard)
- SOX (Sarbanes-Oxley Act)
- FISMA, GLBA, ISO 27001, NIST, and others

MFT platforms provide technical capabilities that enforce compliance and generate audit-ready evidence.

1.2.5 Integration

In modern enterprise environments, systems rarely operate in isolation. Businesses run on a complex ecosystem of platforms ERP, CRM, databases, cloud services, APIs, SaaS applications, and legacy systems all of which must exchange data efficiently and securely. Integration is the bridge that connects MFT platforms to these internal and external systems, enabling seamless, automated, and intelligent data flows across the enterprise.

At its core, Managed File Transfer is about moving data from one system to another in a secure, reliable, and policy-driven manner. But in order to truly deliver value, MFT must be able to integrate with the systems that generate, consume, or process data. Without integration, file transfers become siloed, manual, and disconnected from business processes.

1.2.6 Scalability and High Availability

As organizations grow and digital ecosystems become more complex, file transfer systems must be able to handle increasing volumes of data and user demands without performance degradation or downtime. Two key architectural pillars that support this are Scalability and High Availability (HA). Together, they ensure that MFT platforms remain responsive, resilient, and dependable even under pressure.

Scalability refers to an MFT system's ability to grow in capacity to meet increased workload demands either by adding more resources (scale-up) or adding more nodes/instances (scale-out).

Key Features of a Scalable MFT System:

- **Horizontal scaling**: Adding more servers or instances to balance load and handle more transfers in parallel.
- **Vertical scaling**: Enhancing server resources (CPU, RAM, disk) to support larger files or more users.
- **Load balancing**: Distributing traffic and transfer tasks across multiple servers or components automatically.

- **Elasticity** (in cloud environments): Dynamically scaling up/down based on usage patterns or thresholds.

Why Scalability Matters:

- Supports increased users and partners without redesigning the system.
- Handles larger and more frequent file transfers without performance degradation.
- Enables global file exchange across distributed teams, regions, or cloud platforms.

1.3 History and Evolution from FTP/SFTP/FTPS/HTTPS to MFT

1.3.1. The Beginning of FTP (File Transfer Protocol)

The history of Managed File Transfer (MFT) is deeply rooted in the evolution of network communication protocols that enabled the secure, reliable exchange of data over digital systems. The journey from basic File Transfer Protocols (FTP) to sophisticated AI-augmented MFT platforms represents a transformation driven by business needs for security, compliance, automation, and visibility.

This section traces the path of that evolution from the early days of unencrypted file transfers to the intelligent, policy-driven ecosystems that exist today.

Introduced in the early 1970s as part of the ARPANET project (the precursor to the internet), FTP was one of the earliest standardized protocols used to transfer files between computers on a network.

The original File Transfer Protocol (FTP) operates over the TCP/IP protocol suite, typically using port 21 for commands and port 20 for data transfer. Designed for simplicity and basic functionality, FTP supports essential operations such as file uploads, downloads, and directory browsing, making it a useful tool in early networked environments.

However, one of the major drawbacks of traditional FTP is its lack of security features, making it unsuitable for modern, compliance-driven environments. FTP does not provide encryption, meaning that both data and user credentials are transmitted in plaintext, which leaves them highly vulnerable to interception or man-in-the-middle attacks. Additionally, FTP lacks built-in security mechanisms such as authentication controls, access governance, or encryption policies. The protocol also offers minimal auditing and monitoring capabilities, making it difficult to track user activity or detect unauthorized access. As a result, FTP is not considered safe for transmitting regulated, sensitive, or confidential information, particularly in industries like healthcare, finance, and government where data protection is paramount.

1.3.2 Security Enhancements: SFTP and FTPS

To address the inherent security flaws of FTP, two secure alternatives were developed, one of which is SFTP (SSH File Transfer Protocol). Unlike FTP, SFTP is built on the SSH (Secure Shell) protocol, providing a secure channel for data exchange over an unsecured network. It encrypts all data transmissions, including login credentials and file contents, ensuring confidentiality and integrity throughout the transfer process. SFTP typically operates over a single port (port 22), making it easier to manage through firewalls and network security systems. Additionally, it supports *public key authentication*, offering a stronger and more secure alternative to traditional password-based access. This combination of encryption, authentication, and simplified configuration makes SFTP a preferred choice for secure file transfers in enterprise environments.

1.3.3 HTTPS and Web-Based Transfers

As the internet gained dominance in the early 2000s, HTTPS (Hypertext Transfer Protocol Secure) emerged as a popular and user-friendly method for transferring files both through web browsers and via application programming interfaces (APIs). HTTPS operates over port 443 and secures data transmission using SSL/TLS encryption, making it a widely trusted protocol for secure communication. It caters to both human users, who upload or download files through web interfaces, and machines, which exchange data using RESTful APIs. HTTPS has become especially useful in cloud-based integrations, web portals, and software platforms that require secure data uploads. However, despite its widespread adoption,

HTTPS was not originally designed for large-scale or high-frequency file transfers, and it offers limited built-in automation or workflow management. Additionally, logging and monitoring capabilities are basic unless explicitly extended through API integrations or custom development.

1.3.4 AS2/AS4 – Secure B2B Protocols for EDI

As B2B integration needs expanded, particularly across industries like supply chain, logistics, and manufacturing, more secure and standardized protocols were required to support certified, auditable data exchange. This led to the emergence of protocols such as AS2 (Applicability Statement 2), which enables the secure transmission of EDI (Electronic Data Interchange) documents over HTTP or HTTPS. AS2 leverages S/MIME encryption and digital signatures, providing both data confidentiality and non-repudiation, ensuring that recipients cannot deny having received a message. AS2 quickly became a retail standard with major organizations like Walmart requiring its use from all suppliers. Building on this foundation, AS4 was introduced as a modern evolution of AS2, adopting web services standards and incorporating technologies like SOAP, WS-Security, and XML payloads for more flexible, scalable integrations. The rise of AS2 and AS4 highlighted the growing demand for reliable, policy-driven, and auditable file transfer mechanisms core principles that would later be fully integrated into Managed File Transfer (MFT) platforms.

1.3.5 The Birth of MFT: Need for Enterprise-Grade Solutions

As enterprises began facing increasing regulatory scrutiny driven by frameworks such as HIPAA, GDPR, and SOX alongside escalating cybersecurity threats and growing demands for business process automation, it became evident that traditional file transfer protocols like FTP and its variants were no longer adequate. These legacy tools lacked the essential features modern organizations required to operate securely and efficiently. Among the most pressing limitations were the absence of centralized control and governance, no enforcement of encryption policies, and inability to track service-level agreements (SLAs) or monitor transfers in real-time. Additionally, they offered no integration capabilities with core business systems like ERP or CRM platforms and introduced high operational risks due to undetected failures or incomplete transfers. To address these challenges, Managed File Transfer (MFT) solutions emerged in the late 2000s as a secure, reliable, and policy-driven approach to enterprise data exchange and by the 2010s, MFT had become the mainstream standard for organizations seeking to modernize their file transfer operations.

1.3.6 Managed File Transfer (MFT): A Unified, Secure Framework

Managed File Transfer (MFT) emerged as a comprehensive solution that consolidated multiple file transfer functionalities into a single, centralized platform. Designed to address the limitations of legacy protocols, MFT platforms offer a robust set of core capabilities tailored for modern enterprise needs. These include support for all major secure transfer protocols such as SFTP, FTPS, HTTPS, and AS2 along with end-to-end encryption, strong user authentication, and role-based access control (RBAC) to safeguard sensitive data. MFT systems also enable automated workflows, allowing organizations to streamline and orchestrate data movement with minimal manual intervention. Features like real-time monitoring, alerting, and comprehensive audit logging provide critical visibility and traceability, while policy enforcement tools and compliance templates help meet regulatory mandates such as HIPAA, GDPR, and PCI-DSS. With dashboard-driven SLA tracking and the flexibility to deploy on-premises or in the cloud, MFT not only fills the technical and security gaps of earlier file transfer tools but also aligns seamlessly with corporate objectives for governance, compliance, and operational efficiency.

1.3.7 Modern MFT: Cloud-Native, API-Driven, AI-Enhanced

Modern Managed File Transfer (MFT) platforms have evolved far beyond traditional file delivery mechanisms, emerging as strategic components of enterprise IT ecosystems. Today's MFT solutions are engineered to support hybrid and multi-cloud architectures, offering the flexibility to operate across on-premises data centers, public clouds, and private cloud environments. They embrace containerized deployment models using technologies like Docker and Kubernetes, enabling scalability, portability, and rapid deployment.

Additionally, these platforms are increasingly API-driven, providing RESTful APIs that facilitate seamless integration with enterprise applications, automation tools, and third-party services. A defining shift in next-generation MFT platforms is the integration of artificial intelligence (AI) capabilities. AI-powered features such as predictive analytics, smart routing, anomaly detection, auto-remediation, and transfer forecasting transform MFT from a static utility into an intelligent, adaptive system. These innovations are pushing MFT beyond its infrastructure roots, positioning it as a vital part of modern data architecture, cybersecurity frameworks, and digital transformation strategies

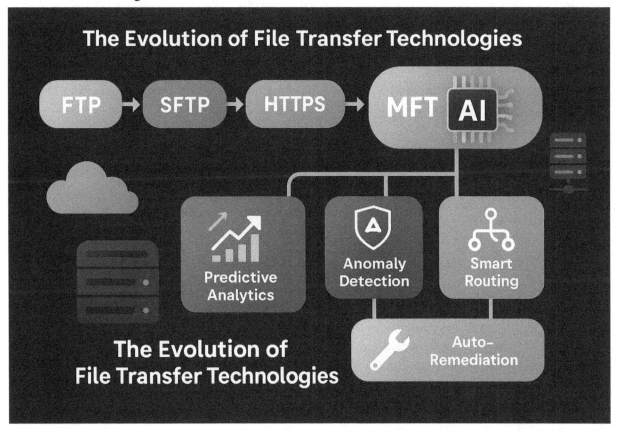

1.4 Key Drivers for Managed File Transfer (MFT) Adoption

One of the most compelling reasons for the growing adoption of Managed File Transfer (MFT) solutions is the increasing need for robust security and data protection. In a landscape of rising cybersecurity threats and frequent data breaches, traditional protocols like FTP are no longer viable. MFT platforms address these concerns by offering end-to-end encryption (such as AES-256 and TLS), secure authentication mechanisms, and granular access control with identity management, ensuring that sensitive data remains protected during transfer and storage. Beyond security, regulatory compliance is a key driver, especially for industries such as healthcare, finance, retail, and government. MFT solutions help meet stringent regulations including HIPAA, GDPR, PCI-DSS, SOX, and FISMA by providing detailed audit trails, comprehensive logging, and policy enforcement for data handling and retention, making it easier for organizations to demonstrate compliance and succeed in audits.

Another major advantage is the automation of file transfer operations, which replaces error-prone, manual processes with schedulers, event-driven workflows, and trigger-based execution. This automation not only reduces human intervention but also enhances processing speed, consistency, and operational efficiency. MFT systems also offer extensive visibility and monitoring capabilities. Unlike legacy tools that provide little to no feedback, modern MFT solutions deliver real-time dashboards, automated alerts, and SLA tracking, empowering IT and business teams with full control and rapid incident response capabilities.

As enterprise ecosystems become increasingly complex, the need for a centralized, secure platform to manage data exchange across internal systems (e.g., ERP, CRM, HRMS), cloud services, and external trading partners becomes critical. MFT platforms support these diverse integrations through standardized protocols like SFTP, FTPS, HTTPS, and AS2, ensuring seamless communication across all touchpoints. In addition, MFT platforms integrate natively with enterprise applications such as SAP, Oracle, and Salesforce, along with databases, data warehouses, APIs, and workflow engines, enabling true end-to-end process automation. For instance, a completed sales order can automatically trigger a secure file transfer or document upload to a cloud repository without any manual input.

As organizations increasingly embrace cloud-first strategies, MFT solutions are designed for hybrid deployments, supporting both on-premises infrastructure and cloud-native environments like AWS, Azure, and Google Cloud Platform. Through containerization technologies such as Docker and Kubernetes, MFT platforms offer scalable, agile, and resilient deployments that align with modern DevOps practices.

To maintain business continuity and uphold service-level agreements (SLAs), MFT systems include built-in mechanisms for transfer validation, automated retries, high availability configurations, and disaster recovery support. These features are especially crucial for critical workflows like financial reporting, regulatory submissions, and time-sensitive communications.

Finally, today's MFT solutions are laying the foundation for AI-driven intelligence. By integrating predictive load balancing, anomaly detection, smart file routing, and auto-remediation, MFT platforms are evolving into self-healing, adaptive systems that align with enterprise-wide digital transformation strategies. These capabilities reduce manual oversight, enhance decision-making, and ensure that file transfer operations remain reliable, compliant, and scalable in even the most demanding environments.

1.5 Core Components of MFT

1.5.1 File Transmission Protocol (FTP)

File Transfer Protocol (FTP) is a foundational network protocol used to transfer files between computers over TCP/IP connections. Within the TCP/IP model, FTP operates at the application layer, facilitating the structured exchange of data between client and server systems.

FTP is widely utilized by individuals and organizations alike ranging from everyday users downloading files from the internet, to IT administrators, web developers, and system integrators managing file repositories and website content. Despite the rise of newer transfer technologies and more secure alternatives, FTP continues to be used in many legacy applications and background processes, including automated data flows in banking systems, software downloads, and internal data migrations.

FTP Architecture and Terminology

An FTP transaction typically involves two systems:

- The **local host** – the user's computer or initiating system.
- The **remote host** – the target server that stores the files.

How FTP Works: The Dual-Channel Model

FTP uses a client-server architecture and relies on two separate communication channels:

1. **Control Channel:**
   Used to transmit commands and responses. This channel is persistent throughout the session and operates over TCP port 21.

2. **Data Channel:**
   Used exclusively for transferring files and directory listings. This channel is initiated as needed, and its behavior differs depending on the FTP connection mode (active or passive).

A typical FTP session includes operations such as:

- Authentication (with username and password, or anonymous access)

- File and directory listing

- File uploads and downloads

- Renaming, copying, or deleting files on the remote server

FTP Modes: Active vs. Passive

FTP supports two connection modes that define how the data channel is established:

Active Mode:

In this mode:

- The client opens the control channel to the server on port 21.
- When a data transfer is needed, the server initiates the data connection back to the client using TCP port 20.
- This requires the client to open a listening port, which can pose problems when firewalls or NAT (Network Address Translation) are in place.

Passive Mode:

In passive mode:

- The client initiates both the control and data connections.
- Upon a PASV command, the server responds with a random port number for the client to use for the data transfer.

- This method is more firewall- and NAT-friendly, as it avoids inbound server-to-client connections.

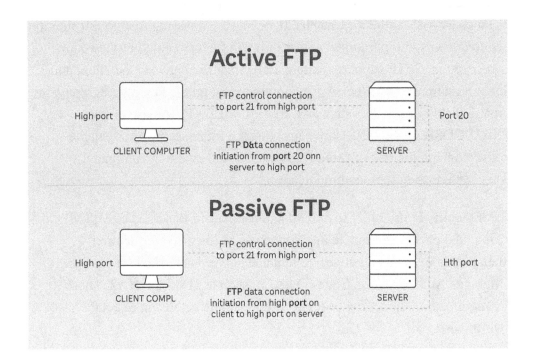

1.5.2 SFTP – SSH File Transfer Protocol

SFTP (SSH File Transfer Protocol) is a secure network protocol used for transferring files over a reliable connection, typically SSH (Secure Shell). Unlike FTP and FTPS, which operate on separate command and data channels, SFTP uses a single encrypted channel, providing confidentiality, integrity, and authentication in one streamlined session. It is defined as part of the SSH-2 protocol suite and is widely adopted for secure, scriptable, and firewall-friendly file transfers in enterprise environments.

Security Model of SFTP

The Security Model of SFTP (SSH File Transfer Protocol) is one of its defining strengths, making it a preferred choice for secure file transfer in compliance-critical and highly regulated environments. Built on top of the SSH (Secure Shell) protocol, SFTP inherits a robust and well-established security framework designed to ensure confidentiality, integrity, and authenticity of the transmitted data. Unlike traditional FTP or even FTPS, which rely on multiple ports and can be difficult to secure consistently, SFTP operates over a single, encrypted connection (typically on TCP port 22), significantly simplifying firewall configuration and reducing attack surface.

SFTP provides end-to-end encryption of both command and data streams using strong cryptographic ciphers (such as AES-128/256, ChaCha20, or 3DES), ensuring that no information be it file contents, user credentials, or operational commands can be intercepted or viewed in transit. In addition to encryption, SFTP supports mutual authentication between the client and server. This can be done through username/password combinations, public key cryptography, or integration with enterprise identity providers such as Kerberos or LDAP. The use of public key authentication (via RSA, ECDSA, or Ed25519 key pairs) offers a more secure and scalable alternative to passwords, reducing the risk of brute-force attacks and enabling automated, password-less access for system-to-system communications.

A critical part of SFTP's security is its ability to defend against man-in-the-middle (MITM) attacks, session hijacking, and packet sniffing, thanks to the use of integrity verification mechanisms. Every data packet exchanged between client and server is checked for tampering using cryptographic Message Authentication Codes (MACs), such as HMAC-SHA2. These MACs ensure that any modification, injection, or replay attempt is detected and rejected, preserving data trustworthiness.

How SFTP Works

SFTP (SSH File Transfer Protocol) is a secure, packet-based protocol that operates over TCP port 22, using the same transport channel as SSH (Secure Shell) to establish encrypted sessions and authenticate users. Unlike traditional FTP or FTPS which separate control and data channels SFTP communicates through a single, persistent, and encrypted connection, enhancing both security and simplicity in firewall and NAT environments.

The SFTP session begins with an SSH handshake, during which the client and server negotiate cryptographic algorithms (ciphers, MACs, and key exchange methods) to secure the communication channel. Once this secure tunnel is established, the client authenticates using either a username/password combination or more securely, via public key cryptography (e.g., RSA, ECDSA, Ed25519 keys). If the authentication is successful, the SFTP subsystem is invoked, effectively launching the file transfer capabilities on top of the SSH connection.

File transfer commands in SFTP are handled quite differently from FTP. Rather than using plain-text command-response syntax, SFTP uses a binary message-based protocol, where client and server exchange structured data packets. Each packet contains a specific operation code (such as SSH_FXP_OPEN, SSH_FXP_READ, SSH_FXP_WRITE, SSH_FXP_RENAME, or

SSH_FXP_REMOVE) along with relevant metadata. This design is machine-optimized, allowing for better performance, consistent behavior across platforms, and easier automation in script-based environments.

The protocol supports random file access, allowing files to be read or written at specific byte offsets, which is especially useful for resumable or partial transfers. It also provides built-in commands for directory listing, symbolic link handling, file attribute manipulation, and permission setting making it a versatile solution for complete remote file system interaction.

How SFTP Works

SFTP operates over TCP port 22 by default and uses an SSH connection for both authentication and encrypted data exchange.

> SSH handshake initiates the session and negotiates ciphers

↓

> Client authenticates using password or public/private key

↓

> SFTP subsystem is started over the secure channel

↓

> Client and server exchange binary protocol packets for commands like open, read, write, rename, delete, etc.

Unlike FTP, which transmits text-based commands, SFTP uses binary packet-based messaging, making it machine-optimized and consistent across platforms.

Due to its robust security model, support for modern cryptography, and cross-platform consistency, SFTP has become the de facto standard for secure file transfer in both enterprise-grade MFT platforms and standalone automation scripts. Its design minimizes complexity while maximizing compatibility and security offering a clean alternative to legacy protocols without compromising on functionality or control.

Furthermore, SFTP's encrypted tunnel makes it resilient to protocol-level attacks that plague older file transfer systems, such as command injection or protocol downgrade attacks. Its single-channel design not only simplifies secure deployment but also eliminates vulnerabilities caused by the control/data channel separation found in FTP and FTPS.

This multi-layered security model makes SFTP highly suitable for compliance-driven sectors such as financial services, healthcare, government, and e-commerce, where the confidentiality and traceability of data transfers are mission-critical. Whether used for transmitting personal health information (PHI), financial transactions, or sensitive operational files, SFTP provides a trusted, standards-based foundation for secure enterprise file exchange particularly when integrated into Managed File Transfer (MFT) platforms that extend its capabilities with policy enforcement, audit logging, and intelligent automation.

SFTP Subsystem Versions

While SFTP (SSH File Transfer Protocol) runs over the SSH-2 transport layer, it operates as a distinct subsystem protocol, with its own versioning independent of the SSH protocol itself. The SFTP protocol versions currently range from version 3 to version 6, each introducing incremental enhancements to file transfer capabilities and remote file system interactions. Among these, version 3 is the most widely implemented and supported, particularly due to its integration with OpenSSH, which has become a de facto standard across Unix/Linux environments.

Version 3, as implemented by OpenSSH, forms the basis for the majority of SFTP interactions seen in the wild. It supports essential operations such as file upload/download, permission handling, file renaming, and directory management. It also defines a straightforward binary packet structure and command set, making it suitable for both scripting and integration into larger platforms like MFT systems.

Subsequent versions, such as SFTP version 4, 5, and 6, introduce a number of technical improvements. These include enhanced file attribute handling, allowing for the manipulation of metadata like creation and modification times, user/group ownership, and extended permissions. Symbolic link resolution is another enhancement in later versions, which enables clients to resolve and follow symlinks securely and accurately across different server filesystems.

Later protocol versions also support richer directory listing formats, enabling clients to retrieve file metadata in a more structured, extensible manner critical for automation and synchronization tools. Additionally, extended attributes which allow storage of custom metadata such as access control lists (ACLs), security labels, or digital signatures can be used to enforce fine-grained access and integrity policies, particularly in environments where regulatory compliance or digital rights management is a concern.

However, due to inconsistent support for newer versions across different server implementations, many enterprise systems and MFT platforms standardize on version 3 to maintain broad compatibility. While version 3 may lack some of the more advanced features of later iterations, it remains sufficiently powerful for most secure file transfer use cases.

Understanding the differences between these protocol versions is essential for developers, security architects, and integration teams who aim to build or interact with custom SFTP solutions. It also plays a role in capability negotiation between client and server, as the SFTP protocol version supported by the server may limit or enable certain advanced operations during runtime.

Authentication Methods in SFTP

SFTP (SSH File Transfer Protocol) supports a range of robust authentication methods, allowing organizations to tailor security based on their operational and compliance requirements. Authentication in SFTP is handled by the underlying SSH protocol, which facilitates secure identity verification before any file transfer operation can occur. The three most common authentication mechanisms supported by SFTP are password-based authentication, public key authentication, and GSSAPI/Kerberos-based single sign-on (SSO).

Password Authentication is the most basic and widely used method, where the user provides a username and password during session initiation. While simple to implement, this method is also the least secure, especially when used without multi-factor authentication (MFA) or without additional safeguards such as rate limiting or account lockouts. Passwords are susceptible to brute-force attacks, phishing, and credential stuffing if not managed properly. For this reason, password authentication is often disabled by default on hardened systems, or reserved for low-privilege automation scripts operating within trusted environments.

Public Key Authentication is a far more secure and scalable option, particularly in automated or high-volume environments. In this method, the client generates a cryptographic key pair consisting of a private key (kept secret) and a public key (shared with the server). Supported key types include RSA, ECDSA, and Ed25519, with Ed25519 being the preferred option in modern systems due to its faster performance, stronger security, and smaller key size. During authentication, the client proves possession of the private key without revealing it, and the server validates the digital signature using the stored public key. This process ensures non-repudiation, as only the rightful key owner can initiate the session. Public key authentication also eliminates the need for interactive logins, making it ideal for automated scripts, system integrations, and MFT workflows.

GSSAPI/Kerberos Authentication is commonly used in enterprise environments, particularly those built on Windows Active Directory or MIT Kerberos realms. This method enables single sign-on (SSO), allowing users or systems to authenticate to the SFTP server using tickets issued by a central Key Distribution Center (KDC), rather than transmitting credentials directly. GSSAPI-based authentication supports mutual authentication, ticket delegation, and centralized identity lifecycle management, making it especially attractive for environments with strict auditing, access control, and federated identity requirements. This is particularly useful in federated environments, multi-domain enterprises, and government or defense sectors where trust domains are separated.

Within a Managed File Transfer (MFT) platform, these authentication mechanisms are typically abstracted and centralized, offering administrators a unified interface for managing access. Key and credential management systems within MFT platforms allow for automatic key rotation, revocation, expiration alerts, and partner-specific credentials, ensuring operational integrity and compliance with security policies such as ISO 27001, PCI-DSS, and NIST 800-53. These platforms may also integrate with certificate authorities (CAs), vault solutions (like HashiCorp Vault), or identity providers (IdPs) for managing and securing credentials at scale.

Ultimately, choosing the right authentication method in SFTP depends on a combination of security requirements, automation needs, and integration complexity. In modern enterprise contexts, public key authentication and GSSAPI/Kerberos have become the de facto standards, offering a high-security, low-maintenance alternative to traditional password-based access and serving as the backbone for secure, compliant, and scalable file transfer systems.

SFTP and Firewalls

One of the key architectural advantages of SFTP (SSH File Transfer Protocol) over legacy file transfer protocols like FTP and FTPS is its firewall-friendliness and network simplicity. SFTP operates exclusively over a single TCP port (port 22), which is used for both control commands and data transfer. This unified communication channel is established during the SSH handshake and remains encrypted and persistent throughout the session. In contrast, traditional FTP opens separate ports for control (port 21) and dynamic ports for data transfer, while FTPS may involve additional complexity with multiple TLS negotiation steps and dynamically allocated ports, making them more difficult to manage in secure environments.

From a firewall configuration perspective, SFTP's single-port model significantly simplifies network security rules. There is no need to configure and maintain port ranges for passive or active data connections, as is required with FTP and FTPS. This not only reduces administrative overhead but also minimizes the surface area exposed to external threats, which is particularly important in regulated and high-security environments.

SFTP is also highly compatible with NAT (Network Address Translation) environments. Since the client initiates and maintains the connection to the server, NAT devices and firewalls can easily track and maintain session state without complex connection tracking rules or application-layer gateways (ALGs). This makes SFTP an excellent choice for cloud-native architectures, containerized applications, secure file transfer gateways, and DMZ (Demilitarized Zone) deployments, where strict perimeter controls and stateful inspection firewalls are common.

Furthermore, in cloud-hosted environments (such as AWS, Azure, and GCP), where network security groups (NSGs) or security rules are tightly managed, SFTP's consistent use of port 22 ensures predictable and easily auditable access configurations. This predictability enhances security posture and enables rapid deployment of secure file transfer workflows without needing to punch holes through firewalls for arbitrary high ports, something that often leads to misconfigurations and potential vulnerabilities in FTP-based solutions.

In short, the SFTP protocol not only simplifies network design but also aligns closely with modern firewall architectures, zero trust models, and security best practices, making it a reliable and scalable choice for secure file transfer across distributed enterprise infrastructures.

Feature	SFTP	SCP	FTPS
Security	Encrypted (SSH)	Encrypted (SSH)	Encrypted (TLS/SSL)
Protocol Type	Subsystem of SSH (v2)	Command-line copy tool	Extension of FTP
Port	22	22	21 (control), 990/others (data)
Channel Separation	Single channel	Single channel	Separate command/data channels
Firewall/NAT Friendly	Yes	Yes	Often difficult
Interactive Commands	Yes	No	Yes
Logging/Audit	Yes (platform-dependent)	Minimal	Yes

1.5.3 File Transmission Protocol FTP(SSL)

FTPS, also known as FTP Secure or FTP-SSL, is an extension of the traditional File Transfer Protocol (FTP) enhanced with Transport Layer Security (TLS) or its predecessor Secure Sockets Layer (SSL). Unlike SFTP, which is a completely separate protocol built on SSH, FTPS retains the traditional FTP architecture including its control and data channels but adds a security layer via encryption and digital certificates. FTPS was developed to help organizations continue using their FTP-based infrastructure while meeting modern data protection requirements through encrypted communication.

FTPS Communication Channels: Control and Data

FTPS (FTP Secure), as an extension of the standard FTP protocol, relies on a dual-channel architecture to manage its communication flow specifically, a control channel and a data channel. The control channel, typically operating over TCP port 21, is responsible for session establishment, user authentication, and the transmission of FTP commands such as LIST (directory listing), RETR (retrieve/download file), and STOR (store/upload file). In implicit FTPS, encryption is initiated immediately upon connection, meaning the client and server begin the session within a pre-encrypted TLS tunnel usually over port 990. In explicit FTPS, the session begins as plain FTP and is then upgraded to a secure TLS session after the client explicitly sends the AUTH TLS command. This provides more flexibility and is the more commonly used mode in modern secure environments.

The data channel, on the other hand, is used exclusively for transferring file contents and directory listings. It is dynamically negotiated, that is, when a data transfer command is issued, the server allocates a new TCP port (often in the ephemeral high-numbered range) and informs the client to initiate the connection. This connection may be either encrypted or unencrypted depending on server and client configurations. FTPS supports independent encryption settings for the data channel, allowing some implementations to enforce TLS for both control and data traffic, while others may choose to encrypt only the control channel to simplify performance or compatibility.

While this separation of channels allows for efficient parallel command execution and data streaming, it also introduces complexity, particularly in firewall and NAT traversal, since dynamic port allocation requires precise rule configuration or the use of application-aware firewalls capable of interpreting and rewriting FTP control commands in real time. Proper configuration of both channels along with secure certificate management and policy enforcement is essential for maintaining data confidentiality and session integrity in FTPS deployments.

Explicit vs. Implicit FTPS Modes

FTPS (FTP Secure) extends the traditional FTP protocol by adding TLS (Transport Layer Security) to secure data and command channels. FTPS supports two distinct modes of operation: Explicit FTPS and Implicit FTPS. Though both serve the same fundamental purpose of securing FTP sessions they differ in how and when encryption is initiated, what ports are used, and how compatible they are with modern network security architectures.

Explicit FTPS

Explicit FTPS, also known as FTPES, is the modern and preferred method for securing FTP communications. In this mode, the connection starts on the standard FTP port (TCP 21). Upon initiating the session, the client explicitly requests the use of TLS by sending the AUTH TLS command to the server over the unencrypted control channel. If the server supports FTPS, it acknowledges the request, and from that point forward, all subsequent communications including credentials, commands, and responses are encrypted within a secure TLS tunnel.

This approach is flexible and firewall-friendly, as it maintains compatibility with legacy systems while enabling encryption when supported. Additionally, administrators can configure Explicit FTPS to fall back to plain FTP if encryption is unavailable, though in secure environments this fallback is typically disabled by policy to avoid downgrading to insecure communication. Explicit FTPS also allows clients to negotiate encryption settings and cipher suites, which makes it more adaptable to modern security standards.

From a firewall perspective, since the control connection remains on port 21 and is TLS-encrypted post-handshake, firewalls with FTP inspection modules can still operate effectively. However, like all FTP-based protocols, data channels still use dynamic ports (unless explicitly configured), which can introduce challenges with NAT traversal and security group management unless a fixed passive port range is defined and allowed through the firewall.

Implicit FTPS

Implicit FTPS is the older and now largely deprecated mode of encrypted FTP. In this configuration, the client initiates the connection on TCP port 990 and immediately enters a TLS-encrypted session without any negotiation or plain FTP fallback. If the client does not initiate TLS immediately upon connecting, the server will terminate the session. There is no AUTH TLS negotiation step; encryption is assumed from the start.

This design ensures enforced encryption by default, which can be advantageous in strictly controlled environments. However, the rigid nature of Implicit FTPS, along with its use of a non-standard port, has made it less compatible with modern firewall and proxy configurations. Additionally, the lack of negotiation flexibility can lead to interoperability issues with clients and servers that only support Explicit FTPS.

Despite being deprecated by RFCs and no longer actively developed in many FTP libraries, Implicit FTPS still exists in some legacy systems, particularly in older banking, logistics, or industrial platforms where upgrading is non-trivial due to compliance or vendor restrictions.

Explicit vs. Implicit FTPS Modes

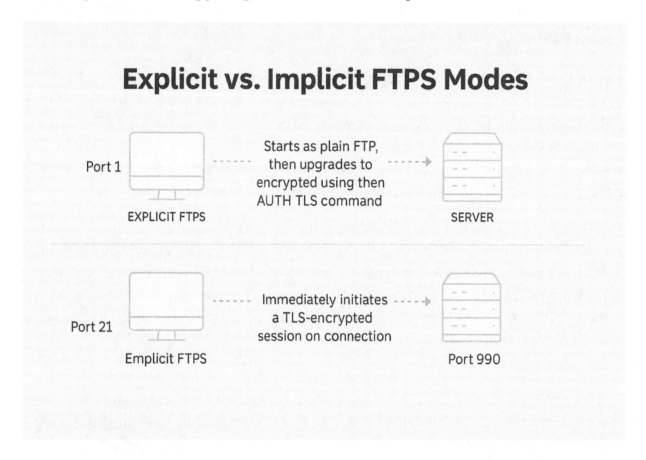

Port 1
EXPLICIT FTPS

Starts as plain FTP, then upgrades to encrypted using then AUTH TLS command

SERVER

Port 21
Emplicit FTPS

Immediately initiates a TLS-encrypted session on connection

Port 990

Why Explicit FTPS Is Preferred Today

In contemporary enterprise environments, Explicit FTPS has become the preferred mode of encrypted FTP communication, particularly within Managed File Transfer (MFT) platforms and modern secure FTP clients. One of its greatest strengths lies in its flexibility and standards compliance. Explicit FTPS begins the session on the standard FTP port 21, allowing clients to initiate a plain FTP connection and then explicitly request an upgrade to a secure session using the AUTH TLS command. This model enables negotiation of TLS parameters, such as protocol version (e.g., TLS 1.2 or 1.3), supported cipher suites (e.g., AES-GCM, ChaCha20-Poly1305), and certificate authentication policies all of which are essential for aligning with evolving IETF standards and enterprise security requirements.

Moreover, Explicit FTPS offers superior compatibility with firewalls and NAT devices compared to Implicit FTPS. By retaining port 21 for initial handshakes and allowing organizations to define fixed passive port ranges for data channels, it significantly simplifies firewall rule management. This predictability is critical in cloud-hosted deployments, DMZ architectures, and zero trust network models, where administrators must tightly control inbound and outbound port access without sacrificing transfer performance or reliability.

Another major advantage is the ability to integrate certificate-based authentication using X.509 digital certificates, which enhances identity assurance and supports mutual authentication between client and server. Modern FTPS implementations enforce support for strong encryption algorithms and TLS 1.2+, ensuring data in transit is protected against eavesdropping, tampering, and downgrade attacks. Additionally, many enterprise-grade MFT systems layer advanced capabilities such as TLS session reuse, forward secrecy, and OCSP stapling to further harden the security posture of Explicit FTPS connections.

While Implicit FTPS may still be required to maintain interoperability with legacy trading partners or outdated FTP servers, it is increasingly considered obsolete by security professionals. Its lack of negotiation, use of non-standard port 990, and rigid session initialization behavior make it less adaptable to modern infrastructure and incompatible with many firewall and proxy configurations. Furthermore, Implicit FTPS is not included in the current RFCs governing FTP over TLS, which discourages its use in new deployments.

In summary, Explicit FTPS strikes the right balance between security, compatibility, and manageability, making it the protocol of choice for secure file transfers in modern MFT architectures. It supports both legacy FTP workflows and modern security controls ensuring secure transmission without disrupting existing integrations or requiring extensive reconfiguration.

Encryption and Certificates in FTPS

Encryption and identity verification are at the core of FTPS (FTP Secure), which leverages TLS (Transport Layer Security) or its predecessor SSL (Secure Sockets Layer) to secure data communications over traditional FTP. FTPS relies on X.509 digital certificates to authenticate the server, and optionally the client, creating a trust model that ensures the integrity and confidentiality of the session. When a client connects to an FTPS server, the server presents its digital certificate either signed by a trusted Certificate Authority (CA) or self-signed which the client then validates. This validation process helps prevent man-in-the-middle (MITM) attacks by confirming the server's identity and ensuring that the connection has not been intercepted or spoofed.

Once authentication is established, FTPS uses industry-standard encryption algorithms to protect the data in transit. Supported ciphers include AES (Advanced Encryption Standard) for symmetric encryption, ChaCha20-Poly1305 for high-performance, stream-based encryption with authenticated data integrity, and RSA or Elliptic Curve Diffie-Hellman (ECDHE) for secure key exchange and forward secrecy. The use of TLS 1.2 or higher is strongly recommended, as older versions of SSL/TLS (such as SSLv3 or TLS 1.0) are considered deprecated and vulnerable to known exploits like POODLE or BEAST attacks.

FTPS also supports mutual authentication, often referred to as mutual TLS (mTLS), where the client presents its own certificate in addition to verifying the server's certificate. This bidirectional trust model is particularly common in financial services, government systems, and regulated industries, where identity assurance on both ends of the connection is critical for non-repudiation and compliance with frameworks such as PCI-DSS, HIPAA, and ISO/IEC 27001. In such environments, client certificates must be issued and managed through a central public key infrastructure (PKI), and administrators must enforce certificate expiration, renewal, and revocation policies to maintain trust.

In Managed File Transfer (MFT) platforms, certificate management is often integrated with automation tools to handle certificate rotation, expiry notifications, and trust store updates, thereby reducing the risk of service disruption and ensuring ongoing compliance. Additionally, modern FTPS implementations may support TLS session reuse, Perfect Forward Secrecy (PFS), and OCSP stapling, which further strengthen the security of encrypted sessions and reduce handshake overhead.

Ultimately, FTPS combines strong encryption with identity verification via digital certificates to deliver a secure, authenticated communication channel. When properly implemented, these features make FTPS a powerful option for secure file exchanges particularly in environments that demand both robust encryption and traceable, certificate-based trust mechanisms.

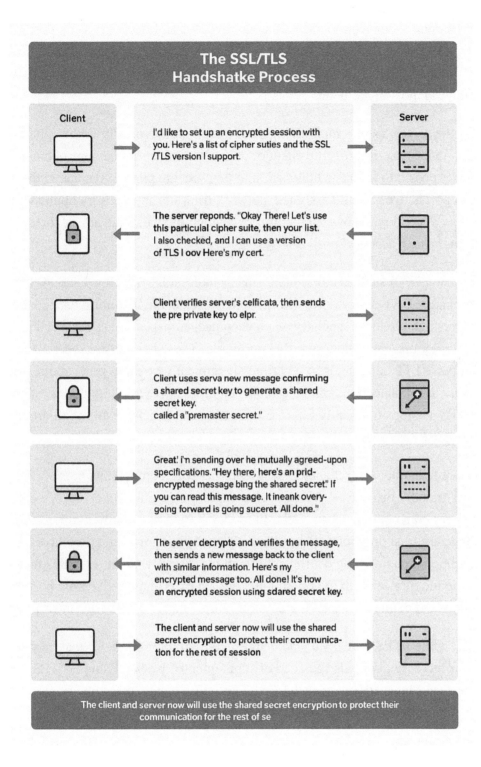

Firewall and Port Challenges in FTPS

While FTPS (FTP Secure) offers robust encryption and secure authentication through the use of TLS/SSL, it retains the traditional FTP architecture of separating the control and data channels, which introduces significant complexity in firewall and NAT (Network Address Translation) environments. The control connection in FTPS is relatively straightforward using port 21 in Explicit FTPS or port 990 in Implicit FTPS and is generally easy to accommodate in firewall rules. However, the data channel poses more substantial challenges, particularly in passive mode, which is the default in most modern deployments.

In passive mode, the server opens a random high-numbered port (typically in the ephemeral port range, e.g., 1024–65535) and informs the client of the port number via the control connection. The client is then expected to initiate a connection to this specific port for the actual data transfer. Because this data port is dynamically assigned, network firewalls and security appliances must be configured to allow a broad range of ephemeral ports, which increases the attack surface and makes it harder to manage access control policies.

In environments using NAT, such as cloud platforms or internal DMZs, this behavior becomes even more problematic. NAT devices often struggle to associate the incoming data connection with the existing control session, especially when deep packet inspection (DPI) or FTP-aware firewall helpers are not present or not properly configured. These helpers are specialized components that parse FTP commands in real time, dynamically opening ports and rewriting IP addresses to ensure data connections can be established across network boundaries. Without them, passive FTPS sessions frequently fail to establish data channels, resulting in dropped transfers or incomplete sessions.

This inherent unpredictability and reliance on auxiliary network components makes FTPS less firewall- and NAT-friendly than SFTP, which uses a single, persistent, and encrypted connection over TCP port 22 for both commands and data. In modern cloud-native environments, especially those built around zero trust principles, microservices, or strict ingress/egress controls, FTPS often requires additional engineering overhead to function correctly. Security teams must balance the need for secure file transfer with the operational burden of managing dynamic port ranges, certificate handling, and connection tracking across multiple layers of network infrastructure.

For these reasons, while FTPS remains a viable and secure protocol in traditional on-premises environments, it is increasingly being replaced or supplemented by SFTP and HTTPS-based alternatives in modern Managed File Transfer (MFT) platforms, where simplicity, firewall compatibility, and centralized access control are paramount.

FTPS in Managed File Transfer (MFT) Platforms

Despite its architectural complexities, FTPS (FTP Secure) continues to play a relevant role in many enterprise-grade Managed File Transfer (MFT) platforms, particularly in environments that maintain legacy FTP-based integrations or require strict regulatory compliance. Organizations often have long-standing relationships with trading partners, vendors, or government systems that rely on FTP tooling, and FTPS allows these workflows to remain operational while introducing encryption and authentication via TLS/SSL. This makes FTPS a practical bridge between legacy infrastructure and modern security expectations.

MFT platforms that support FTPS typically embed robust configuration and policy management capabilities to overcome the protocol's limitations. One of the most important components is centralized certificate management, which handles the issuance, renewal, expiration alerts, and revocation of X.509 certificates used for FTPS sessions. This centralization ensures continuity and trust across multiple endpoints while minimizing administrative overhead and human error especially when managing client certificates for mutual TLS (mTLS) authentication.

To meet security best practices and regulatory requirements such as PCI-DSS (Payment Card Industry Data Security Standard), HIPAA (Health Insurance Portability and Accountability Act), and SOX (Sarbanes-Oxley Act), MFT platforms enforce policies around encryption strength, including minimum supported versions of TLS (1.2 or 1.3), approved cipher suites, and certificate authority validation. These policies ensure that only compliant, hardened connections are permitted, helping organizations demonstrate adherence to encryption-in-transit mandates during audits.

Furthermore, enterprise MFT solutions provide extensive logging and audit trails for all FTPS activity. This includes records of TLS handshake negotiations, certificate validity, session duration, data transfer integrity, and IP-level connection tracing. These logs are critical for forensics, compliance reporting, SLA tracking, and security incident response, especially in regulated sectors such as banking, healthcare, and government.

While FTPS may not offer the same simplicity or firewall compatibility as SFTP or HTTPS-based transfers, its inclusion in modern MFT platforms ensures backward compatibility with partners who rely on FTP-based systems. Through centralized governance, automated workflows, and security policy orchestration, MFT platforms effectively mitigate FTPS's limitations transforming it into a viable and compliant component of today's hybrid and transitional data ecosystems.

1.5.4 HTTPS – Hypertext Transfer Protocol Secure

HTTPS (Hypertext Transfer Protocol Secure) is the secure version of HTTP, designed to provide confidentiality, integrity, and authentication over digital communications, particularly web-based transactions. It operates over TCP port 443 and is widely used for web services, APIs, and browser-based interactions, including secure file uploads and downloads. HTTPS integrates HTTP with TLS (Transport Layer Security) to encrypt the entire session between a client (such as a browser or an application) and a server, ensuring that sensitive data transmitted over the network like login credentials, personal information, or financial records cannot be intercepted, altered, or spoofed by unauthorized parties.

From a technical standpoint, an HTTPS session begins with the TLS handshake, during which the client and server exchange cryptographic parameters. The server presents an X.509 digital certificate, often issued by a trusted Certificate Authority (CA), to verify its identity. Once the handshake is successful, a shared symmetric session key is derived and used to encrypt all subsequent communication using strong ciphers such as AES (Advanced Encryption Standard) or ChaCha20-Poly1305. This layered security model not only secures the transport channel but also allows for Perfect Forward Secrecy (PFS) and certificate pinning, which significantly improve resilience against replay attacks, session hijacking, and certificate forgery.

HTTPS is firewall-friendly and extremely scalable, as it uses a single, predictable port (443) and follows a stateless, request-response communication model, making it ideal for integration into RESTful APIs, cloud-native microservices, and web-based portals. It is also fully compatible with proxy servers, load balancers, NAT devices, and modern security architectures like Zero Trust Networks and Web Application Firewalls (WAFs). Unlike FTP-based protocols that require multiple ports and complex configurations, HTTPS can be securely deployed with minimal effort across diverse infrastructure landscapes.

In the context of Managed File Transfer (MFT), HTTPS is increasingly being used to facilitate secure, browser-accessible file exchanges, self-service portals for partners and clients, and automated data integration with cloud storage providers and SaaS applications. MFT platforms often extend HTTPS with features like token-based authentication, multi-factor login, rate limiting, and access expiration controls to ensure compliance with standards like GDPR, HIPAA, and ISO/IEC 27001. Additionally, HTTPS is well-suited for handling large file transfers, chunked uploads, and resumable sessions via advanced HTTP extensions such as HTTP/1.1 keep-alive and HTTP/2 multiplexing.

Due to its widespread support, simplicity, and robust security posture, HTTPS has become a foundational protocol not only for secure web browsing but also for enterprise-grade data exchange, automation, and file transfer especially in scenarios that require tight integration with web-based platforms, mobile clients, or public APIs.

1.5.5 AS2 – Applicability Statement 2

AS2 (Applicability Statement 2) is a widely adopted protocol for securely transmitting structured business data, such as EDI (Electronic Data Interchange) documents, over the internet using HTTP or HTTPS. Defined by the IETF and governed by RFC 4130, AS2 enables the real-time exchange of business-critical files between trading partners, ensuring not just confidentiality and integrity but also non-repudiation of delivery, which is a key requirement in regulated industries like retail, manufacturing, finance, and healthcare.

AS2 wraps payloads typically in formats such as X12, EDIFACT, XML, or CSV in S/MIME (Secure/Multipurpose Internet Mail Extensions)-encoded messages. These messages are then transmitted over HTTP or HTTPS as MIME attachments. The use of S/MIME enables end-to-end encryption and digital signing, ensuring that the data is protected from interception or tampering and that the identity of the sender can be authenticated with a digital certificate. Encryption algorithms commonly used include AES, 3DES, and RSA-based public key cryptography, depending on the certificate and configuration.

One of AS2's hallmark features is its support for Message Disposition Notifications (MDNs), which function like delivery receipts. An MDN is digitally signed and returned by the recipient upon successful processing of the message, providing proof of receipt and establishing non-repudiation of a legal assurance that the message was received exactly as sent and cannot be denied by the recipient. This feature makes AS2 particularly useful in industries like retail (e.g., Walmart mandates AS2 for all suppliers), where auditability, transaction traceability, and regulatory compliance are critical.

AS2 is firewall-friendly, as it transmits over standard HTTP(S) ports (80/443), eliminating the need for complex port management. However, it does require both trading partners to exchange digital certificates and pre-configure endpoints, making onboarding somewhat manual unless automated via a Managed File Transfer (MFT) platform. Most enterprise-grade MFT systems provide built-in AS2 support, enabling centralized certificate management, partner profile configuration, logging, retry handling, and MDN tracking, all of which simplify the deployment and operation of AS2-based integrations.

In modern IT environments, AS2 continues to be a reliable and secure protocol for B2B file exchanges, especially when regulatory compliance, data integrity, and delivery assurance are non-negotiable. Though more contemporary API-based approaches are emerging, AS2 remains a standards-driven, mature, and widely supported protocol that integrates well with ERP systems, EDI gateways, and supply chain platforms.

1.5.6 IBM Connect:Direct

IBM Connect:Direct originally known as NDM (Network Data Mover) is a robust, point-to-point Managed File Transfer (MFT) solution engineered for high-volume, high-performance, and mission-critical data movement between enterprises or within large organizations. Designed to replace traditional FTP with a more secure, reliable, and automated alternative, Connect:Direct has become a foundational tool in industries like banking, government, insurance, and retail, where guaranteed delivery, auditability, and performance are non-negotiable.

At its core, IBM Connect:Direct operates on a peer-to-peer architecture, meaning two nodes communicate directly without relying on an intermediary gateway. This architecture allows for uninterrupted file transfer, even in the face of intermittent network outages, through checkpoint/restart capabilities where a transfer can resume from the last successful point rather than restarting from scratch.

One of the distinguishing features of Connect:Direct is its cross-platform support. It can run seamlessly across mainframes (z/OS), midrange systems (iSeries), UNIX/Linux, and Windows platforms, making it ideal for heterogeneous enterprise environments. The protocol is optimized for throughput and reduced latency, enabling bulk file movements across WANs with minimal overhead. Performance tuning, like parallel sessions, data compression, and priority queuing, further enhances large-scale data transfers.

Security is deeply integrated into the Connect:Direct framework. It supports TLS/SSL for encrypted sessions, Secure+ add-on for compliance with FIPS 140-2, and granular user authentication and authorization policies. Audit trails are comprehensive, offering non-repudiation, logging of all activity, and integration with SIEM tools for enterprise-wide monitoring.

From an automation standpoint, Connect:Direct offers sophisticated scheduling, conditional logic, and process scripting via its proprietary language (Process Language). This facilitates intelligent workflows where file movements are conditional on specific triggers or post-processing actions (e.g., archiving, renaming, transformation).

Administrators and integration architects benefit from IBM Sterling Control Center, a centralized console for monitoring, managing, and reporting across Connect:Direct nodes, which enhances governance and operational control.

In summary, IBM Connect:Direct is a high-throughput, secure, and resilient MFT solution that aligns well with organizations requiring deterministic, scalable, and compliant file transfers across diverse systems. Its technical maturity and deep integration into critical enterprise workflows make it a cornerstone of modern B2B and internal data exchange infrastructures.

1.5.7 PeSIT Protocol

PeSIT (*Protocol d'Echanges pour un Système Interbancaire de Télécompensation*) is a specialized file transfer protocol originally developed in the 1980s by the French Interbank Teleclearing System (SIT), now overseen by STET (Systèmes Technologiques d'Échange et de

Traitement). Its initial objective was to support secure, reliable, and traceable file exchanges between banks and financial institutions participating in interbank clearing and settlement processes within France and across Europe.

Technically, PeSIT operates as an application-layer protocol that supports both synchronous and asynchronous file transfers. It is highly transaction-oriented, built to guarantee end-to-end integrity, non-repudiation, and delivery confirmation. It emphasizes structured messaging and detailed status reporting at each phase of the file exchange process, from connection initiation to final acknowledgment. These characteristics make it ideal for use in financial systems where data consistency, auditability, and traceability are essential.

The protocol is defined by a modular architecture that allows for flexible integration into a wide variety of systems. It supports multiple file transfer modes, including:

- Block mode for optimized high-speed transfers.

- Record mode for structured file formats.

- Resume mode to support fault-tolerant transfers, allowing restarts from the last known good point.

PeSIT supports robust session management using stateful negotiation, and its protocol stack allows for encryption and authentication mechanisms to be embedded or handled externally. Although PeSIT itself does not prescribe a specific encryption standard, implementations often incorporate SSL/TLS, IPSec, or network-layer encryption tools to ensure data confidentiality and integrity in transit.

Another key technical strength is its extensive logging and audit capabilities. Every transaction can be logged with a unique identifier, time-stamped, and linked to both the sending and receiving systems. This provides comprehensive traceability an essential requirement in regulated environments like banking and government sectors.

PeSIT is predominantly used in France and French-speaking regions, but it has also been adopted in sectors like insurance, public administration, and utilities. Despite the rise of newer, more globally adopted protocols like AS2, SFTP, or HTTPS, PeSIT remains in active use in legacy systems, especially where long-standing regulatory compliance and interoperability with national clearing systems are required.

Today, PeSIT implementations are available through various vendors and middleware solutions, including those from Axway, Sterling, and niche European providers, often integrated into MFT platforms or middleware buses that support multi-protocol interoperability.

In conclusion, PeSIT is a legacy yet highly dependable protocol, specifically designed for secure, traceable, and structured data exchanges in critical financial ecosystems. It remains an important component in the European managed file transfer landscape, particularly where historical interoperability and compliance are essential

1.5.8 Security in MFT: Encryption, Authentication, and Compliance

Security is a foundational pillar of any Managed File Transfer (MFT) solution, encompassing robust encryption, authentication mechanisms, and strict compliance alignment with global data protection regulations. Unlike traditional file transfer protocols that offer minimal or optional security, MFT platforms are purpose-built to secure data both in transit and at rest, ensuring that sensitive files exchanged between systems, users, and partners are protected against unauthorized access, tampering, and interception. MFT systems use strong encryption algorithms such as AES-256, TLS 1.2/1.3, and RSA-based public key infrastructure (PKI) to ensure end-to-end confidentiality. Data in transit is secured using transport protocols like SFTP, FTPS, HTTPS, and AS2, while encryption at rest is enforced using FIPS 140-2 compliant cryptographic modules, protecting stored files on disk or in cloud storage.

Authentication in MFT is equally sophisticated. Beyond basic username-password access, enterprise MFT solutions support multi-factor authentication (MFA), public key authentication, OAuth, SAML-based single sign-on (SSO), and integration with LDAP/Active Directory for centralized identity management. Role-based access control (RBAC) ensures that users only have access to the data and workflows they are authorized to handle, preventing privilege escalation and enforcing least-privilege security principles. Many platforms also offer IP whitelisting, device fingerprinting, and session timeouts to further harden user access and eliminate attack vectors such as brute force attempts or session hijacking.

On the compliance front, MFT platforms are designed to address the increasingly complex landscape of data privacy laws and industry regulations. This includes built-in support for HIPAA (healthcare), GDPR (EU personal data protection), PCI-DSS (payment card industry), SOX (financial reporting), and FISMA (federal systems). Features such as detailed audit logs, automated file tracking, digital signing, non-repudiation controls, and data retention policies ensure that all file activity is traceable, verifiable, and compliant with internal and external governance mandates. Moreover, many MFT platforms undergo third-party security audits and offer certifications like SOC 2 Type II and ISO/IEC 27001 to validate their ability to manage data securely.

In essence, security in MFT is not an add-on; it is deeply embedded across every layer of the platform, providing organizations with a centralized, policy-driven, and audit-ready framework for secure data exchange. This makes MFT an indispensable solution for enterprises that require resilient, compliant, and scalable methods of transferring files in a digital economy defined by cyber threats and regulatory complexity.

1.5.9 Automation and Scheduling in MFT

Automation and scheduling are core capabilities of modern Managed File Transfer (MFT) solutions, designed to eliminate manual intervention, reduce operational risk, and streamline complex file movement workflows. Unlike traditional file transfer methods that rely on ad-hoc scripting or human-triggered processes, MFT platforms offer intelligent, rule-driven automation engines that can initiate, monitor, and respond to file transfers in a fully unattended fashion. At the heart of this functionality lies the ability to define event-driven triggers (e.g., a file arrives in a directory, a database is updated, or an HTTP API call is received) or time-based schedules (e.g., hourly, daily, weekly, or cron-like advanced expressions) to execute predefined workflows.

These workflows can include multi-step sequences involving file encryption/decryption, compression, renaming, conditional routing, metadata tagging, PGP signing, or even integration with downstream systems such as ERP, CRM, or cloud storage platforms. Advanced MFT platforms allow administrators to build visual workflow diagrams using drag-and-drop tools or define them as reusable templates in XML or JSON formats. This enables both technical and non-technical users to configure sophisticated automation chains that handle thousands of transactions daily with zero-touch reliability.

Furthermore, MFT systems support concurrency management, load balancing, and resource scheduling, allowing large volumes of files to be processed efficiently across distributed nodes. Job queuing and prioritization features ensure that mission-critical transfers take precedence over lower-priority jobs, while dependency-based execution ensures files are only moved or processed when upstream conditions are met, preventing premature actions that might lead to data corruption or process failures.

On the administrative side, robust audit logging and execution history tracking give full transparency into when and how each automated process ran, whether it succeeded or failed, and what data was moved. If errors occur, MFT platforms can automatically retry failed jobs, send real-time alerts via email, SMS, or webhooks, or execute custom remediation scripts minimizing downtime and eliminating the need for human escalation. Many solutions also integrate with SIEM (Security Information and Event Management) systems and IT service management tools (e.g., ServiceNow) to ensure that anomalies and exceptions are handled as part of broader enterprise operations.

In summary, automation and scheduling in MFT are about more than just moving files on a timer; they represent a mission-critical orchestration layer that empowers organizations to build secure, compliant, and responsive data pipelines. These capabilities not only enhance operational efficiency and reduce error rates but also allow businesses to respond quickly to data-driven events in a real-time, policy-governed, and fully auditable environment.

1.5.10 Monitoring and Auditing in MFT

Monitoring and auditing are mission-critical functions in any enterprise-grade Managed File Transfer (MFT) solution, providing organizations with real-time visibility, historical traceability, and compliance assurance over all file transfer activities. While traditional FTP-based tools offer minimal or no insight into operational behavior, modern MFT platforms are designed with centralized monitoring dashboards, automated alerting, and granular audit trails that track every file, user, and transaction across the system. These platforms continuously monitor the status of scheduled jobs, ad hoc transfers, workflows, endpoints, and network connections, offering live insights into file movement, queue states, resource usage, and system health metrics.

At a technical level, MFT monitoring systems support real-time telemetry through dashboards that display transfer success/failure states, job duration, throughput, SLA adherence, and transfer delays. They also track user activity logs, connection attempts, encryption protocols used, and authentication events critical for detecting unauthorized access, policy violations, or data anomalies. Some advanced MFT solutions even integrate with AI or machine learning models to detect patterns in transfer behavior and flag anomalies, such as unexpected spikes in file size, frequency, or destination, helping prevent data exfiltration or misuse.

On the auditing side, MFT platforms maintain immutable logs that document every interaction within the system who sent or received what, when, where, and how. These logs typically include metadata such as file names, sizes, hash values, protocol used (e.g., SFTP, FTPS, AS2), IP addresses, digital signature verification, and TLS handshake records. Logs are timestamped, digitally signed, and stored in tamper-proof repositories to ensure data integrity and legal defensibility. Many MFT systems also offer log export and integration with third-party SIEM tools (like Splunk, logstash, Datadog, IBM QRadar, or ArcSight) for consolidated security analysis, compliance reporting, and forensic investigation.

From a regulatory standpoint, robust monitoring and auditing are essential for demonstrating compliance with data protection regulations and industry standards, including HIPAA, GDPR, SOX, FISMA, and PCI-DSS. These frameworks often require organizations to maintain auditable records of all data movements, define retention policies, and provide reporting capabilities during security audits or investigations. MFT solutions streamline this by offering pre-built compliance templates, customizable reporting engines, and automated log retention schedules aligned with policy mandates.

In summary, monitoring and auditing within MFT platforms go far beyond basic operational oversight; they deliver end-to-end governance, compliance readiness, and proactive security controls, enabling organizations to manage data transfers with full accountability, transparency, and operational intelligence.

1.6 MFT Use Cases

1.6.1 Managed File Transfer in Banking and Financial Services

In the banking and financial services sector, where data sensitivity, compliance mandates, and transaction velocity are exceptionally high, Managed File Transfer (MFT) plays a critical role in enabling secure, automated, and auditable exchange of financial data. Banks, payment processors, clearinghouses, and financial technology (FinTech) firms rely on MFT platforms to handle large volumes of time-sensitive data flows including payment instructions, SWIFT messages, clearing and settlement reports, customer statements, transaction logs, and regulatory filings. These transfers must meet stringent security, compliance, and performance standards, and MFT platforms are designed to deliver on all three fronts.

From a security perspective, MFT ensures that financial data is protected in transit and at rest using FIPS 140-2 certified encryption, such as AES-256, and secure transport protocols like SFTP, FTPS, AS2, and HTTPS. Transactions are authenticated using multi-factor authentication (MFA), public key infrastructure (PKI), and role-based access controls (RBAC), ensuring that only authorized users and systems can access sensitive information. MFT systems also support digital signing and hash validation to maintain data integrity and non-repudiation across file exchanges critical for high-value interbank and cross-border transfers.

Operationally, financial institutions leverage MFT to orchestrate complex workflow automation between internal systems such as core banking, treasury management, anti-fraud engines, risk models, and enterprise data warehouses (EDWs). Transfers can be triggered based on business events, settlement windows, or regulatory deadlines, and are often executed in near real-time with SLA guarantees. MFT platforms support advanced scheduling, retry logic, error notifications, and failover capabilities, ensuring continuous availability and rapid recovery in the event of system failures or network outages.

From a compliance and auditability standpoint, MFT platforms are instrumental in helping financial organizations meet the requirements of global regulations such as PCI-DSS, SOX, GDPR, GLBA, FINRA, and Basel III. MFT solutions generate detailed audit logs, transaction histories, access reports, and exception tracking, which are used by internal audit teams and regulators to validate the secure handling of confidential data. These logs are typically immutable, timestamped, and cryptographically protected for evidentiary value.

Additionally, as financial services increasingly move toward cloud adoption and API-first ecosystems, modern MFT platforms support hybrid deployments, RESTful integration, token-based authentication, and secure file-sharing portals, enabling seamless collaboration with FinTech partners, regulatory bodies, and third-party service providers without compromising security or governance.

In summary, MFT is not just a back-end utility in banking it is a strategic infrastructure layer that supports secure transaction processing, regulatory compliance, and digital innovation, while ensuring that every file transfer adheres to the industry's highest standards of confidentiality, integrity, availability, and traceability.

1.6.2 MFT in Healthcare – Enabling HIPAA-Compliant Secure Data Exchange

In the highly regulated and privacy-sensitive world of healthcare, Managed File Transfer (MFT) plays an indispensable role in enabling secure, auditable, and policy-driven data exchange, particularly when it involves electronic protected health information (ePHI). With the introduction of the Health Insurance Portability and Accountability Act (HIPAA), covered entities and business associates such as hospitals, insurance providers, labs, clinics, and health IT vendors are legally required to implement administrative, technical, and physical safeguards to ensure the confidentiality, integrity, and availability of ePHI during transmission and storage. MFT platforms are designed to meet these requirements by offering end-to-end encryption, authentication controls, detailed audit trails, and automated compliance workflows.

At the core of HIPAA compliance is secure transmission, and MFT supports this by enforcing TLS 1.2+, AES-256 encryption, and FIPS 140-2 validated cryptographic modules for both data-in-transit and data-at-rest. Protocols like SFTP, FTPS, and HTTPS are standard in MFT platforms, allowing healthcare organizations to securely exchange sensitive files such as patient medical records, lab results, imaging files, insurance claims, prescription data, and telehealth transcripts across internal systems and with external partners (e.g., payers, labs, health information exchanges). Some MFT solutions also support AS2 and AS4 protocols for secure EDI transactions, commonly used in claims processing and provider-payer communications.

Authentication mechanisms are equally robust, including multi-factor authentication (MFA), public key infrastructure (PKI), and LDAP/Active Directory integration, all of which help enforce user access controls in alignment with HIPAA's technical safeguards. Role-based access control (RBAC) ensures users and systems have access only to the files and operations necessary for their role, minimizing the risk of unauthorized exposure. Additionally, MFT platforms support session timeouts, IP whitelisting, and digital signatures to further fortify endpoint-to-endpoint trust.

One of the most critical aspects of HIPAA is the requirement for complete auditability of ePHI-related events. MFT platforms provide immutable logs and real-time monitoring that track who accessed which files, when, from where, using what protocol, and whether the transmission succeeded, failed, or was interrupted. These logs are often stored in tamper-evident formats with timestamping and digital verification, making them suitable for forensic analysis and audit reviews by internal security teams and regulatory bodies like OCR (Office for Civil Rights).

MFT systems also automate Business Associate Agreement (BAA) compliance workflows and integrate with Data Loss Prevention (DLP), antivirus scanning, and email gateway systems to prevent unauthorized file sharing, accidental exposure, or malware transmission. Some platforms enable data classification and tagging of ePHI files, ensuring that files containing sensitive healthcare information are handled with elevated security rules across hybrid environments whether on-premises, in the cloud, or in multi-tenant SaaS applications.

With the growing adoption of telemedicine, remote care, and interoperability mandates like FHIR and HL7, healthcare organizations are expanding the scope of digital file transfers across systems and organizations. MFT platforms are increasingly being integrated with EHR systems (e.g., Epic, Cerner), medical imaging platforms (PACS/RIS), healthcare APIs, and mobile applications, facilitating secure, standards-compliant, and automated file exchanges that scale with demand while maintaining compliance.

In summary, MFT in healthcare is not just about moving files, it is about providing a comprehensive, policy-enforced, and audit-ready infrastructure for managing the secure exchange of ePHI. By aligning deeply with HIPAA's technical safeguards and operational best practices, MFT enables healthcare organizations to deliver patient-centric care, meet regulatory obligations, and maintain trust in an increasingly digital and interconnected healthcare ecosystem.

1.6.3 MFT in Retail and Supply Chain

In the retail and supply chain industry, where speed, accuracy, and visibility are critical to operational success, Managed File Transfer (MFT) plays a central role in enabling secure, automated, and traceable data exchanges across a diverse ecosystem of suppliers, distributors, warehouses, point-of-sale (POS) systems, e-commerce platforms, and logistics providers. Retailers routinely exchange massive volumes of transactional and operational data including purchase orders (POs), invoices, advance ship notices (ASNs), product catalogs, pricing files, inventory updates, shipping confirmations, and EDI documents that must flow seamlessly across both internal systems (e.g., ERP, WMS, CRM) and external trading partners. MFT platforms facilitate these exchanges with high reliability, security, and scalability, ensuring that business-critical workflows are executed in real-time or near-real-time, without disruption.

One of MFT's key advantages in retail lies in its support for standards-based protocols such as SFTP, AS2, FTPS, and HTTPS, all of which provide end-to-end encryption and data integrity guarantees critical for securing sensitive customer information, vendor contracts, and supply chain transaction records. AS2, in particular, is widely used in retail EDI networks, especially in supplier onboarding and order fulfillment, and is mandated by large retailers like Walmart, Target, and Amazon. MFT platforms not only support these protocols but also offer advanced EDI translation, message validation, and non-repudiation through digital signatures and MDNs (Message Disposition Notifications), which are essential for audit trails and regulatory compliance.

Retail MFT implementations also heavily emphasize automation and scheduling to optimize supply chain workflows. MFT platforms can automate the entire lifecycle of file transfer events, such as triggering a shipping label generation after receiving an order confirmation, or initiating a product replenishment notification once inventory thresholds are breached. These workflows are designed with conditional logic, event-based triggers, and real-time exception handling, allowing the system to dynamically reroute transfers, retry failed jobs, or escalate alerts when SLA violations are detected. This enables businesses to maintain just-in-time (JIT) inventory levels, reduce stock outs or overstock, and respond to demand fluctuations with greater agility.

From a security and compliance standpoint, retail environments must adhere to PCI-DSS (Payment Card Industry Data Security Standard), GDPR, SOX, and in some cases, CIS and ISO 27001, especially when handling customer payment data, loyalty programs, and international supplier records. MFT platforms enforce secure user authentication, role-based access control (RBAC), data loss prevention (DLP), and real-time monitoring of all data flows. Built-in logging and auditing features track every file movement, user action, and protocol session, enabling detailed compliance reporting, incident response, and forensic investigation.

As the retail industry continues its shift to omnichannel commerce, global fulfillment, and cloud-first operations, MFT platforms provide native support for hybrid deployments, allowing secure and orchestrated file transfers between on-premises applications (like SAP or Oracle Retail) and cloud services (like AWS S3, Microsoft Azure Blob, or Google Cloud Storage). Integration with REST APIs, e-commerce platforms (e.g., Shopify, Magento), and logistics APIs (e.g., FedEx, UPS, DHL) enables real-time synchronization of product availability, delivery tracking, and customer notifications making MFT a critical enabler of supply chain visibility and customer satisfaction.

In conclusion, Managed File Transfer is not just an IT tool in retail and supply chain, it is a strategic operational backbone that connects people, systems, and partners in a secure, automated, and auditable manner. By streamlining data exchanges across the entire value chain, MFT ensures that retailers and distributors can operate at scale, meet ever-evolving customer expectations, and maintain data compliance and trust in a highly competitive and fast-paced market.

1.6.4 MFT in Government and the Public Sector

In the government and public sector, where the transmission of sensitive citizen data, inter-agency communication, and national security information must adhere to the highest levels of confidentiality, integrity, and availability, Managed File Transfer (MFT) has emerged as a mission-critical solution. Government agencies from local and state governments to national ministries and defense institutions rely heavily on MFT platforms to securely exchange data such as citizen records, tax files, financial disclosures, healthcare information, public safety reports, law enforcement intelligence, procurement documents, census data, and more. These transfers must not only be encrypted and tamper-proof but must also be traceable, policy-governed, and compliant with regulatory mandates such as FISMA (Federal Information Security Management Act), NIST 800-53, CJIS (Criminal Justice Information Services) standards, GDPR, and FedRAMP (for cloud-based platforms).

MFT solutions in government environments provide end-to-end data protection using FIPS 140-2 validated encryption algorithms such as AES-256, TLS 1.2/1.3, and SHA-2 hashing. Secure transport protocols like SFTP, FTPS, AS2, and HTTPS ensure that data exchanges between agencies, contractors, third-party systems, and cloud platforms remain confidential and authenticated. These platforms also support digital signing, non-repudiation, and certificate-based authentication, which are especially critical in sensitive workflows such as court record submissions, inter-agency task forces, defense data sharing, or national healthcare coordination.

Security and access control are tightly managed through role-based access control (RBAC), multi-factor authentication (MFA), smart card and CAC/PIV integration, and directory service integration (e.g., Active Directory, LDAP). MFT platforms allow system administrators to apply granular permissions, enforce zero-trust principles, and isolate file zones or tenant environments, ensuring that users and departments can only access the data they are authorized to handle. Additionally, geo-fencing, IP whitelisting, and audit logging enable real-time threat detection and facilitate internal and external audits, while supporting compliance with government-specific cybersecurity frameworks.

The automation capabilities of MFT are especially valuable in the public sector, where efficiency and consistency are paramount. Agencies use MFT to automate the ingestion and distribution of grants data, tax reports, financial aid documents, background checks, FOIA requests, and more triggered by time-based schedules or business events. These workflows eliminate manual errors, ensure adherence to SLAs, and accelerate service delivery to citizens and stakeholders. MFT can also integrate with legacy systems (e.g., COBOL-based mainframes) and modern platforms (e.g., Salesforce for Government, ServiceNow), bridging the gap between traditional infrastructure and cloud-first strategies.

From a visibility and compliance standpoint, government MFT solutions provide detailed audit trails, immutable log retention, real-time monitoring dashboards, and anomaly detection engines that can flag unauthorized behavior or suspicious transfer patterns. These capabilities are essential not only for security operations centers (SOCs) but also for demonstrating compliance during OIG audits, Inspector General reviews, and regulatory assessments. Moreover, some MFT vendors offer air-gapped deployment options, containerized environments, and FedRAMP-authorized SaaS offerings, enabling agencies to securely deploy MFT solutions in accordance with evolving cloud and edge strategies.

In summary, Managed File Transfer is a foundational component of secure digital transformation in the government and public sector. It enables agencies to exchange sensitive data securely, automate critical processes, and comply with stringent legal and regulatory mandates all while maintaining public trust and national resilience. As governments continue to modernize their IT ecosystems, MFT serves as a secure, scalable, and compliant backbone for inter-agency collaboration, public service delivery, and digital governance.

1.7 Traditional MFT Tools and Vendors

Over the past two decades, a wide range of Managed File Transfer (MFT) tools and vendors have emerged to address the limitations of legacy file transfer protocols like FTP, offering enterprises a more secure, automated, and auditable means to exchange data internally and with external partners. These traditional MFT tools became essential as organizations recognized the need to go beyond basic point-to-point file transfers and adopt centralized, policy-driven platforms capable of meeting regulatory, operational, and scalability demands.

1.7.1 Overview of industry-leading tools

IBM Sterling Secure File Gateway

IBM Sterling Integrator and Sterling File Gateway are cornerstone technologies in the Managed File Transfer (MFT) and B2B integration landscape, known for their scalability, reliability, and compliance readiness. Their roots trace back to the late 1990s and early 2000s, when enterprise integration and secure data exchange between business partners began to outgrow the capabilities of traditional FTP and EDI (Electronic Data Interchange) point solutions.

The origins of these platforms lie with Sterling Commerce, a pioneer in B2B integration, supply chain collaboration, and secure file exchange. Sterling Commerce was initially part of SBC Communications (now AT&T) and became an independent software company known for its Gentran Integration Suite (GIS), a robust integration engine built to support EDI mapping, document routing, and protocol-agnostic communication. GIS was rebranded as Sterling Integrator to better reflect its capabilities as a centralized integration platform that supported not only EDI but also non-EDI file formats, XML, APIs, and custom data transformations.

To address the growing need for secure, large-scale, partner-facing file exchange, Sterling Commerce introduced Sterling File Gateway (SFG) as a component of the Sterling suite. SFG was designed specifically to handle partner onboarding, protocol translation, mailbox routing, and high-volume file movement with full support for encryption, auditing, non-repudiation, and service-level agreement (SLA) monitoring. SFG integrates tightly with Sterling Integrator, using its business process engine (BPEL-based) for routing, transformation, and orchestration of file flows across complex B2B ecosystems.

In 2010, IBM acquired Sterling Commerce from AT&T for approximately $1.4 billion, recognizing the strategic value of its integration technology in supporting multi-enterprise collaboration and supply chain digitization. Post-acquisition, Sterling Integrator and File Gateway were incorporated into IBM's B2B and MFT portfolio, aligned under the IBM Sterling brand, which also includes products like IBM Control Center, Sterling Secure Proxy, SEAS (Sterling External Authentication Server), and Connect:Direct.

Since then, IBM has continued to evolve the Sterling suite to support modern deployment models, including containerization (Docker, Kubernetes), hybrid cloud, REST APIs, and enterprise security enhancements. IBM Sterling Integrator today is widely used in industries such as retail, banking, healthcare, logistics, and government, where mission-critical file exchanges, regulatory compliance, and partner interoperability are non-negotiable.

IBM Sterling Secure File Gateway is one of the most mature, robust, and enterprise-focused Managed File Transfer (MFT) solutions on the market, designed specifically for high-volume, secure, B2B data exchange across complex and highly regulated environments. As part of the broader IBM Sterling suite, which also includes IBM B2B Integrator and IBM Control Center, the Secure File Gateway provides a centralized, policy-driven platform that enables large organizations to connect, authenticate, route, transform, and monitor file-based transactions with internal systems, trading partners, and cloud applications while maintaining strict compliance with industry regulations such as HIPAA, PCI-DSS, GDPR, and SOX.

At its core, IBM Sterling SFG supports a wide array of secure transfer protocols including SFTP, FTPS, HTTPS, AS2, and Connect:Direct, enabling compatibility with diverse partner environments and legacy systems. Its protocol translation capabilities allow it to act as a universal data bridge, converting file formats or communication methods to meet partner-specific requirements. One of its key architectural strengths lies in its store-and-forward engine, which decouples the file receipt process from delivery, ensuring fault tolerance, queuing, and retry mechanisms in the event of network or endpoint failure. This is crucial in environments where delivery assurance and SLAs must be guaranteed regardless of real-time availability.

Sterling Secure File Gateway excels in partner onboarding and management. Through its Partner Management Console, administrators can define partner profiles, authentication credentials, data format preferences, and communication protocols. It supports both user-based and certificate-based authentication, and integrates with directory services like LDAP and Active Directory, as well as external identity providers for federated access control. Granular role-based access control (RBAC) ensures that users and partners have only the permissions necessary to execute their specific functions, reducing security risk and supporting internal segregation of duties.

Security is deeply embedded into the platform, with features like FIPS 140-2 certified encryption, TLS 1.2/1.3, digital signatures, PGP/GPG file encryption, and support for non-repudiation mechanisms. Administrators can enforce policy-based encryption, data retention, access auditing, and compliance reporting, which is especially critical in financial services, healthcare, and government deployments. All file movements, user actions, and system-level events are captured in tamper-evident logs, with integration to IBM Control Center for centralized monitoring, SLA tracking, alerting, and analytics.

Sterling SFG is designed to scale horizontally and support high availability (HA) and disaster recovery (DR) architectures, making it suitable for global enterprises that need to manage millions of file transfers per day. It supports clustered deployments, load balancing, and multi-node processing, ensuring that performance is optimized and failure domains are isolated. Moreover, IBM provides deep integration with IBM MQ, IBM DataPower, and other middleware components, creating a seamless ecosystem for secure integration with ERP systems (e.g., SAP, Oracle), databases, cloud storage providers, and custom applications.

With its rich automation, visual workflow modeling, and support for hybrid cloud deployments, IBM Sterling Secure File Gateway is evolving to meet modern enterprise needs. It offers support for containerized deployments (e.g., Kubernetes), RESTful APIs for partner integration, and emerging features such as data visibility dashboards, metadata tracking, and AI-driven anomaly detection (when integrated with IBM's AI Ops solutions).

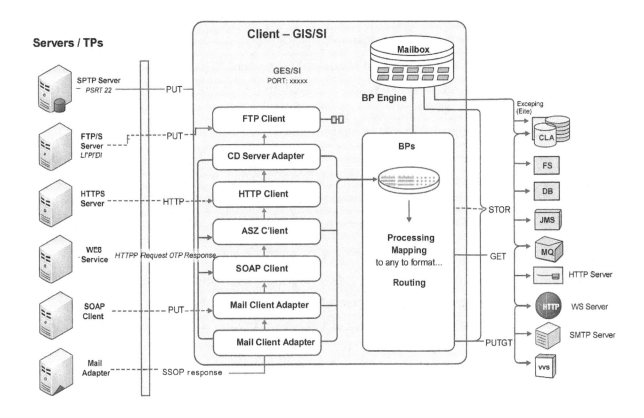

GoAnywhere MFT – Secure, Scalable, and User-Friendly Managed File Transfer

GoAnywhere MFT, now a flagship solution under the Fortra (formerly HelpSystems) brand, has evolved into one of the most accessible, reliable, and secure Managed File Transfer (MFT) platforms for enterprises of all sizes. Its origins trace back to the mid-2000s, during a period when organizations were seeking more streamlined alternatives to traditional script-based file transfer systems and ad hoc FTP servers. The original GoAnywhere suite was developed by Linoma Software, a Nebraska-based company that specialized in data encryption, file transfer automation, and secure integration between platforms. Linoma's goal was to create a product that could reduce the complexity of file movement across the enterprise while maintaining strong security controls and regulatory compliance.

The initial GoAnywhere releases quickly gained traction due to their user-friendly web-based interface, cross-platform compatibility, and built-in automation features qualities that made the solution particularly attractive to IT teams looking to eliminate manual scripting and FTP management overhead. As industries like finance, healthcare, logistics, and retail began facing stricter compliance regulations (such as HIPAA, PCI-DSS, and SOX), GoAnywhere emerged as a go-to solution for organizations needing to secure, audit, and streamline sensitive file exchanges internally and externally.

In 2016, Linoma Software was acquired by HelpSystems, a well-established enterprise IT software company. This acquisition allowed GoAnywhere to benefit from HelpSystems' broader portfolio of IT management, cybersecurity, and automation tools. Under HelpSystems (which rebranded as Fortra in 2022), GoAnywhere expanded its capabilities even further, introducing features like agent-based architecture, cloud connectors (for AWS, Azure, Google Cloud), RESTful APIs, and centralized job scheduling across distributed environments. It also introduced high availability (HA) clustering, secure file sharing portals, data encryption at rest and in transit, and deep audit logging, aligning the product with the evolving needs of digital transformation, hybrid cloud, and zero-trust security models.

What sets GoAnywhere apart in today's MFT landscape is its commitment to providing powerful capabilities through an intuitive, low-code interface making it accessible to both technical and non-technical users. Whether deployed on-premises, in the cloud, or through its SaaS offering (GoAnywhere MFTaaS), the platform continues to empower organizations to centralize and secure their file transfers, comply with global regulations, and automate mission-critical workflows with confidence and ease.

Axway Secure Transport

Axway SecureTransport is one of the most mature and widely adopted Managed File Transfer (MFT) platforms in the enterprise IT ecosystem, renowned for its security, scalability, and extensibility across complex B2B environments. The roots of SecureTransport can be traced back to Tumbleweed Communications, a California-based software company that, in the late 1990s and early 2000s, was a pioneer in secure messaging, file transfer, and digital certificate management. Tumbleweed developed the early versions of SecureTransport as a secure gateway for organizations to exchange files over the internet using standards-based protocols and strong encryption, at a time when traditional FTP was still the norm and enterprise security concerns were on the rise.

In 2008, French enterprise software company Axway, a subsidiary of Sopra Steria Group, acquired Tumbleweed Communications, gaining access to SecureTransport and integrating it into its growing portfolio of data integration, B2B communication, and API management solutions. This acquisition positioned Axway as a serious global contender in the MFT space, allowing it to offer a unified solution that not only provided secure file transfer capabilities but also supported complex hybrid integration patterns, cloud migration initiatives, and regulatory compliance requirements for highly regulated industries such as financial services, healthcare, energy, and public sector.

Axway SecureTransport has since evolved into a highly configurable, multi-protocol MFT gateway capable of supporting file-based, API-based, and hybrid data exchange workflows. It enables secure, reliable, and policy-driven file transfers using protocols like SFTP, FTPS, HTTPS, AS2, AS4, and Connect:Direct, and supports both push and pull models for data exchange. A key strength of SecureTransport is its ability to scale horizontally, support high availability and disaster recovery, and manage thousands of concurrent partner connections making it ideal for large enterprises with global trading networks.

One of SecureTransport's most significant differentiators is its policy-based routing and transfer orchestration engine. Organizations can define advanced rules for encryption, user authentication, directory scanning, filtering, throttling, data validation, file routing, and integration with external systems such as databases, message queues, cloud storage, and enterprise applications. The platform also supports integration with Axway's broader AMPLIFY platform, allowing customers to extend their MFT infrastructure with API management, real-time visibility, centralized logging, analytics, and hybrid integration capabilities bridging the gap between legacy B2B infrastructure and modern cloud-native services.

In terms of compliance and governance, Axway SecureTransport is designed to help enterprises meet stringent regulatory mandates such as PCI-DSS, GDPR, HIPAA, SOX, and ISO 27001. It provides detailed audit logging, role-based access controls (RBAC), certificate-based mutual authentication, and integration with identity management systems such as LDAP, Active Directory, and SAML-based SSO providers. It also supports OpenPGP and FIPS 140-2 compliant encryption, ensuring that both data in transit and data at rest remain protected.

Today, Axway SecureTransport is widely regarded as a battle-tested, enterprise-ready MFT platform that supports mission-critical file exchanges across cloud, hybrid, and on-premise environments. With native support for DevOps, containerization (Docker/Kubernetes), REST APIs, and event-based triggers, it continues to evolve to meet the needs of organizations undergoing digital transformation, without sacrificing the robust security and reliability it has always been known for.

TIBCO MFT

TIBCO Managed File Transfer (MFT) is a product of TIBCO Software Inc., a California-based enterprise software company founded in 1997 and known globally for its innovations in data integration, messaging, real-time analytics, and enterprise application integration (EAI). The origins of TIBCO MFT trace back to its strategic expansion into B2B communication and secure data movement in the early 2000s, when enterprises increasingly needed reliable, auditable, and secure ways to transfer large volumes of files across departments, business partners, and geographically distributed systems.

TIBCO's entry into the MFT domain was solidified through a combination of internal development and acquisitions. One of the key catalysts was the integration of MFT capabilities into its broader enterprise integration suite, enabling customers to extend traditional service bus and messaging frameworks with file-based transport mechanisms. The MFT solution was specifically designed to complement TIBCO's flagship products like BusinessWorks (BW) and EMS (Enterprise Message Service), bridging the gap between application messaging, file transfer, and end-to-end process automation.

Unlike many MFT solutions that began with a client-server architecture, TIBCO took a unique approach by building an agent-based, event-driven model. This allowed for distributed deployments where file transfer agents could be installed directly on source and destination systems, reducing reliance on centralized control servers and increasing resilience, scalability, and flexibility. This architecture proved ideal for industries like financial services, telecom, logistics, and government, where high-volume file movement, low-latency requirements, and mission-critical operations demand near real-time performance with guaranteed delivery.

TIBCO MFT continued to evolve in response to rising security and compliance pressures. It integrated FIPS 140-2 certified cryptography, digital signing, multi-factor authentication, and fine-grained access control, making it suitable for use cases governed by HIPAA, PCI-DSS, SOX, GDPR, and FedRAMP. Its ability to handle large, distributed file systems, perform automated retries and resume transfers, and compress/encrypt data on the fly gave it a performance edge over conventional MFT systems, particularly for organizations operating across low-bandwidth or high-latency environments.

Over the years, TIBCO has continued to enhance its MFT offering by incorporating support for hybrid cloud deployments, containerization (Docker/Kubernetes), REST APIs for integration, and centralized dashboards for governance and auditing. These enhancements ensure that TIBCO MFT remains not only a tool for secure file transfer but also a core integration component in digital transformation initiatives.

Today, TIBCO MFT is used by enterprises around the world as a backbone for secure, scalable, and policy-driven data movement, enabling file-based workflows to interoperate seamlessly with API-based services, real-time data pipelines, and event-driven architectures all within a unified platform governed by centralized security and compliance frameworks.

Cleo Integration Cloud

Cleo Integration Cloud (CIC) is the flagship integration platform developed by Cleo, a company with decades of expertise in secure data movement, B2B integration, and file-based communication. Founded in 1976, Cleo began as a provider of data communications and mainframe connectivity solutions, building a strong foundation in file transfer protocols, EDI (Electronic Data Interchange), and secure communications. Over time, as global commerce and supply chain ecosystems became more digitized and interconnected, Cleo recognized the need for a more flexible, scalable, and cloud-ready solution that could support both traditional MFT workflows and modern API-based integrations.

In response, Cleo launched Cleo Integration Cloud (CIC) in the mid-2010s as a next-generation hybrid integration platform-as-a-service (iPaaS) that combines MFT, EDI, and API integration capabilities in a single, unified environment. Unlike conventional MFT tools that focused solely on secure file exchange, CIC was built to address the broader challenges enterprises face in ecosystem integration that is, the ability to connect not only systems within the enterprise, but also customers, suppliers, logistics providers, and cloud services in a real-time, end-to-end, and governed manner.

One of the distinguishing aspects of CIC is its cloud-native, multi-tenant architecture, which enables rapid deployment, elastic scalability, and seamless partner onboarding. The platform supports all major file transfer protocols (SFTP, FTPS, AS2, HTTPS), while also offering pre-built connectors for popular ERP systems (e.g., SAP, NetSuite, Oracle), CRM tools, cloud storage (AWS S3, Azure Blob), and e-commerce platforms (Shopify, Magento, BigCommerce). This extensibility allows organizations to create integration flows that combine file-based batch transfers with real-time API transactions, enabling supply chain agility and digital transformation without disrupting legacy operations.

Cleo also focused on enhancing visibility and control, one of the primary limitations of traditional MFT tools. CIC offers rich operational dashboards, real-time analytics, and customizable alerts to provide business and IT users with complete end-to-end transparency into all data flows, including file status, message tracking, SLA violations, and exception handling. This business-driven integration model empowers users to troubleshoot proactively, manage trading partner relationships, and align integration performance with key business outcomes.

From a security and compliance standpoint, CIC adheres to FIPS 140-2, TLS 1.2/1.3, AES-256 encryption, and supports data residency controls, digital signing, and secure onboarding practices all essential for complying with HIPAA, PCI-DSS, GDPR, SOX, and other global regulations. It is also available in SaaS, private cloud, and hybrid deployments, offering the flexibility needed to support enterprise modernization, cloud migration, and edge-to-cloud connectivity.

Today, Cleo Integration Cloud serves thousands of organizations across retail, manufacturing, logistics, distribution, and healthcare, and is particularly valued for its ability to help enterprises connect, transform, and orchestrate ecosystem data flows from EDI and flat files to APIs and real-time webhooks. With a vision centered around integration without limits, Cleo continues to position CIC as a composable, future-ready integration platform that bridges the gap between legacy MFT systems and modern, agile digital ecosystems.

1.7.2 Comparison: Open-Source vs Commercial Tools

As organizations seek to secure and automate their file transfer workflows, they are often faced with the decision of choosing between open-source and commercial Managed File Transfer (MFT) tools. While both categories offer mechanisms for transferring data between systems, users, and partners, they differ significantly in terms of features, security, compliance, support, scalability, and enterprise-readiness.

Open-source MFT tools such as FileZilla Server, OpenSSH/SFTP, vsftpd, and Apache Mina are attractive primarily due to their zero-cost licensing, community-driven development, and modular flexibility. These tools are often lightweight, scriptable, and easily deployable in Unix/Linux environments. For organizations with strong in-house technical expertise, open-source solutions allow for high customization, integration via shell scripts or cron jobs, and freedom from vendor lock-in. However, these advantages come at a cost: open-source MFT solutions typically lack centralized management interfaces, workflow orchestration, compliance auditing, and enterprise-grade features such as role-based access control (RBAC), multi-factor authentication (MFA), automated retries, or visibility dashboards. Security updates and patches may also be infrequent or community-dependent, making them less ideal for regulated industries or mission-critical applications.

On the other hand, commercial MFT solutions like IBM Sterling, GoAnywhere MFT, Axway SecureTransport, Cleo Integration Cloud, and TIBCO MFT are built with enterprise operations and compliance at their core. These platforms provide end-to-end encryption (AES-256, TLS 1.2/1.3, FIPS 140-2), protocol diversity (SFTP, FTPS, HTTPS, AS2/AS4, Connect:Direct), and support for secure user portals, APIs, and partner onboarding. Most include visual workflow designers, automated job scheduling, event-based triggers, SLA tracking, and real-time monitoring dashboards all designed to minimize manual effort, reduce risk, and improve governance.

From a compliance and auditing perspective, commercial MFT tools excel with features like immutable audit logs, policy-based file retention, data loss prevention (DLP) integration, and pre-built templates for frameworks such as HIPAA, PCI-DSS, GDPR, SOX, and ISO/IEC 27001. They are often subject to third-party security audits, include vendor support and SLAs, and offer high availability, clustering, and disaster recovery options for production-grade environments.

Scalability is another key differentiator. While open-source tools can be scaled manually with load balancers or cron-based automation, commercial solutions are architected for large-scale, distributed environments and support multi-node deployments, agent-based remote execution, cloud integration, and containerization (Docker, Kubernetes) for modern DevOps pipelines.

In summary, open-source MFT tools may be suitable for non-regulated, low-complexity environments with experienced DevOps teams who are comfortable with scripting, manual patching, and limited feature sets. In contrast, commercial MFT platforms are the clear choice for enterprises that need centralized governance, compliance assurance, operational efficiency, and 24/7 vendor support. The investment in commercial tools is justified by the security, reliability, and time savings they deliver particularly in financial services, healthcare, government, retail, and supply chain operations, where file transfers are not just a utility, but a core business function.

PART 2: Architecture, Implementation & Best Practices

2 MFT System Architecture

At the heart of any robust Managed File Transfer (MFT) implementation lies a well-designed system architecture that balances security, scalability, resilience, and integration. MFT is no longer a simple conduit for file exchange; it is a mission-critical platform that must support automated workflows, multiple communication protocols, real-time monitoring, and regulatory compliance across on-premises, cloud, and hybrid environments. A typical modern MFT architecture consists of several interconnected layers, each performing a specialized role in the secure, governed, and reliable movement of files.

2.1 Perimeter & Security Layer (DMZ Zone)

The Perimeter & Security Layer, often referred to as the DMZ (Demilitarized Zone) or boundary zone, is a critical component in any secure Managed File Transfer (MFT) architecture. It acts as the first layer of defense between external entities (such as trading partners, clients, or third-party systems) and the internal corporate network. This zone is designed to safely terminate inbound and outbound connections, inspect traffic, enforce access controls, and segregate high-risk protocols, all while ensuring that no sensitive data or business logic is directly exposed to the public internet.

From a network perspective, the DMZ is typically positioned between two firewalls:

1. The external firewall controls inbound traffic from the internet or partner networks into the DMZ.

2. The internal firewall governs what traffic is allowed to pass from the DMZ into the protected internal network where the core MFT engine resides.

Within this DMZ zone, several key architectural components and design patterns are used to maintain security, control, and regulatory compliance.

2.1.1 Secure Proxy Servers / Reverse Proxies

To maintain a strong security posture in Managed File Transfer environments, organizations rely heavily on secure proxy servers or reverse proxies to create a robust boundary between external users and internal systems. Solutions such as IBM Sterling Secure Proxy, Axway Gateway, and GoAnywhere Gateway serve as critical perimeter components that ensure sensitive internal MFT servers remain isolated from direct internet exposure.

These secure proxies are typically deployed in the DMZ and are designed to terminate external client sessions at the edge. Instead of passing connections directly to the internal MFT server, they initiate a new, independent outbound connection into the internal network. This technique often referred to as connection decoupling or session bridging ensures that internal systems never directly receive inbound traffic from untrusted sources, greatly reducing the risk of intrusion.

One of the core advantages of secure proxies is their ability to offload protocol-specific responsibilities. For instance, they handle TLS/SSL termination, SFTP session negotiation, HTTPS header parsing, and other low-level protocol intricacies. This offloading not only improves performance on the internal MFT servers by freeing them from computational overhead, but also simplifies the overall architecture by centralizing protocol management at the edge.

Another essential feature is IP address masking or IP masquerading. Secure proxies ensure that external clients never see internal IP addresses, DNS hostnames, or server metadata. This obfuscation adds a critical layer of security by preserving infrastructure anonymity and making it significantly more difficult for attackers to map the internal network topology.

Many advanced secure proxy solutions also incorporate load balancing functionality. In large-scale MFT deployments, reverse proxies can intelligently distribute incoming client sessions across a pool of internal MFT nodes, optimizing resource utilization and ensuring high availability. This built-in traffic management enables horizontal scalability and resilience without the need for additional infrastructure components.

By providing a secure and transparent relay between external users and internal systems, secure proxy servers play a foundational role in the modern MFT security model. They offer a blend of traffic isolation, protocol handling, anonymization, and performance optimization, all while maintaining the core principle of keeping internal servers safely behind the firewall.

2.1.2 Authentication Delegation and SEAS

In enterprise-grade Managed File Transfer (MFT) environments, especially those powered by platforms like IBM Sterling, secure authentication of external trading partners is a critical concern. To address this, organizations often deploy a component known as the Sterling External Authentication Server (SEAS) in the DMZ. SEAS is purpose-built to manage authentication delegation, enabling secure, scalable identity verification at the network perimeter without exposing internal identity systems to direct access.

SEAS acts as a front-line authentication gateway. When an external partner attempts to initiate a file transfer session, SEAS handles the authentication request within the DMZ. It validates user credentials, digital certificates, or other identity artifacts without needing to store sensitive data locally. Instead, it securely relays authentication requests to the internal MFT server or associated identity infrastructure for final validation. This design adheres to the principles of least privilege and zero trust, ensuring that the internal network remains insulated from untrusted external connections.

One of SEAS's key strengths lies in its ability to offload security-intensive authentication operations. These include password validation, X.509 certificate checks, and certificate revocation list (CRL) or OCSP-based status verification. SEAS can also enforce multi-factor authentication (MFA) policies at the edge, increasing security for partner access without compromising internal system integrity.

Furthermore, SEAS is capable of integrating with a variety of enterprise identity services such as LDAP, Active Directory (AD), RADIUS, or external SSO/federated identity providers. This flexibility enables organizations to maintain centralized identity governance while decentralizing authentication logic. As a result, external users can authenticate against trusted corporate identity sources indirectly through SEAS without those sources ever being exposed directly to the internet.

Importantly, SEAS is stateless. It does not retain session data, credentials, or authentication results beyond the scope of a single transaction. This not only supports scalability allowing SEAS nodes to be horizontally scaled but also enhances security by minimizing the attack surface and preventing unauthorized data persistence.

By moving authentication functions into the DMZ, SEAS helps enforce robust access control while simplifying compliance with internal security policies, industry standards, and regulatory mandates. It plays a vital role in enabling secure, delegated authentication in next-generation MFT deployments.

2.1.3 Perimeter (Edge) Servers

In modern Managed File Transfer (MFT) architectures, security is increasingly enforced at the network edge using lightweight, stateless perimeter nodes also known as DMZ agents or protocol handlers. These specialized servers are typically deployed in the demilitarized zone (DMZ) and act as the first point of contact for external connections. Their primary role is to handle inbound and outbound traffic over secure file transfer protocols such as SFTP, FTPS, AS2, and HTTPS, without exposing the internal network to direct access.

These edge nodes serve as intelligent relays. When a file arrives from an external source, the node negotiates the protocol, authenticates the connection, and initiates a secure, outbound-only tunnel to relay the data to the internal MFT system. At no point is the file permanently stored on the edge node; instead, it is held only briefly in memory buffers during transit. This stateless design is intentional; it minimizes the system's attack surface and significantly reduces the potential impact of a breach. Even if an edge node were compromised, the lack of persistent storage and internal access limits an attacker's ability to move laterally within the network.

Beyond protocol handling, these perimeter agents also perform essential pre-processing tasks. They often include built-in antivirus scanning, schema or file format validation, content filtering, and bandwidth throttling. This ensures that only clean, well-formed, and policy-compliant files are passed into the core MFT infrastructure. Such early-stage sanitization not only improves security but also helps maintain operational integrity within the internal network.

A key security advantage of these perimeter nodes is their architectural design: internal servers never have to open inbound ports to receive files. Instead, they establish outbound connections to the DMZ agent, which relays files securely using a predefined, encrypted backchannel. This approach aligns with zero-trust principles, as it enforces strict control over data ingress and egress, and ensures that the internal environment remains shielded from unsolicited external communication.

Scalable and resilient, these stateless nodes can be clustered or distributed across geographic locations to support high availability, regulatory compliance, and low-latency file delivery. In enterprise-grade deployments, multiple edge nodes may be configured to handle specific protocols, customer segments, or regional data flows, making them a foundational component of secure, flexible, and modern MFT ecosystems.

2.1.4 TLS Offloading and Certificate Management at the Edge

In modern MFT deployments, TLS offloading is a critical function performed by perimeter gateways or DMZ-based proxies. These components are strategically positioned to handle TLS/SSL termination, offloading the computational burden of encryption and decryption from internal MFT servers. By managing these cryptographic tasks at the edge, organizations can significantly enhance both performance and security, while simplifying certificate lifecycle management.

TLS offloading gateways are engineered to support the latest versions of the protocol, including TLS 1.2 and TLS 1.3, and are equipped to negotiate robust cipher suites such as AES-GCM, ChaCha20-Poly1305, and key exchange mechanisms like Elliptic Curve Diffie-Hellman Ephemeral (ECDHE). These algorithms offer strong encryption, forward secrecy, and protection against modern cryptographic attacks.

Another core responsibility of these gateways is certificate management. They integrate seamlessly with certificate authorities (CAs) and enterprise Public Key Infrastructure (PKI) systems, facilitating the issuance, renewal, and revocation of X.509 certificates. Many solutions also support automation tools such as Let's Encrypt or ACME-based workflows, enabling the secure and timely rotation of certificates without administrative overhead. This is essential in maintaining uninterrupted service and preventing certificate expiration-related outages.

Advanced deployments also leverage mutual TLS (mTLS), which introduces two-way authentication using digital certificates. With mTLS enabled, not only does the client validate the server's identity, but the server also verifies the client's certificate before proceeding with the connection. This bidirectional trust model is especially vital in high-assurance B2B integrations, where identity verification and non-repudiation are required.

Maintaining certificate hygiene at the network edge is imperative. Expired, misconfigured, or weakly signed certificates can lead to denial of service, broken integrations, or even security vulnerabilities. Regular certificate audits, automated expiration alerts, and centralized trust store management are all best practices that help avoid operational disruptions and uphold secure communication standards.

By handling TLS termination and certificate operations at the DMZ layer, organizations benefit from centralized control, enhanced security visibility, and scalable encryption management making it a cornerstone of resilient, policy-driven MFT infrastructures.

2.1.5 Firewall Configuration and Port Management

An effective Managed File Transfer (MFT) security architecture begins with rigorous firewall configuration and port management, especially in environments utilizing a demilitarized zone (DMZ). The objective is to control traffic flow between external entities, the DMZ, and the internal network with precision, following the principle of least privilege. Every open port is a potential vector for attack, and every protocol allowed must be explicitly justified and tightly controlled.

A well-architected DMZ minimizes exposure by limiting both the number of open ports and the protocols permitted through each network boundary. Firewalls at both the outer (internet-facing) and inner (DMZ-to-internal) edges of the DMZ are configured to allow only known, expected traffic. This includes restricting connections by IP address, domain name, protocol type, and port.

One of the fundamental practices is the allow-listing of specific partner IPs or domains. Only pre-approved external entities are granted access to the MFT services, reducing the surface area exposed to unknown actors or bots. Traffic from all other sources is automatically blocked, effectively mitigating many opportunistic scanning and exploitation attempts.

Equally important is the restriction of protocols to specific, whitelisted ports. For example:

- SFTP traffic is limited to TCP port 22

- HTTPS connections use port 443

- AS2 communications may be confined to custom ports like 4080 or 8443

For more complex or legacy protocols such as FTPS or passive FTP, firewalls must support dynamic port forwarding or use protocol-aware inspection tools (e.g., FTP helpers) to open data channels on-the-fly in a controlled manner. Without this capability, passive mode transfers can fail due to blocked ephemeral ports, undermining interoperability with partners.

To further bolster network defenses, many organizations deploy Intrusion Prevention Systems (IPS) and Intrusion Detection Systems (IDS) at DMZ boundaries. These systems monitor traffic patterns for anomalies, exploit attempts, or known attack signatures in real-time. When combined with rate limiting and throttling mechanisms, they provide a strong defense against Distributed Denial-of-Service (DDoS) attacks and brute-force intrusions.

In summary, firewall and port management is not simply about connectivity it is about policy enforcement, segmentation, and threat containment. When implemented correctly, it provides the first layer of defense in a multi-tiered MFT security model, ensuring that only legitimate, intended traffic can traverse the boundary between the internet, the DMZ, and the protected internal MFT infrastructure.

2.1.6 Security Hardening and Monitoring: Fortifying the DMZ Layer

In any enterprise Managed File Transfer (MFT) deployment, components residing in the Demilitarized Zone (DMZ) represent the first line of defense against external threats. Because these systems are directly exposed to the internet, they are prime targets for scanning, probing, and exploitation attempts. As such, security hardening and continuous monitoring of DMZ assets are non-negotiable pillars of a resilient MFT architecture.

A core tenet of DMZ design is that no sensitive data or authentication credentials are ever stored on perimeter nodes. These systems operate in a stateless and transient mode, relaying traffic and enforcing security controls without persisting any business-critical information. By ensuring that DMZ components do not hold long-term secrets, organizations can dramatically reduce the potential impact of a breach.

To further minimize risk, all DMZ systems are hardened according to industry-standard security benchmarks, such as the CIS (Center for Internet Security) guidelines. This includes disabling unused services and ports, enforcing strict user permissions, enabling mandatory access controls (MAC), and applying regular operating system and software patches. Every unnecessary service is a potential vulnerability, and every outdated package a possible entry point so minimizing the attack surface is paramount.

Security monitoring and visibility are also central to maintaining a defensible posture. DMZ components are typically integrated with centralized logging and threat detection systems. Logs are forwarded in real time using protocols like Syslog, SNMP traps, or agent-based collectors to Security Information and Event Management (SIEM) platforms such as Splunk, IBM QRadar, or

Elastic Security. These tools allow security teams to correlate events, detect anomalies, and respond swiftly to potential threats or indicators of compromise (IOCs).

For advanced perimeter defense, many organizations implement layered controls such as:

- **Port knocking** to obscure open services until a specific connection sequence is executed

- **GeoIP-based filtering** to block traffic from high-risk or non-relevant geographic regions

- **Threat intelligence integration**, allowing real-time blocking of IPs, domains, or behaviors associated with known attack campaigns

These proactive strategies help transform the DMZ from a simple relay point into an **intelligent, adaptive defense layer**, capable of detecting and deflecting sophisticated threats before they reach internal systems.

Ultimately, a hardened and monitored DMZ is not just a security best practice, it is an operational requirement in any serious MFT deployment. It ensures that internet-facing components maintain the integrity, availability, and confidentiality expected in regulated and mission-critical environments.

2.2 Protocol Handling & Communication Layer

This layer manages connectivity and protocol-level processing for both inbound and outbound file transfer sessions. The MFT platform must support a diverse set of secure transport protocols, including:

- SFTP (SSH File Transfer Protocol) – Secure, firewall-friendly, and widely used. *(for more information on SFTP, please refer to 1.5.2)*

- FTPS (FTP over SSL/TLS) – Offers encryption but requires multiple ports and firewall rules. *(for more information on FTPS, please refer to 1.5.3)*

- HTTPS – Useful for web-based portals and RESTful API exchanges. *(for more information on HTTPS, please refer to 1.5.4)*

- AS2/AS4 – Industry-standard protocols for EDI document exchange and B2B file exchange, with built-in support for non-repudiation. *(for more information on AS2, please refer to 1.5.5)*

- Connect:Direct / PeSIT – Legacy protocols still heavily used in banking and government sectors. *(for more information on Connect:Direct/PeSIT, please refer to 1.5.6 and 1.5.7)*

This layer ensures secure authentication (via passwords, keys, certificates), session initiation, and data streaming between endpoints.

2.3 File Processing and Orchestration Layer: The Intelligent Core of MFT

At the heart of every Managed File Transfer (MFT) system lies the File Processing and Orchestration Layer the operational backbone that governs the full lifecycle of file movement, transformation, and delivery. This layer is responsible for executing complex, policy-driven workflows that automate how files are ingested, validated, secured, transformed, and routed within the enterprise or across external systems.

The orchestration process begins with file intake, which can be triggered by scheduled polling, event-based listeners, file system monitors, or real-time API calls. Once a file is detected, it enters a validation pipeline, where the system enforces business and security rules. These checks may include filename pattern verification, format and schema validation (e.g., XSD or JSON Schema), digital signature verification, and virus or malware scanning using integrated antivirus engines.

Following validation, the MFT engine may apply file transformation routines, converting data from one structured format to another. Common use cases include converting EDI documents into XML, transforming CSV files into JSON, or enriching flat files with metadata before transmission. These transformations are essential for interoperability between heterogeneous systems and trading partners.

Security operations such as encryption and decryption are also executed within this layer. Files may be encrypted using standards like PGP or AES before transmission to ensure confidentiality, or decrypted upon receipt for further internal processing. Key management is typically handled through integrated keystores or external HSMs (Hardware Security Modules), ensuring compliance with enterprise security policies and data protection regulations.

Once processed, files are routed to their final destinations, which can include external trading partners, internal applications, cloud storage providers (e.g., AWS S3, Azure Blob), or databases. The routing logic is often dynamic and driven by file metadata, content, or external business rules.

A key strength of the orchestration layer is its workflow automation capabilities. Administrators can define visual or script-based workflows that encode business logic, such as conditional branching, retries, error handling, notifications, and rollback procedures. This flexibility ensures operational resilience, even in complex or failure-prone data exchange environments.

To support enterprise-grade operations, this layer must be highly configurable and scalable, with features like parallel processing, transaction auditing, workflow versioning, and end-to-end tracking. These capabilities enable organizations to meet performance requirements, maintain regulatory compliance, and quickly troubleshoot issues when they arise.

2.4 File Storage and Retention Layer: Securing Data at Rest Across Its Lifecycle

The File Storage and Retention Layer plays a critical role in a Managed File Transfer (MFT) system by ensuring that all file data whether in transit, awaiting processing, or stored long-term is securely managed, auditable, and compliant with enterprise data governance policies. This layer provides the foundational storage infrastructure that supports both operational performance and regulatory obligations.

At the core of this layer are staging areas, which act as temporary, high-availability holding zones for files that are pending further actions such as validation, transformation, or delivery. These areas are optimized for short-lived, high-speed access and are typically isolated from persistent storage to reduce risk and improve processing efficiency.

For more sensitive or critical files, vaulted storage is used. These are encrypted repositories that enforce strict access controls, multi-factor authentication, and role-based permissions. Files stored here are often subject to regulatory requirements such as HIPAA, GDPR, or SOX, and the use of encryption standards like AES-256 ensures confidentiality even in the event of physical or logical compromise.

Organizations that require long-term retention for compliance or audit readiness utilize archival storage tiers. These are designed for immutable, tamper-resistant storage of historical file data, often integrated with WORM (Write Once, Read Many) technologies. Archival files are indexed, timestamped, and logged in detail to ensure chain-of-custody traceability and to support regulatory audits or eDiscovery processes.

Modern MFT platforms also support cloud-based storage integration, enabling scalable, redundant storage across services such as Amazon S3, Microsoft Azure Blob Storage, and Google Cloud Storage. These integrations allow organizations to take advantage of geo-redundancy, cost-effective tiering, and automatic failover, while still maintaining centralized visibility and control over data assets.

Administrators are empowered to define granular data retention policies that align with business and legal requirements. These include automated deletion schedules, expiration rules, retention windows, and legal hold exceptions. Every action whether a file is stored, moved, expired, or deleted is captured in an audit log, enabling full accountability and traceability across the file lifecycle.

By combining secure storage mechanisms with intelligent policy enforcement and auditability, the File Storage and Retention Layer ensures that file data remains protected, compliant, and operationally accessible throughout its lifecycle in the MFT ecosystem.

2.5 Integration and Application Connectivity Layer: Bridging MFT with the Enterprise Digital Core

In modern digital ecosystems, Managed File Transfer (MFT) platforms are no longer isolated utilities that simply move files from point A to point B. Instead, they must operate as deeply integrated components of the enterprise architecture, orchestrating the seamless flow of data across business-critical applications and platforms. The Integration and Application Connectivity Layer serves as the interface between the MFT engine and the broader enterprise technology stack, ensuring that file-based data is not just delivered, but is also processed, consumed, and acted upon by relevant business systems in real time.

At the forefront of this layer is native integration with ERP and CRM systems, which are the operational backbone of most enterprises. Modern MFT platforms offer pre-built connectors and adapters for systems such as SAP (via IDoc, RFC, or BAPI), Oracle E-Business Suite, NetSuite, and Salesforce. These connectors ensure that inbound files such as invoices, purchase orders, or customer data can be automatically mapped and ingested into transactional workflows without manual intervention. Conversely, outbound data generated by these systems can be extracted, transformed into required formats (e.g., EDI, XML, CSV), and securely transferred to trading partners or downstream platforms.

In addition to application-layer integration, this layer provides robust database connectivity through industry-standard protocols such as ODBC (Open Database Connectivity) and JDBC (Java Database Connectivity). This allows MFT workflows to interact directly with databases like Microsoft SQL Server, Oracle Database, MySQL, PostgreSQL, and others for tasks such as:

- Metadata enrichment

- Data validation or lookups

- Logging of file transfer events

- Inserting or retrieving business records based on file content

To enable modern API-driven architectures, the MFT platform exposes and consumes RESTful and SOAP-based APIs through built-in API gateways. These APIs allow other enterprise applications, microservices, and cloud-native workloads to programmatically initiate transfers, retrieve status updates, upload/download files, or trigger processing workflows. This is especially useful in hybrid environments, where integration across on-premises, cloud, and third-party services is required.

Furthermore, MFT systems increasingly integrate with messaging middleware and event-driven platforms, providing support for JMS (Java Message Service), Apache Kafka, IBM MQ, RabbitMQ, and similar event bus technologies. This enables the MFT platform to both publish and subscribe to business events, allowing files to be processed or transferred in response to real-time triggers. For example, a new customer record inserted into a CRM system could emit an event to Kafka, which in turn triggers a file transfer containing onboarding data to an external partner or system.

Crucially, this layer transforms MFT from a standalone system into a connected data exchange hub, one that's capable of driving automated business outcomes. It facilitates bidirectional data exchange, ensures data consistency and synchronization, and eliminates silos by making file-based exchanges an active part of enterprise integration patterns.

Whether integrating with monolithic ERP suites or modern, distributed microservices architectures, the Integration and Application Connectivity Layer ensures that every file transfer is intelligently routed, contextually enriched, and operationally aligned with the business processes it supports.

2.6 Monitoring, Logging, and Governance Layer: Ensuring Visibility, Compliance, and Operational Control

The Monitoring, Logging, and Governance Layer represents the final, but arguably most critical, tier of a modern Managed File Transfer (MFT) architecture. While upstream layers focus on execution and data movement, this layer ensures operational visibility, audit readiness, and compliance enforcement functions that are essential in regulated industries and enterprise environments where data flows must be both reliable and accountable.

At the forefront of this layer are real-time operational dashboards, which provide administrators and operations teams with at-a-glance visibility into system health and file transfer activity. These dashboards typically display active job status, queued or pending transfers, processing durations, throughput metrics, and SLA adherence indicators. By monitoring these key performance metrics, organizations can proactively detect bottlenecks, delays, or abnormal patterns in file flow before they escalate into service disruptions.

To complement real-time visibility, this layer includes a robust alerting and notification framework. Administrators can configure automated alerts via email, SNMP traps, or webhook integrations to signal failures, unauthorized access attempts, file validation errors, and SLA breaches. These alerts support rapid incident response and can be integrated into existing IT service management (ITSM) platforms, enabling coordinated remediation efforts across support teams.

A cornerstone of governance is the generation of immutable, tamper-proof audit logs. Every file movement, user action, system event, and security-related transaction is recorded with detailed metadata such as timestamps, usernames, IP addresses, protocol used, and file hashes. These logs are often cryptographically signed or stored in write-once repositories to prevent tampering, ensuring the integrity and forensic reliability of audit trails.

For enterprises operating under strict regulatory mandates, MFT platforms provide built-in compliance modules. These include predefined report templates and log formats tailored to frameworks such as HIPAA, PCI-DSS, GDPR, SOX, and FISMA. Organizations can generate periodic compliance reports for internal governance, external auditors, or regulatory bodies, significantly reducing the effort required to demonstrate adherence to industry standards.

Finally, this layer integrates with Security Information and Event Management (SIEM) platforms such as Splunk, IBM QRadar, ArcSight, or Elastic Security. By exporting logs and event streams to a centralized SIEM, the MFT platform becomes a part of the broader enterprise threat detection and response ecosystem. Security analysts can correlate MFT activities with network events, user behaviors, and known threat indicators to detect anomalies, investigate breaches, and enforce enterprise-wide security policies.

In essence, the Monitoring, Logging, and Governance Layer elevates MFT from a utility into a trustworthy, compliant, and audit-ready enterprise service ensuring that data transfers are not only successful but also transparent, traceable, and secure.

2.7 Deployment Patterns: Adapting MFT Architecture to Enterprise Needs

Modern Managed File Transfer (MFT) solutions offer flexible deployment patterns designed to meet the diverse architectural, regulatory, and operational requirements of today's enterprises.

The choice of deployment model significantly impacts performance, scalability, governance, and integration, making it a strategic decision in the overall data flow architecture.

In a **Centralized Architecture**, all file transfers, workflows, user authentications, and routing decisions are handled by a single MFT server or clustered environment. This model is ideal for organizations seeking unified visibility, simplified policy enforcement, and centralized governance. It streamlines auditing and security management by consolidating logs, access control, and configurations within a single system. High-availability clustering and load balancing can be employed to ensure resilience and scalability under growing workloads.

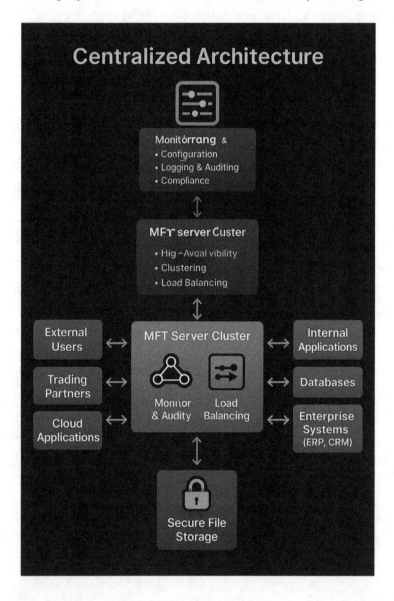

The **Agent-Based or Distributed** Architecture introduces lightweight MFT agents at remote locations such as branch offices, cloud virtual machines, or partner sites. These agents perform local file pickup, delivery, preprocessing, or validation, and relay results back to the central MFT engine. This model excels in edge computing scenarios, where bandwidth optimization, network segmentation, or local processing requirements are critical. It also supports offline file queuing and autonomous operation, enabling robust performance in intermittent or low-connectivity environments. Centralized orchestration ensures that enterprise-wide policies, workflows, and compliance controls remain intact, even as execution is distributed.

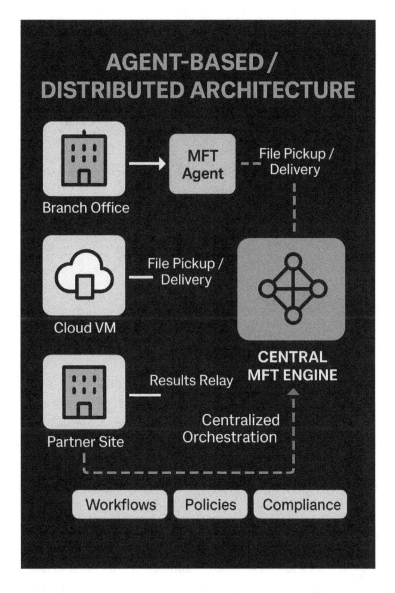

For organizations embracing cloud strategies, the Hybrid Cloud Architecture blends on-premises control with cloud-native scalability. In this model, internal data transfers and sensitive operations remain within the enterprise perimeter supporting data residency, sovereignty, and low-latency requirements while partner-facing or high-volume exchanges are offloaded to the cloud. Cloud-based components can scale elastically, provide geographically distributed endpoints, and integrate with cloud object storage and SaaS applications. This pattern is particularly useful for global enterprises, multi-cloud environments, and B2B integration hubs needing both flexibility and control.

Hybrid Cloud and-Onprem MFT Architecture

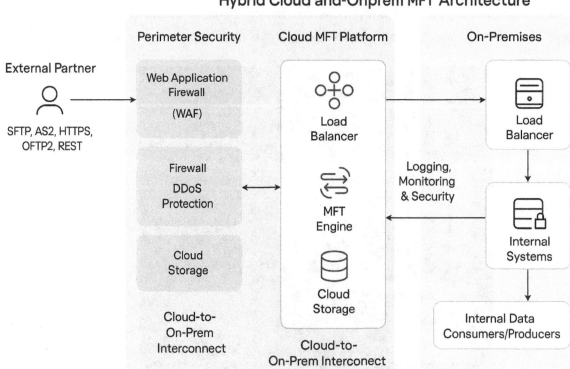

Each deployment pattern offers unique strengths, and in many advanced use cases, a blended strategy is employed leveraging centralized management, distributed agents, and cloud-native components in concert. The ability of MFT platforms to support these varied architectures is essential for aligning data transfer strategies with evolving business and infrastructure needs.

2.7.1 Centralized vs. Decentralized MFT Architectures – A Deep Technical Comparison

When designing a Managed File Transfer (MFT) architecture, one of the most critical architectural decisions is choosing between a centralized and a decentralized (often agent-based) deployment model. Both approaches have distinct advantages and are selected based on organizational size, security posture, compliance obligations, operational complexity, and scalability requirements.

Centralized MFT Architecture

A centralized MFT architecture consolidates all file transfer operations whether internal or external through a single, central MFT platform or cluster. This model is the most common in enterprise environments that prioritize uniform control, simplified governance, and centralized auditing.

Technical Characteristics:

- All external trading partners, applications, and internal systems connect to a central server or high-availability cluster.

- All workflows, encryption/decryption tasks, scheduling, and routing are orchestrated from one location.

- Centralized logging, monitoring, and SLA tracking are streamlined through a single point of visibility.

Advantages:

- Unified control plane for administration, configuration, and compliance enforcement.

- Easier to enforce data governance policies, such as encryption standards, retention rules, and access controls.

- Simplifies audit readiness, with all logs and file activity centralized in one repository.

- Reduces administrative overhead to only one instance of the platform to maintain, patch, and secure.

Limitations:

- Scalability bottlenecks may arise if the centralized node becomes overloaded with high volumes of concurrent transfers or workflows.

- Introduces a single point of failure if HA/DR strategies are not properly implemented.

- May struggle in multi-region or latency-sensitive deployments, where all data must be routed through the central hub.

This architecture is ideal for organizations with a controlled IT environment, such as banks, healthcare providers, or government agencies, where tight compliance controls and full audit traceability are mandatory.

Decentralized (Agent-Based) MFT Architecture

A decentralized MFT architecture distributes processing across multiple lightweight agents deployed at remote locations, edge sites, or partner endpoints. These agents initiate and manage file transfers autonomously, while being orchestrated centrally.

Technical Characteristics:

- Agents are installed on remote servers, branch offices, cloud VMs, or trading partner environments.

- Each agent handles its own encryption, automation, file movement, and local retry mechanisms.

- A central controller or orchestration engine coordinates policies, workflows, and visibility across all agents.

Advantages:

- Reduces network load by enabling local processing and peer-to-peer transfers, rather than routing all traffic through a central node.

- Ideal for hybrid or distributed enterprises, such as global supply chains, logistics firms, or retailers with hundreds of remote locations.

- Improves performance and resiliency, especially in regions with intermittent connectivity or limited bandwidth.

- Increases operational agility, as agents can be updated or configured remotely via central orchestration.

Limitations:

- Greater complexity in deployment and lifecycle management each agent must be monitored, updated, and secured.

- Log aggregation and compliance tracking can become fragmented unless consolidated into a central SIEM or monitoring solution.

- May introduce inconsistency in configurations or security controls if governance is not enforced uniformly.

This model is preferred by organizations with highly distributed infrastructures, where local autonomy, resilience to connectivity issues, and data proximity are more valuable than centralized control.

Comparison:

Feature	Centralized MFT	Decentralized MFT (Agent-Based)
Control & Governance	High – single control point	Moderate – policy push to agents
Scalability	Limited by central resources	Horizontally scalable via agents
Latency & Performance	May introduce delays over distance	Optimized for remote and branch operations
Fault Tolerance	Requires HA/DR architecture	Built-in via distributed nodes
Deployment Complexity	Simpler setup and management	More complex due to agent management
Security Control	Centralized enforcement	Must enforce uniform security policies
Use Cases	Compliance-heavy, regulated sectors	Logistics, retail chains, global enterprises

Hybrid Architectures – The Best of Both Worlds

Modern MFT platforms (e.g., GoAnywhere, Cleo Integration Cloud, IBM Sterling) often support hybrid deployment models, allowing organizations to use central orchestration with decentralized agents where needed. This enables:

- Centralized visibility and governance for compliance.

- Decentralized processing for performance and regional autonomy.

- Seamless integration with cloud, SaaS, and edge environments.

2.8 High availability and Disaster Recovery

As file transfers evolve into mission-critical operations for modern enterprises, ensuring continuous availability and rapid recoverability of the MFT infrastructure becomes paramount. Downtime of even a few minutes can disrupt supply chains, delay transactions, violate SLAs, and jeopardize compliance with regulatory standards such as HIPAA, PCI-DSS, or SOX. This makes High Availability (HA) and Disaster Recovery (DR) indispensable components of a resilient and enterprise-grade MFT deployment.

High Availability in MFT refers to the system's ability to maintain **uninterrupted operations and service continuity**, even in the event of hardware, software, or network component failures. The goal is to **eliminate single points of failure** and **ensure consistent uptime**, often targeting 99.99% or higher.

2.8.1 Clustering and Load Balancing: Ensuring High Availability and Scalability in MFT

In enterprise-grade Managed File Transfer (MFT) environments, clustering and load balancing are foundational architectural strategies designed to deliver high availability, fault tolerance, and horizontal scalability. By deploying MFT servers in a clustered configuration, organizations can distribute processing workloads across multiple nodes, ensuring consistent performance even as file volumes and concurrent sessions grow.

A typical MFT cluster consists of two or more active nodes, each capable of handling connections, executing workflows, and processing file transfers independently, but operating in coordination with a shared backend such as a centralized database, message bus, or distributed file system. This shared infrastructure ensures that all nodes remain state-aware, meaning session metadata, user credentials, file status, and audit logs are consistently synchronized across the cluster. This is critical for enabling session handoff and recovery during failover scenarios.

To optimize traffic distribution and prevent bottlenecks, MFT clusters are fronted by a load balancer commonly used by solutions like F5 BIG-IP, HAProxy, NGINX, or cloud-native equivalents such as AWS ELB or Azure Application Gateway. The load balancer manages incoming client connections and intelligently routes them to the appropriate node using algorithms such as:

- **Round Robin** (evenly rotating across all nodes),

- **Least Connections** (routing to the node with the fewest active sessions),

- **IP Hashing** (to maintain client affinity),

- Geographic Routing (directing clients to the nearest datacenter or node based on location).

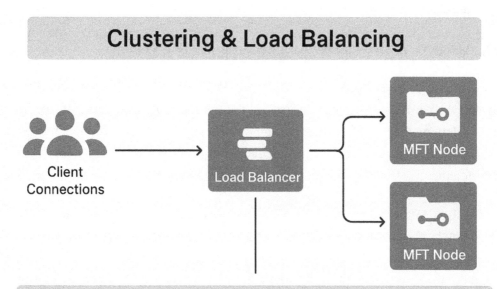

Advanced configurations may leverage health checks and monitoring hooks to detect node health and responsiveness in real time. If a node becomes unresponsive or fails, the load balancer will automatically reroute sessions to healthy nodes without requiring client-side changes. This failover capability ensures that active transfers or login attempts are not disrupted, maintaining service continuity and upholding SLAs (Service Level Agreements).

Some MFT platforms also support active-active clustering, where all nodes process requests simultaneously, and session stickiness, which maintains session continuity across multiple HTTP/S requests from the same user. Others may use message queues (e.g., Kafka, RabbitMQ) or distributed workflow engines to coordinate task execution and job distribution.

Moreover, clustering enables elastic scalability, allowing organizations to dynamically scale out (add more nodes during peak loads) or scale in (reduce resource usage during off-peak hours), particularly when deployed in containerized environments using Kubernetes or Docker Swarm.

In summary, clustering and load balancing are essential for building resilient, performant MFT systems. They ensure that file transfer operations are not only fast and efficient, but also fault-tolerant, scalable, and ready for enterprise demands, regardless of geographic distribution or workload variability.

2.8.2 Active-Active vs. Active-Passive Architectures in MFT Systems

When architecting high-availability (HA) Managed File Transfer (MFT) environments, the choice between Active-Active and Active-Passive configurations plays a crucial role in determining system resilience, performance, and complexity. These two models represent distinct strategies for ensuring service continuity in the face of hardware failure, software crashes, or planned maintenance.

In an Active-Active Architecture, multiple MFT nodes operate concurrently, each actively processing connections, executing workflows, and handling data transfers in parallel. Load balancing mechanisms distribute incoming requests across all available nodes using algorithms such as round-robin, least connections, or application-aware metrics. This configuration maximizes system throughput, improves scalability, and ensures seamless failover if one node becomes unavailable, its workload is redistributed in real time to the remaining active nodes without disrupting ongoing sessions. Shared storage or session replication is typically required to maintain state consistency across nodes, enabling session affinity or "stickiness" for protocols like HTTPS or SFTP. Active-active clusters are ideal for mission-critical MFT environments with high transaction volumes and strict SLA (Service Level Agreement) requirements.

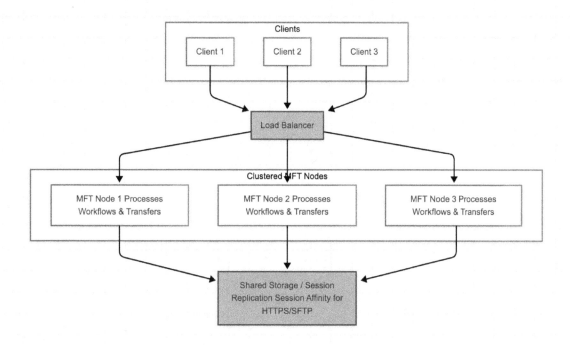

In contrast, an Active-Passive Architecture features a primary (active) node that handles all MFT operations under normal conditions, while one or more secondary (passive) nodes remain idle or in a "hot standby" state. These standby nodes continuously monitor the health of the primary system via heartbeat protocols or cluster management software and are triggered to take over only in the event of a failure. Upon detection of an outage, the passive node promotes itself to active status, mounts the necessary storage, and resumes services. Although this architecture is simpler to implement and manage, particularly for small- to mid-sized deployments, it involves a delay during failover, typically ranging from seconds to a few minutes depending on how quickly services can be restored. Additionally, since the passive node is not utilized under normal conditions, this model offers lower resource efficiency and can represent higher total cost of ownership if hardware is underutilized.

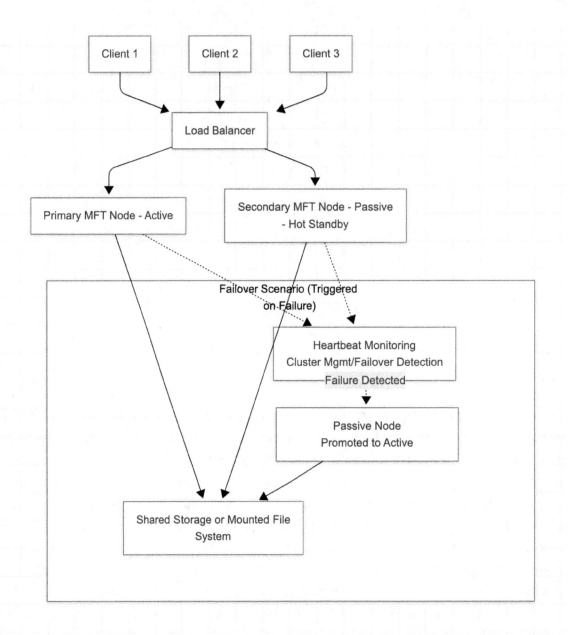

From a deployment standpoint, Active-Active configurations usually require:

- A load balancer with health checks and failover awareness

- Shared session management (via a database, distributed cache, or stateful file system)

- Cluster-aware MFT software capable of horizontal scaling

Whereas Active-Passive setups often use:

- A failover clustering service (e.g., Windows Server Failover Clustering, Pacemaker/Corosync)

- Virtual IPs (VIPs) for endpoint consistency

- A shared file system or replicated data volumes between nodes

In summary, Active-Active architectures provide superior performance and availability but demand greater investment in infrastructure and orchestration. Active-Passive designs are more straightforward and cost-effective, but introduce latency in failover and may not scale well under peak load conditions. The decision between the two should align with the organization's tolerance for downtime, transactional throughput needs, and operational complexity limits.

2.8.3 Session Persistence in High-Availability MFT Environments

In high-availability (HA) Managed File Transfer (MFT) deployments, session persistence also known as session stickiness is a critical requirement for maintaining stateful protocol connections, especially for SFTP, FTPS, and HTTPS. These protocols establish secure, long-lived sessions that involve authentication handshakes, encryption key negotiations, and transactional state management. If a client session is terminated or redirected mid-transfer due to a failover or load balancing event, it can result in transfer failures, data corruption, or user disruption unless handled with precision.

To address this, MFT platforms designed for HA environments often implement session-aware clustering mechanisms. This involves the use of session replication or state synchronization, where session-related data (e.g., session tokens, keys, metadata, transfer progress) is actively shared among nodes in the cluster typically via a distributed cache (like Redis or Hazelcast), shared database, or in-memory session store. This allows other nodes to seamlessly resume an interrupted session in the event of node failure or network interruption, without requiring the client to reauthenticate or restart the transfer.

From an infrastructure standpoint, load balancers play an essential role in enforcing session persistence. They are configured to support source IP affinity, application-layer cookie-based stickiness, or SSL session ID affinity, ensuring that all requests from a given client are consistently routed to the same MFT node for the duration of the session. In HTTPS scenarios, for example, SSL session IDs or tokens stored in cookies can be used by the load balancer to bind a user to a specific server node. For SFTP or FTPS, which rely on long-lived TCP connections, load balancers must maintain TCP connection affinity to prevent session disruption.

Advanced MFT platforms may also offer graceful failover capabilities, which delay failover operations until in-flight sessions have completed, or replicate session state proactively so that switchover is imperceptible to the client. This level of resilience is especially important in B2B integrations, where large file transfers or high-volume automation workflows require non-disruptive continuity.

In summary, session persistence is a cornerstone of reliable and secure MFT operation in clustered and HA environments. It ensures that the user experience remains seamless and that critical file transfers can complete successfully even during infrastructure transitions or failover scenarios.

2.8.4 Shared Configuration and Storage in Clustered MFT Deployments

In high-availability (HA) and clustered Managed File Transfer (MFT) environments, shared configuration and storage is a foundational architectural element that ensures consistency, resilience, and operational integrity across multiple MFT nodes. Rather than maintaining individual configurations on each server which can lead to configuration drift, synchronization issues, and administrative overhead, key operational artifacts are centralized in shared repositories that are accessible to all nodes in the cluster.

These shared repositories may consist of network file systems (e.g., NFS, SMB), clustered or replicated relational databases (e.g., Oracle RAC, PostgreSQL with streaming replication), or cloud-based object storage platforms (such as Amazon S3, Azure Blob Storage, or Google Cloud Storage). Depending on the deployment model (on-premises, cloud, or hybrid), organizations may also use distributed configuration services like HashiCorp Consul, etcd, or AWS Systems Manager Parameter Store to store runtime configurations in a secure and highly available manner.

The types of data stored in shared configuration systems typically include:

- Workflow definitions and orchestration rules

- User accounts, authentication policies, and access control lists

- Encryption keys and TLS/SSL certificates

- Connection profiles and routing logic

- File retention policies, metadata schemas, and logging parameters

- Custom scripts or pre/post-processing handlers

By centralizing this information, all nodes in the MFT cluster operate using identical business logic, user entitlements, and security constraints, regardless of where the file transfer job is executed. This eliminates inconsistencies that might otherwise arise when scaling out horizontally or during failover scenarios. It also simplifies maintenance and change management, since updates to configuration files or credentials need only be applied once, in the shared location, rather than individually across each server.

In more advanced implementations, shared configuration layers are paired with version control systems (e.g., Git) and CI/CD pipelines (e.g., Jenkins, GitHub Actions, Azure DevOps) to manage deployment of changes through controlled, auditable workflows. This enables infrastructure-as-code (IaC) practices and allows for automated configuration promotion across environments (dev, test, prod), improving both agility and governance.

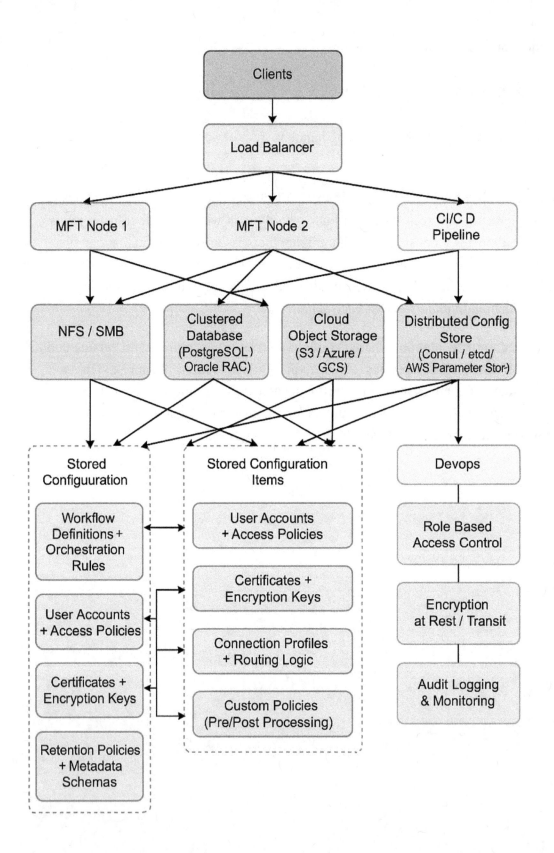

From a security and performance perspective, access to shared configuration and storage repositories is tightly controlled through RBAC (role-based access control), network segmentation, and encryption at rest and in transit. Read/write access is granted only to authorized nodes and administrators, and activity is often logged and monitored for audit and compliance purposes.

In summary, shared configuration and storage is essential for delivering a scalable, reliable, and centrally managed MFT platform. It ensures that all nodes in a clustered or HA deployment function cohesively, maintain policy consistency, and can be maintained efficiently with minimal operational risk.

2.8.5 Health Monitoring and Self-Healing in MFT Platforms

In high-availability and mission-critical Managed File Transfer (MFT) environments, health monitoring and self-healing mechanisms play a vital role in ensuring continuous service availability, operational resilience, and rapid recovery from failures. These capabilities are especially critical in environments that demand non-stop file movement, regulatory compliance, and strong service-level agreements (SLAs).

At the core of health monitoring is heartbeat-based status detection, where MFT nodes are continuously polled or self-report their operational state at regular intervals. A heartbeat mechanism may include agent-based monitoring, API-driven health endpoints, or cluster-aware orchestration tools that check critical service components such as file listeners, workflow engines, database connections, and protocol services (e.g., SFTP, HTTPS, AS2). If a node fails to respond within a defined threshold, it is flagged as unhealthy and removed from the active load balancer pool to avoid routing new traffic to it.

Modern MFT platforms such as Axway SecureTransport, GoAnywhere MFT, IBM Sterling, and others go beyond basic monitoring by offering self-healing automation. These platforms include built-in routines that can automatically attempt to:

- Restart failed services or daemons (e.g., protocol listeners, database connections, workflow schedulers)

- Retry failed or interrupted file transfers, with exponential backoff or retry limits

- Trigger alerts or escalation workflows if auto-recovery is unsuccessful

Self-healing logic is often managed through policy-based configuration or event-driven rule engines, which define how specific failure scenarios should be handled. For example, if a file transfer job fails due to a temporary remote server issue (e.g., a partner SFTP endpoint is down), the system can pause the job and retry it after a specified interval. If the issue persists beyond the allowed retry count, the system may escalate the incident by sending notifications via email, SNMP, webhook, or ITSM integration (e.g., ServiceNow, PagerDuty).

To further enhance resilience, MFT platforms may be integrated with external monitoring and observability stacks, such as:

- Prometheus + Grafana (for metrics collection and alerting)

- Nagios, Zabbix, or SolarWinds (for infrastructure monitoring)

- ELK Stack, Datadog, logstash, Splunk, or QRadar (for log aggregation and anomaly detection)

These tools can provide real-time dashboards, trend analysis, and automated response triggers for CPU spikes, memory leaks, disk utilization, and protocol-level error patterns.

Additionally, some advanced platforms support cluster-wide awareness, where if one node goes down, its in-flight sessions, queued jobs, or pending workflows can be resumed or rerouted to other healthy nodes using session replication or distributed job queues. This ensures that service continuity is maintained without data loss or user disruption.

In summary, health monitoring and self-healing mechanisms are essential to delivering robust, intelligent, and autonomous MFT environments. They minimize downtime, reduce manual intervention, and enable platforms to respond proactively to failures ensuring consistent data delivery, even in unpredictable or degraded infrastructure conditions.

2.8.6 Disaster Recovery (DR)

Geographically Redundant Deployments for MFT Systems

In today's globally distributed, always-on digital landscape, Managed File Transfer (MFT) platforms are increasingly deployed in geographically redundant configurations to ensure business continuity, regulatory compliance, and operational resilience. A geographically redundant deployment involves provisioning the MFT solution across multiple data centers or cloud regions, where one location serves as the primary production site, and others act as secondary or standby nodes for failover, disaster recovery, or regional access optimization.

This architectural pattern is particularly valuable for enterprises with a global footprint or for those operating in highly regulated sectors such as finance, healthcare, and government, where uptime guarantees, data sovereignty, and failover readiness are mandated by service-level agreements (SLAs) and compliance frameworks.

Deployment Models and Data Synchronization

In a typical setup, the primary region handles all active file transfer operations, user authentications, workflow executions, and system orchestration. The secondary site, which can be another physical data center or a logically isolated cloud region (e.g., AWS Availability Zone, Azure Region), remains passive or in hot standby mode, continually synchronized with the primary.

Data consistency and state synchronization across sites are achieved using:

- Database replication mechanisms like PostgreSQL streaming replication, Oracle Data Guard, or SQL Server Always On to mirror configuration, user accounts, and transaction logs in real time.

- Object storage replication across cloud regions (e.g., Amazon S3 cross-region replication, Azure Geo-Redundant Storage) to ensure that file payloads and metadata remain available in both primary and secondary locations.

- Filesystem-level tools like rsync, DRBD, or distributed file systems (e.g., GlusterFS, Ceph) to sync configuration files, scripts, certificates, and logs.

Advanced MFT platforms also support real-time job replication and stateful session synchronization, enabling an active session at one site to resume at the secondary site in the event of a failure without requiring the user to restart the file transfer process.

Failover & Traffic Redirection Strategies

Failover mechanisms are typically orchestrated using:

- Global Server Load Balancing (GSLB) with DNS-based failover, directing clients to the healthiest region.

- BGP-based route control, allowing ISPs to shift traffic to the backup site when a primary region becomes unreachable.

- Cloud-native tools such as AWS Route 53, Azure Traffic Manager, or Google Cloud Load Balancing, which monitor health probes and shift workloads automatically when a region becomes unhealthy.

Some MFT solutions provide auto-switchover capabilities, while others require manual intervention or orchestration via CI/CD pipelines and infrastructure-as-code tools (e.g., Terraform, Ansible) to rehydrate infrastructure and services in the secondary location.

Security & Compliance Considerations

Geographical redundancy introduces new security challenges, such as ensuring:

- Consistent identity and access management across regions

- End-to-end encryption of data at rest and in transit

- Audit log synchronization for regulatory tracking

- Geo-fencing or data residency controls to comply with GDPR, HIPAA, or country-specific data protection laws

To address these, organizations often deploy federated identity systems, centralized SIEM platforms, and data classification policies that govern cross-region operations.

Data and Configuration Backups in MFT Systems

In any secure and enterprise-grade Managed File Transfer (MFT) deployment, implementing a robust data and configuration backup strategy is essential for ensuring operational resilience, disaster recovery readiness, and compliance with internal policies and industry regulations. MFT platforms are responsible not only for transferring mission-critical files but also for enforcing security, executing automation workflows, and maintaining audit trails making the loss of configuration or operational metadata potentially catastrophic.

A well-designed backup plan includes regularly scheduled backups of all key components such as:

- Configuration files (protocol settings, connection profiles, system parameters)

- User metadata and authentication policies (user accounts, roles, access control lists)

- Audit logs and transaction history (for regulatory reporting and forensic analysis)

- Encryption keys and certificate stores (critical for decrypting archived or in-transit data)

- Workflow definitions and job schedules (including pre/post-processing scripts and triggers)

These backups must be stored in encrypted formats using strong algorithms such as AES-256, and must be transferred to secure, offsite locations such as cloud-based object storage (e.g., AWS S3 with server-side encryption), remote backup servers, or air-gapped appliances. To protect against data corruption or compromise, many organizations use immutable storage options (e.g., S3 Object Lock, WORM-compliant storage) that prevent deletion or modification for a defined retention period.

Advanced backup strategies often include differential or incremental backups to optimize storage and bandwidth, as well as point-in-time snapshots for quick recovery from configuration errors or ransomware attacks. Modern MFT platforms may offer native tools or APIs for exporting system state or support integration with third-party backup solutions like Veeam, Commvault, Rubrik, or cloud-native services such as AWS Backup, Azure Backup, and Google Cloud Backup & DR.

Just as important as creating backups is ensuring their restorability. Backups should be tested regularly through scheduled restore drills or automated recovery simulations, verifying that critical services including file transfer workflows, user access, and encrypted data handling can be restored without data loss or misconfiguration. These tests are vital for passing audits, validating RTO/RPO objectives, and maintaining business continuity under real-world failure conditions.

Access to backup data must be strictly governed using role-based access controls (RBAC), audit logging, and multi-factor authentication (MFA) to prevent unauthorized recovery or exfiltration of sensitive assets. Additionally, backup retention policies must align with regulatory and legal obligations, such as GDPR, HIPAA, PCI-DSS, and SOX, which may impose specific requirements for data storage duration, encryption, and geographic location.

In summary, effective data and configuration backup practices are a non-negotiable aspect of secure and resilient MFT operations. They ensure that even in the face of catastrophic failures whether due to system crashes, cyberattacks, or human error organizations can quickly recover, preserve compliance, and maintain uninterrupted business operations.

Failover and Switchover Mechanisms in MFT Environments

Ensuring service continuity is a critical requirement for enterprise Managed File Transfer (MFT) systems, particularly in environments where downtime impacts revenue, compliance, or partner trust. To address this, modern MFT platforms incorporate failover and switchover mechanisms that allow systems to recover rapidly from infrastructure outages, application failures, or site-level disasters. These mechanisms enable seamless redirection of traffic and reallocation of workloads between primary and disaster recovery (DR) sites, maintaining uninterrupted data flows even under failure conditions.

Failover typically refers to the automated transition of services from a failed or degraded primary system to a healthy standby system, while switchover is often a planned, manual process used during maintenance or testing that gracefully transfers active operations to a secondary system. Depending on the MFT platform and deployment architecture, failover can occur at various levels: application layer, database layer, file storage, or even network routing.

Advanced MFT solutions such as Axway SecureTransport, GoAnywhere MFT, and IBM Sterling File Gateway may include native high-availability clustering and site-awareness features that support automatic failover across data centers or cloud regions. In these setups, health checks and heartbeat signals are continuously exchanged between nodes or orchestrated by external systems (e.g., Kubernetes, Pacemaker, or cloud-native services like AWS Auto Scaling Groups). When a node or region becomes unavailable, the orchestrator reroutes sessions and workflows to the standby site, often with session replication and job queue preservation to minimize transfer disruptions.

Where automatic failover is not natively supported, organizations must rely on manual switchover procedures, triggered through disaster recovery runbooks, CI/CD pipelines, or infrastructure-as-code tools like Terraform, Ansible, or CloudFormation. In such cases, the recovery time objective (RTO) is longer and more dependent on operational readiness and administrative intervention.

A critical component of any failover strategy is traffic redirection, and this is most commonly handled at the DNS or load balancing layer. MFT endpoint URLs such as SFTP hostnames or HTTPS APIs must be managed through:

- Dynamic DNS (DDNS) services or short TTL values that allow rapid DNS updates when the active region changes.

- Global Server Load Balancing (GSLB) appliances or cloud-based tools (e.g., AWS Route 53, Azure Traffic Manager, Cloudflare Load Balancer) that perform health checks and redirect traffic automatically based on node availability or geographic proximity.

- Virtual IPs (VIPs) managed by failover clusters to provide seamless endpoint continuity within LAN or hybrid architectures.

To ensure reliability, regular failover testing and validation drills are essential. These exercises confirm not only the technical efficacy of the failover logic but also the coordination between systems, DNS propagation, and operational procedures. Additionally, logs and metrics should be captured and sent to centralized SIEM platforms to ensure visibility and auditability during transition events.

RTO and RPO in MFT Disaster Recovery Planning

In enterprise Managed File Transfer (MFT) environments, designing for disaster recovery (DR) and high availability (HA) requires a precise understanding of two key metrics: Recovery Time Objective (RTO) and Recovery Point Objective (RPO). These parameters define the operational expectations for restoring service and minimizing data loss in the event of a system failure, infrastructure outage, or regional disaster.

RTO (Recovery Time Objective) refers to the maximum allowable duration of downtime before the MFT system must be fully restored and operational again. It represents the time window within which critical file transfer capabilities such as job execution, protocol services (e.g., SFTP, HTTPS), user authentication, and routing workflows must be brought back online to avoid unacceptable business impact. In practical terms, an RTO of 15 minutes means the organization can tolerate up to 15 minutes of system unavailability before experiencing serious operational or contractual consequences.

RPO (Recovery Point Objective), on the other hand, defines the maximum acceptable age of data that may be lost during a recovery scenario. It is typically measured in seconds or minutes and determines how much transaction or file data the system can afford to lose without breaching compliance standards or disrupting business workflows. An RPO near zero implies that real-time or near-real-time replication of configuration data, workflow states, and file payloads is in place, ensuring that no meaningful data is lost during a failover or restore process.

Leading MFT platforms, such as Axway, IBM Sterling, GoAnywhere, and MOVEit, can be configured to achieve aggressive RTO and RPO targets through a combination of architectural strategies:

- Real-time database replication (e.g., Oracle Data Guard, SQL Server Always On, PostgreSQL streaming replication) ensures that configuration data, audit logs, and user sessions are mirrored between active and standby nodes with minimal delay.

- Session persistence and job checkpointing allow transfers in progress to resume without reprocessing the entire file or restarting workflows.

- Distributed file systems or cross-region object storage replication maintain a consistent copy of inbound/outbound files and metadata across geographic locations.

- Automated failover orchestration using tools like Kubernetes, HAProxy with health checks, cloud-native failover services (e.g., AWS Route 53, Azure Traffic Manager), or infrastructure-as-code automation (Terraform, Ansible) accelerates recovery operations and reduces manual intervention.

Organizations that demand sub-15-minute RTOs and near-zero RPOs must not only implement the right technology stack, but also enforce disciplined operational practices, such as:

- Continuous health monitoring and alerting

- Frequent DR testing and validation drills

- Immutable and encrypted backups

- Configuration and code versioning via CI/CD pipelines

Achieving tight RTO/RPO objectives is especially critical for sectors like finance, healthcare, and supply chain, where even brief disruptions in file transfer operations can result in regulatory penalties, SLA breaches, or data integrity issues. Moreover, aligning these recovery objectives with business impact analysis (BIA) helps prioritize recovery investments based on the criticality of specific MFT workflows.

Disaster Recovery Testing for MFT Systems

In a highly interconnected and compliance-driven enterprise environment, Disaster Recovery (DR) testing is a critical operational discipline that ensures the resilience, recoverability, and continuity of Managed File Transfer (MFT) systems. While implementing failover infrastructure and replication technologies is essential, regular and structured DR testing is the only way to validate whether these mechanisms will function as expected during a real-world disaster scenario.

Disaster Recovery testing involves the deliberate simulation of failure events such as infrastructure outages, application-level crashes, network partitioning, or regional unavailability to assess how quickly and accurately the MFT environment can recover. The objective is to verify that Recovery Time Objectives (RTO) and Recovery Point Objectives (RPO) are being met, while also identifying gaps in configuration, orchestration, or operational procedures that could impede recovery efforts.

Typical DR test scenarios in an MFT context include:

- Site failover simulation, where the primary data center or cloud region is declared unavailable, triggering automatic or manual switchover to a secondary site.

- DNS cutover drills, in which endpoint hostnames (e.g., SFTP, HTTPS URLs) are redirected to alternate environments via dynamic DNS, Global Server Load Balancing (GSLB), or cloud-based routing platforms like AWS Route 53 or Azure Traffic Manager.

- Session resumption and job replay testing, which validates the platform's ability to preserve or recover in-flight transfers, pending workflows, and scheduled jobs using checkpointing, transaction logs, or workflow history.

- Backup restore validation, where configuration snapshots, user metadata, certificates, and encryption keys are restored from encrypted backups to confirm data integrity and platform functionality.

- Network isolation exercises, which simulate connectivity failures to critical components like authentication services (LDAP/AD), databases, or cloud storage buckets, ensuring that fault tolerance is not just site-specific but also component-resilient.

In more advanced environments, DR tests are integrated into DevSecOps pipelines using Infrastructure-as-Code (IaC) tools like Terraform or Ansible to automate the provisioning, teardown, and validation of DR environments. This not only accelerates testing cycles but also ensures configuration consistency across primary and secondary regions. Additionally, SIEM and observability platforms (e.g., Splunk, ELK Stack, Prometheus + Grafana) are used to track DR test outcomes, correlate logs, and identify anomalies during the simulated recovery process.

Organizations that take DR readiness seriously also implement structured documentation and audit trails as part of the test. These include step-by-step execution logs, success/failure metrics, lessons learned, and change recommendations. Such documentation is invaluable for internal governance and is often required for demonstrating compliance with regulatory standards like ISO 27001, SOC 2, HIPAA, and PCI-DSS.

2.9 MFT On-Premises Architectures

An on-premises Managed File Transfer (MFT) architecture is deployed entirely within an organization's own data centers, private infrastructure, or virtualized environments. Despite the rise of cloud-based platforms, on-premises MFT remains a strategic choice for enterprises that require complete control over data, infrastructure, compliance enforcement, and internal integration. It is especially prevalent in heavily regulated sectors such as banking, government, manufacturing, and healthcare, where data sovereignty, network isolation, and custom security postures are paramount.

2.9.1 Full Infrastructure Control

For security-conscious and highly regulated organizations, the ability to exercise full infrastructure control over their Managed File Transfer (MFT) environment is not just a preference, it's a critical architectural requirement. Full control means the organization retains end-to-end ownership and governance over every infrastructure component that supports the MFT platform, including compute resources, storage backends, networking configurations, encryption modules, and disaster recovery systems. This model is typically implemented in on-premises, private cloud, or hybrid cloud environments where compliance mandates, data sovereignty, and internal security policies prohibit the use of fully managed or shared cloud services.

One of the core advantages of full infrastructure control is the ability to customize the network and security perimeter to meet exacting internal standards. Organizations can define granular firewall rules, enforce subnet segmentation, and deploy intrusion detection and prevention systems (IDS/IPS) that are tightly integrated with their broader cybersecurity framework. This level of control is especially important for industries governed by regulations such as HIPAA, FISMA, SOX, PCI-DSS, and GDPR, where data ingress and egress must be tightly monitored and controlled.

From a compute and deployment model perspective, organizations with full control can choose the infrastructure paradigm that best aligns with their operational, cost, and scalability goals. This includes running the MFT platform on bare-metal servers for maximum performance and hardware-level encryption support, on virtual machines (VMware, Hyper-V, KVM) for flexibility and isolation, or within containerized environments (e.g., Docker, Podman) orchestrated by platforms such as Kubernetes or OpenShift for scalability and automation. This flexibility allows MFT systems to seamlessly integrate into existing CI/CD pipelines, observability stacks, and DevSecOps workflows.

Full control also enables deep integration with enterprise identity management systems, such as Microsoft Active Directory (AD), LDAP directories, OAuth2 providers, or SAML-based federated identity platforms. This ensures that MFT systems can align with Single Sign-On (SSO) strategies, multi-factor authentication (MFA) policies, role-based access control (RBAC), and group-based policy enforcement, providing consistent identity governance across the enterprise.

Furthermore, organizations can dictate the encryption standards used for both data in transit and at rest, selecting and managing their own TLS certificates, PGP keyrings, HSM-integrated key vaults, or FIPS 140-2 validated modules. With full control over these cryptographic components, organizations eliminate dependence on third-party key management services and can enforce compliance-grade encryption policies throughout the data lifecycle.

Disaster recovery and high availability strategies also benefit from this model, as organizations can architect multi-region, active-passive or active-active failover environments, define custom RTO/RPO targets, and implement self-healing infrastructure orchestration using tools like Terraform, Ansible, or Cloud-native operators ensuring recovery readiness is fully aligned with internal risk profiles.

In essence, full infrastructure control transforms the MFT platform from a point solution into a fully governed, policy-aligned enterprise system. It empowers organizations to tailor every aspect of the deployment to meet stringent internal standards, maximize performance, and ensure security and compliance across the entire data exchange ecosystem.

2.9.2 Protocol and Access Management

On-prem MFT servers support a wide range of secure protocols:

- SFTP, FTPS, and HTTPS for encrypted transfer.

- AS2, AS4, and Connect:Direct for structured B2B integrations.

- Support for DMZ proxies, perimeter servers, and reverse proxy configurations to handle inbound and outbound traffic securely through the DMZ.

Role-based access control (RBAC), multi-factor authentication (MFA), and certificate-based access policies are applied natively, often with integration to existing PKI infrastructures.

2.9.3 On-Prem Deployment Topologies – A. Single-Node Architecture (Basic)

The Single-Node Architecture represents the most fundamental deployment model in on-premises Managed File Transfer (MFT) environments. In this topology, all core MFT components including the protocol listeners (e.g., SFTP, FTPS, HTTPS), workflow automation engine, user authentication modules, file storage, encryption services, and logging/auditing systems are hosted on a single physical or virtual server. This compact deployment style is commonly used in low-volume environments, such as small-to-mid-sized businesses, development labs, or internal departments that handle non-critical file exchanges without stringent uptime or performance requirements.

The simplicity of the single-node model offers several immediate advantages: easy setup, minimal infrastructure footprint, straightforward maintenance, and lower licensing and operational costs. It's an ideal choice for internal integrations, such as automated job schedulers moving files between local systems or uploading data from remote field offices into a central system. Additionally, it allows IT administrators to quickly prototype MFT configurations or test workflows before scaling into more complex topologies.

However, this architecture comes with inherent scalability and resilience limitations. Because all MFT services share the same computer, memory, storage, and network interface, performance bottlenecks can arise as transfer volumes increase, especially with concurrent users, large files, or complex workflows. Furthermore, a single point of failure exists: if the host server or operating system encounters hardware failure, configuration corruption, or resource exhaustion (e.g., full disk, memory leak), the entire MFT environment can become unavailable.

To mitigate this risk, some organizations implement local failover mechanisms such as:

- Virtual Machine snapshots and rollback policies

- Local backup and restore scripts for configuration and certificates

- RAID-protected storage and uninterruptible power supplies (UPS)

- Scheduled configuration exports and encrypted backups for disaster recovery

While these safeguards add a layer of protection, they do not offer the real-time failover or horizontal scalability required for enterprise-grade uptime guarantees. Therefore, single-node architectures are generally not recommended for production workloads involving external partners, regulatory compliance, or service-level agreements (SLAs) without an accompanying disaster recovery plan or a migration roadmap to multi-node or cluster configurations.

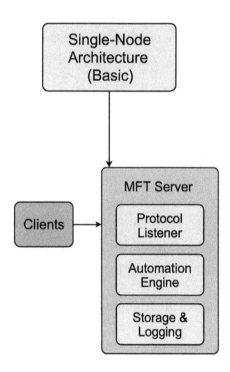

2.9.4 Multi-Tier Architecture (Standard Enterprise Deployment)

In enterprise-grade environments where scalability, security, and compliance are paramount, the Multi-Tier Architecture is the recommended deployment model for Managed File Transfer (MFT) platforms. This architecture organizes the MFT environment into distinct, logically separated layers, each responsible for specific functional responsibilities ensuring modularity, better fault isolation, and compliance with defense-in-depth security principles.

DMZ Layer: Perimeter Security and Protocol Handling

The outermost layer of this architecture resides in the Demilitarized Zone (DMZ) and includes Secure Proxies or Perimeter Servers, such as IBM Sterling Secure Proxy, GoAnywhere Gateway, or Axway Gateway. These components terminate external client connections (e.g., SFTP, FTPS, HTTPS) and relay traffic to internal systems via secure, outbound-only connections. They act as protocol translators, enforce session control, and apply edge-layer protections such as virus scanning, rate limiting, or GeoIP filtering. Importantly, no files are permanently stored in the DMZ; it serves strictly as a controlled entry point that protects the internal MFT server from direct internet exposure.

Application Layer: Core MFT Engine

Sitting behind the firewall in the internal trusted zone is the application layer, where the central MFT server operates. This node or cluster of nodes is responsible for managing user authentication, workflow orchestration, encryption/decryption, file transformation, routing logic, and protocol negotiation. It integrates tightly with identity providers (e.g., LDAP, Active Directory, SAML), implements business rules, and handles interactions with external systems and internal applications. In multi-node setups, this layer may include a high-availability cluster with load balancing and session replication for performance and fault tolerance.

Database Layer: Configuration and Audit Repository

The application layer is backed by a dedicated relational database layer, typically deployed in a high-availability configuration using platforms like PostgreSQL, Oracle RAC, or SQL Server Always On. This database stores all system configurations, user profiles, workflow metadata, key management records, and audit logs. It plays a critical role in compliance, as every file event, user action, and system interaction must be logged and queryable for regulatory audits (e.g., under PCI-DSS, SOX, HIPAA, GDPR). Data encryption, integrity checks, and backup strategies are enforced at this layer to ensure operational resilience and legal defensibility.

Storage Layer: File Vaulting and Archival

At the base of the stack is the storage layer, where inbound, outbound, and staged files are securely stored. Enterprise MFT systems typically use encrypted vaults, SAN/NAS systems, or object storage platforms such as Amazon S3, Azure Blob, or on-premise archival solutions. These repositories are configured with access control policies, encryption at rest, and retention schedules aligned with legal and business requirements. Some deployments integrate WORM (Write Once Read Many) storage for compliance-driven immutability.

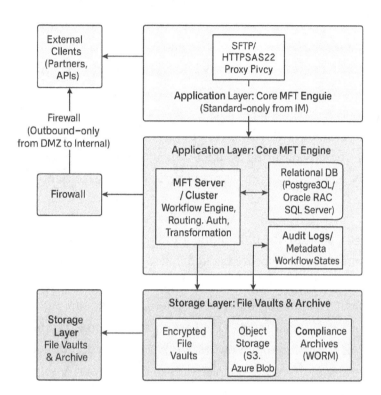

2.9.5 Clustered / High Availability Architecture

- Multiple MFT nodes operate in a cluster behind a load balancer (active-active or active-passive).

- Supports failover, session persistence, and horizontal scaling.

- Configuration data is centralized via shared storage or replicated RDBMS (e.g., Oracle RAC, PostgreSQL clusters).

2.9.6 Security Controls in On-Premises Managed File Transfer (MFT) Environments

TLS/SSL Termination at the DMZ Layer (with Secure Backchannel)

In a secure on-premises MFT deployment, inbound file transfer connections from external partners or users are terminated in a demilitarized zone (DMZ) before reaching the internal network. This is typically achieved by placing a hardened MFT proxy or load balancer in the DMZ to handle TLS/SSL termination for protocols like FTPS, SFTP, or HTTPS. The DMZ-tier system (often called an *MFT Gateway* or reverse proxy) decrypts the incoming encrypted session and then brokers the connection to the internal MFT server over a separate secure channel Crucially, the DMZ proxy is *stateless* with respect to file storage it does not persist any sensitive files or credentials on disk, thereby ensuring no data-at-rest resides in the DMZ segment. The internal MFT server, safely inside the corporate network, handles the actual file storage and business logic.

To maintain a strong security posture, the communication between the DMZ proxy and the internal MFT system is done through a secure backchannel. In practice, this means the internal MFT server initiates an outbound connection to the DMZ proxy (often a persistent, TLS-encrypted control channel), allowing inbound data to be "pulled" in without the DMZ ever opening direct inbound ports into the intranet. This backchannel approach replaces any insecure inbound calls from the DMZ to the internal network with a controlled, internally-originated session. The result is a two-tier architecture that satisfies multiple security requirements: all external connections are terminated in the DMZ, no direct connections from the DMZ to internal servers are allowed (the firewall only permits the internal system's outbound call), and internal server details (like IPs and hostnames) are hidden from outside users. As a best practice, the DMZ termination point should be hardened (minimal services, latest patches, and configured TLS ciphers) and possibly supplemented by a web application firewall or intrusion detection system in front of it for additional scrutiny of the decrypted traffic. This layered approach of TLS offloading at the edge combined with a secure relay to the interior network reduces the attack surface and prevents uninspected traffic from penetrating directly into core systems.

Why it matters: Terminating SSL/TLS in the DMZ and using a backchannel protects the internal network from direct exposure. It allows security teams to inspect and control incoming data at the edge (e.g., apply IP filtering, malware scanning, or DLP checks in the DMZ) before it reaches trusted zones. It also aligns with network segmentation principles: even if the DMZ component were compromised, the attacker gains no direct access to internal servers and finds no sensitive data stored on the DMZ host. Additionally, by not requiring any inbound ports on the internal firewall (the connection is initiated outbound), the design adheres to strict firewall policies and compliance mandates that forbid inbound DMZ-to-intranet connections and storage of sensitive data in the DMZ (for example, PCI DSS requirement.

Data-at-Rest Encryption and Key Management (FIPS 140-2 and HSM Integration)

Protecting files at rest on the MFT servers is just as critical as protecting them in transit. Enterprise-grade MFT solutions encrypt the stored files, configuration secrets, and any sensitive data on disk using strong encryption algorithms (typically AES-256) to mitigate the risk of data exposure if an attacker gains access to the storage. A key aspect of this control is using encryption libraries and modules that are FIPS 140-2 validated. FIPS 140-2 is a U.S. NIST standard that rigorously evaluates cryptographic modules; many regulated industries and government agencies require its use. In practice, running the MFT system in a "FIPS mode" ensures that only approved ciphers and routines are used for encryption operations. For example, vendors often include FIPS-validated cryptographic modules in their products and can configure the software to enforce FIPS-approved algorithms. This gives higher assurance that the data-at-rest encryption meets strict security criteria and has been independently validated. In fact, if you exchange files with U.S. federal systems, **FIPS-compliant encryption is mandatory** – federal agencies are prohibited from using MFT solutions that lack FIPS 140-2 validated cryptography. Even outside of government, using FIPS 140-2 validated ciphers (and the updated FIPS 140-3) is considered a security best practice and is often required by corporate policies and auditors. This means all cryptographic functions (file encryption, TLS ciphers, hashing, etc.) run through certified libraries, reducing the chance of using weak or untested algorithms. Notably, compliance standards like PCI-DSS, HIPAA, and ISO 27001 also call for strong encryption – leveraging FIPS-validated modules helps satisfy those requirements by demonstrating the encryption mechanism itself is industry-approved.

Key management is the other half of the equation. Secure MFT deployments implement robust processes for managing the encryption keys that protect files. Often, the encryption keys (or the master keys that derive file encryption keys) are stored securely, and access to them is tightly controlled. Many enterprises integrate their MFT platforms with Hardware Security Modules (HSMs) or external key management systems to bolster this control. An HSM is a dedicated physical appliance designed to safeguard cryptographic keys and offload cryptographic operations. By using an HSM, the most sensitive keys (like the master encryption key or TLS private keys) never leave the secure hardware – encryption and decryption happen *inside* the HSM's protected environment. This significantly reduces the risk of key compromise: even if an attacker breaches the server, they cannot extract the keys from the HSM. The HSM also provides tamper-resistance (it can detect and react to physical tampering) and can enforce policies like preventing keys from being exported or used in unauthorized ways. In on-prem MFT deployments handling highly sensitive data (financial records, health data, intellectual property), integrating an HSM is considered a best practice for key management. It establishes a hardware root of trust – for example, the MFT software can call the HSM for cryptographic operations or to unwrap file encryption keys on-the-fly, without ever exposing plaintext keys in application memory. At a minimum, if an external HSM is not used, the MFT solution should use a strong internal key management system with role-based access control, secure key storage (encrypted and permissions-restricted on disk), and periodic key rotation. Additionally, all cryptographic modules (whether in software or HSM) should be operated in FIPS-approved mode if compliance requires. By enforcing data-at-rest encryption with strong, validated cryptography and managing keys with the highest levels of security (HSM or equivalent controls), organizations ensure that even if attackers or malicious insiders get access to the MFT file store, the data remains unintelligible and safe from breach. This control not only protects confidentiality but also demonstrates compliance with regulations that mandate encryption of sensitive data at rest (e.g., GDPR, GLBA).

Comprehensive Audit Logging and SIEM Integration

Enterprise MFT systems are expected to maintain a **detailed audit trail** of all activities, providing full visibility into who did what and when. In practice, this means every file transfer event (uploads, downloads), user login/logout, administrator change, permission change, and system error is recorded in an append-only log repository. These logs typically capture attributes like timestamp, user or account ID, client IP address, file names or IDs transferred, success/failure status, and other relevant context. The importance of audit logging is twofold: **security monitoring** and **compliance accountability**. From a security standpoint, robust logging allows detection of suspicious behavior (e.g. multiple failed login attempts, unexpected after-hours downloads) and supports forensic analysis in case of an incident. From a compliance perspective, logs demonstrate control over the system – many frameworks require that organizations can produce records of data access and transfers as evidence of governance.

In secure MFT setups, audit logs are designed to be **tamper-evident** and protected from unauthorized alteration. For example, the MFT software may cryptographically sign or checksum each log entry at write-time. If anyone tries to modify or remove a log entry, the checksum verification will fail, flagging the corruption. This ensures the integrity of the audit trail (i.e., you can trust that the logs haven't been silently manipulated to cover up an action). Best practices also include segregating duties so that no single administrator can alter or delete logs without detection. Often, logs are written to disk in append mode and regularly shipped out to a secure central log server to prevent local tampering. Many MFT solutions provide built-in reporting tools or **out-of-the-box compliance reports** that query these logs. For instance, administrators can run a report showing all file access by a certain user over the past 90 days, or a summary of all failed logins this quarter. These canned reports help demonstrate compliance during audits (e.g., showing adherence to data handling policies). It's common to see requirements that **log records be retained for a minimum period**, such as **7 to 10 years**, especially in heavily regulated industries. Governance, Risk, and Compliance (GRC) policies will dictate the retention schedule based on regulations like SOX, PCI DSS, or internal corporate policy. The MFT environment should therefore be configured to archive logs long-term (often to immutable storage or write-once media for integrity) and to purge older logs only according to the approved retention policy (ensuring old logs are not deleted too soon).

Another critical aspect is integrating MFT logs with enterprise-wide monitoring. Typically, organizations will forward MFT audit logs to a **central Security Information and Event Management (SIEM)** or logging platform (such as Splunk, QRadar, Elastic, etc.) in real time. This is usually accomplished via syslog or a similar log forwarding mechanism that the MFT server supports. By doing so, security operations teams can correlate file transfer events with other security events in the network (for example, correlating a large file download on the MFT with a badge-in entry to the data center, or with an antivirus alert on an endpoint). It also enables real-time alerting e.g., the SIEM can generate an alert if an account initiates an unusual volume of downloads, or if an admin account is used from a new IP address. Piping logs to a SIEM ensures they are centrally collected (preventing an attacker from covering their tracks by only deleting local logs) and retained according to enterprise policy. Additionally, many compliance regimes explicitly or implicitly require centralized log monitoring as part of continuous security monitoring. In summary, **audit logging in an MFT environment should be exhaustive and immutable**, with logs retained as per GRC mandates and continuously exported to a SIEM or log management system for aggregation and analysis. Following these practices provides a trustworthy audit trail that not only helps in meeting controls in frameworks like ISO 27001 (which has controls for logging and monitoring) and NIST 800-53 (Audit and Accountability family controls), but also strengthens the organization's security posture by enabling timely detection of anomalies in file transfer activities.

Enforcement of Security Compliance Frameworks (ISO 27001, NIST 800-53, CIS Benchmarks)

On-premises MFT deployments in large enterprises are typically aligned with well-known security frameworks and benchmarks to ensure a holistic and standardized security posture. Implementing MFT controls in the context of these frameworks means that the file transfer environment isn't secured in isolation, but as part of the organization's broader Information Security Management System (ISMS) and infrastructure hardening program. Three common frameworks/standards referenced are **ISO/IEC 27001**, **NIST SP 800-53**, and **CIS Benchmarks**:

- **ISO/IEC 27001:** This is an international standard for managing information security. It outlines requirements for establishing an ISMS and includes a set of controls (detailed in ISO 27002) that cover areas like access control, cryptography, operations security, and more. In an MFT context, adhering to ISO 27001 means that policies and controls exist for secure file transfer operations – for example, controlling access to MFT systems (account management, least privilege), ensuring data encryption in transit and at rest, maintaining audit logs and monitoring, and handling incidents. Many organizations choose MFT solutions that are developed by vendors with ISO 27001 certification or similar, as a sign that the product meets high security standards. Internally, when deploying the MFT, companies will map its features to ISO 27001 controls: e.g., using its access control features to satisfy ISO control objectives, or using its logging and alerting to satisfy monitoring requirements. By doing so, the MFT becomes a controlled asset under the ISMS, and its security is maintained via regular risk assessments, audits, and continuous improvement in line with ISO 27001 processes.

- **NIST SP 800-53:** NIST Special Publication 800-53 (Rev. 5 being the latest) provides a comprehensive catalog of security and privacy controls for federal information systems, and it's widely used as a benchmark in the private sector as well. Aligning an on-prem MFT deployment with NIST 800-53 means ensuring the relevant controls from various families are implemented. For instance:

  - *Access Control (AC):* MFT should enforce strong user authentication, role-based access control, and session management (mapping to controls like AC-2, AC-7, etc.).

  - *Audit and Accountability (AU):* As discussed, the MFT must generate audit logs and protect them (AU-2, AU-6, AU-9) and retain them per policy (AU-11).

  - *System & Communications Protection (SC):* This includes using TLS for data in transit (SC-8, SC-13), employing cryptographic controls for data at rest (SC-28) with FIPS-validated modules (SC-13(1) for FIPS mode, if applicable).

  - *Identification and Authentication (IA):* MFT user accounts should integrate with enterprise identity (e.g., AD/LDAP or SSO) for centralized management (IA-2) and perhaps use multi-factor authentication for administrative access (IA-2(1)).

  - *Configuration Management (CM):* The MFT server OS and application settings should be securely configured and documented (CM-2, CM-6), and kept up-to-date (SI-2 for flaw remediation).
  By mapping such controls, the organization can demonstrate that the MFT system meets the same rigorous standards as other critical systems. NIST 800-53 compliance enhances security by ensuring no major control gap is overlooked, and it also often underpins other compliance requirements (for example, FedRAMP for cloud or FISMA for federal agencies mandate 800-53 controls). The end goal is a **defense-in-depth implementation** where the MFT environment

has controls covering all key areas: preventative, detective, and corrective, as prescribed by NIST's guidance. This yields a more resilient system and one that auditors can easily assess against a known benchmark.

- **CIS Benchmarks:** The Center for Internet Security (CIS) Benchmarks are a collection of hardening guidelines and best practices for a wide array of technologies – operating systems, databases, network devices, and even some applications. While there may not be a CIS benchmark specifically for every MFT software, the principle here is to apply CIS hardening to the **underlying systems** and any relevant components. For an on-prem MFT server, this means if it runs on Windows or Linux, that OS should be configured according to the appropriate CIS Benchmark (e.g., disabling unnecessary services, using secure configuration settings for accounts, file permissions, network parameters, registry or kernel settings, etc.). Similarly, if the MFT uses a database (to store metadata or audit logs), that database should be hardened per CIS guidelines, and if it uses a web server or application server, those components should also be CIS-hardened. The CIS Benchmarks are widely regarded as the "**gold standard of system hardening**," representing consensus recommendations from security experts. Following them helps eliminate common weaknesses (like default passwords, misconfigured ports, older protocol versions) that attackers often exploit. In many compliance audits, showing that systems are configured to CIS Benchmark Level 1 or 2 can satisfy requirements for secure baseline configurations. Implementing CIS controls for MFT might include steps such as: ensuring only strong ciphers are enabled for TLS (which overlaps with CIS guidelines and NIST recommendations), removing or turning off any default accounts on the server, setting up proper file system permissions for the directories where files are stored, and applying advanced settings like login banner warnings, SSH hardening (if SFTP is used), etc., as detailed in CIS checklists. Additionally, ongoing compliance can be validated by running automated configuration scans or leveraging tools that audit systems against CIS profiles. By enforcing CIS Benchmark recommendations, organizations greatly reduce the attack surface of their MFT infrastructure – it's a proactive measure ensuring that even if the MFT application is robust, the platform it runs on is equally secured and not the weakest link.

In essence, aligning the on-premises MFT environment with frameworks like ISO 27001 and NIST 800-53 provides a *management and controls structure* that ensures that security controls are comprehensive, documented, and continuously evaluated for effectiveness. Adopting CIS Benchmarks provides a *technical configuration baseline*, ensuring the systems are locked down according to industry best practices. Together, these measures address both procedural and technical aspects of security. This layered compliance approach is important not only for passing audits but for real security: it forces discipline in how the MFT system is deployed and maintained. For example, an organization that follows these frameworks will likely have periodic reviews of user access rights (ISO 27001 requirement) on the MFT, will enforce encryption and strong auth (ISO/NIST requirements) by policy, and will have change management for any configuration change (to not drift from the hardened baseline). All of these translate to a lower risk of data leakage or breach. Moreover, many enterprises have to demonstrate compliance with multiple regulations (HIPAA, GDPR, SOX, etc.); mapping MFT controls to broad frameworks makes it easier to show auditors that appropriate controls are in place. In a hardened, well-governed MFT deployment, every aspect from network architecture (DMZ isolation) to encryption to logging is implemented not ad-hoc, but in accordance with these established security frameworks and benchmarks – resulting in an MFT system that can be trusted to safely handle the organization's sensitive file transfers.

References: The practices above are informed by industry sources and vendor guidance for secure managed file transfer. For example, multi-tier MFT reference architectures explicitly recommend DMZ proxies with no data storage and internal call-outs static.spiceworks.comstatic.spiceworks.com. Reputable MFT vendors build in FIPS 140-2 validated encryption to meet federal standards btrade.combtrade.com and often support external HSMs for key management in high-security environments fortinet.com. Logging and reporting capabilities in MFT products are designed to satisfy audit requirements (e.g., file activity tracking, long-term log retention) and facilitate SIEM integration emtmeta.comgoanywhere.com. Finally, organizations frequently align their MFT deployments with overarching security frameworks; they select solutions that help them comply with ISO 27001 or NIST controls and they harden systems per CIS Benchmarks as a matter of policy emtmeta.compro2col.com. By implementing these controls and best practices, enterprises create an MFT environment that is not only functionally robust, but also secure and compliant by design.

2.10 Cloud-based MFT

Implementing Managed File Transfer (MFT) solutions on Google Cloud Platform (GCP) provides organizations with a robust, scalable, and secure framework for automating and managing file exchanges between internal systems, external partners, and cloud-based applications. GCP's comprehensive suite of services enables the deployment of MFT architectures that align with modern enterprise requirements for reliability, compliance, and operational efficiency.

Compute and Deployment Options: MFT applications can be hosted on Compute Engine virtual machines, offering customizable configurations to meet specific performance and workload demands. For containerized deployments, Google Kubernetes Engine (GKE) facilitates orchestration and scalability, allowing for efficient management of microservices-based MFT components.

Data Transfer and Storage: The Storage Transfer Service (STS) is instrumental in transferring large volumes of data between on-premises systems and GCP. STS supports scheduled and event-driven transfers, utilizing agent pools to manage data movement securely and efficiently. For persistent storage, Cloud Storage provides durable and highly available object storage, with features like lifecycle management and fine-grained access controls.

Networking and Security: To ensure secure and reliable connectivity, Cloud VPN and Cloud Interconnect establish encrypted tunnels and dedicated connections between on-premises environments and GCP. Cloud Load Balancing distributes incoming traffic across multiple MFT instances, enhancing availability and performance. Cloud Armor offers protection against distributed denial-of-service (DDoS) attacks and enforces security policies at the edge.

Identity and Access Management: GCP's Identity and Access Management (IAM) provides granular control over user and service permissions, ensuring that only authorized entities can access MFT resources. VPC Service Controls further enhance security by defining perimeters around sensitive data, mitigating the risk of data exfiltration.

Monitoring and Logging: Operational visibility is achieved through Cloud Monitoring and Cloud Logging, which collect metrics and logs from MFT services. These tools enable administrators to set up alerts, visualize performance trends, and conduct root cause analysis. Cloud Audit Logs maintain records of administrative activities, supporting compliance and forensic investigations.

Workflow Automation: GCP offers services like Cloud Scheduler and Cloud Functions to automate MFT workflows. Cloud Scheduler allows for the execution of jobs at specified times, while Cloud Functions can trigger processes in response to events, such as the arrival of new files in Cloud Storage. This automation reduces manual intervention and enhances the responsiveness of file transfer operations.

By leveraging these GCP services, organizations can construct a Cloud-Based MFT solution that meets stringent requirements for data security, compliance, and operational efficiency, while also providing the flexibility to adapt to evolving business needs.

2.11 Real-time Industry Architectures

2.11.1 IBM Sterling File Gateway

Onprem Single Node Architecture

In a secure enterprise Managed File Transfer (MFT) setup utilizing a single-node IBM Sterling File Gateway (SFG) architecture, reliable bi-directional data exchange with external trading partners is achieved through a simplified yet robust network design. This design incorporates key layers such as DMZ-based perimeter control, load balancing via F5, IP filtering through IPTables, and comprehensive encryption mechanisms to safeguard sensitive business data.

At the heart of this architecture lies a standalone SFG instance, deployed within the Secure Zone, which acts as the central hub for processing, validating, encrypting, and routing all file transfers. Inbound file flows begin when external partners initiate secure connections over the internet. These requests pass through an internet-facing firewall, which acts as the first security barrier at the network edge. From there, the traffic is forwarded to an F5 load balancer, which even in a single-node configuration plays a critical role in SSL termination, traffic routing, and preparing the infrastructure for future horizontal scaling.

The load balancer then directs the traffic to a single IBM Perimeter Server, located within the DMZ, typically hosted on a hardened Linux-based virtual machine. This Perimeter Server is secured using IPTables-based IP filtering, allowing only traffic from pre-approved partner IP addresses. This filtering mechanism significantly reduces exposure to unauthorized access and ensures only trusted connections are passed into the internal network.

Once validated, the incoming files are relayed from the Perimeter Server to the SFG node in the Secure Zone, where they undergo partner-specific validation, decryption, and routing. Based on the defined business process rules, the SFG securely forwards the processed files to appropriate internal business systems or applications for consumption.

For outbound transmissions, the flow operates in reverse. Internal applications initiate file submissions to external partners by pushing data to the SFG node. After applying PGP encryption and ensuring compliance with partner-specific configurations, the SFG sends the files to the DMZ-hosted Perimeter Server. The same IPTables filtering logic is applied once more to verify outbound legitimacy before passing the files back through the F5 load balancer, which then delivers them to the intended external recipient using protocols like SFTP, FTPS, or AS2.

Throughout the entire flow, TLS 1.2/1.3 ensures encryption in transit, while optional PGP encryption at rest helps meet data protection requirements. Despite being a single-node deployment, this architecture delivers a strong balance of security, compliance, operational control, and scalability readiness, making it well-suited for midsize organizations or departments with critical file transfer requirements but limited infrastructure complexity.

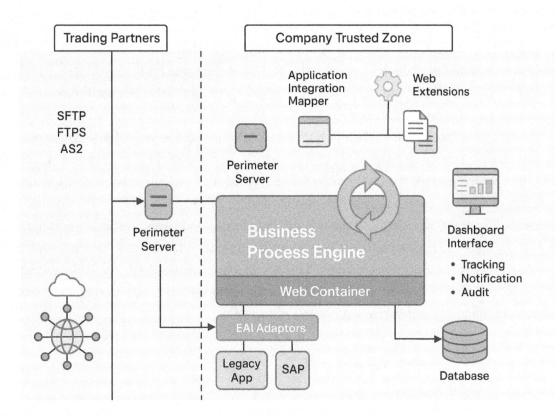

Onprem Two-Node Cluster Architecture

In a robust enterprise MFT architecture leveraging IBM Sterling File Gateway (SFG), secure, bi-directional file exchange with external trading partners is achieved through a layered network design incorporating DMZ-based perimeter defense, load balancing, IP filtering, and encryption controls. The infrastructure is anchored by a two-node IBM Sterling File Gateway cluster deployed in the Secure Zone, serving as the central orchestration point for processing, routing, and encrypting file transmissions. Inbound file transfer begins when external partners initiate connections through internet-facing firewalls, which safeguard the network edge. Traffic is routed to an F5 load balancer that distributes requests across two dedicated IBM Perimeter Servers Perimeter Server1 (hosted on Linux VM1) and Perimeter Server2 (hosted on Linux VM2) both strategically located in the DMZ. These perimeter servers are included as pool members in the F5 load balancer configuration and are hardened with IPTables-based IP filtering, ensuring that only traffic from authorized or whitelisted IPs is allowed, effectively mitigating intrusion risks and protecting the Secure Zone. Upon validation and filtering, these perimeter servers forward the payload to the SFG cluster in the Secure Zone. There, the file decryption, validation, and partner-specific processing occur, after which the files are delivered to the relevant internal business units or downstream systems.

For outbound file transfers, the process is reversed. Internal business units initiate file submissions to external partners by targeting the FQDN of the same F5 load balancer, which in this context is configured to route traffic back to the internal-facing IBM Secure Proxy (SSP) pool members, i.e., the same Perimeter Server VMs (VM1 and VM2) configured for outbound delivery. These VMs receive the outbound traffic and, after passing through IP filtering and compliance checks, forward it to the SFG cluster, which then applies PGP encryption according to the pre-configured partner profile. Finally, the encrypted files are delivered securely to the external trading partners via the appropriate protocol (e.g., SFTP, AS2, FTPS). Throughout both inbound and outbound flows, data-in-transit is protected using industry-standard encryption protocols (e.g., TLS 1.2/1.3), and data-at-rest is optionally encrypted using PGP within the SFG as per regulatory and business requirements. This architecture ensures high availability, deep packet inspection, endpoint-level security, and granular partner-level flow configuration, offering a resilient, compliant, and enterprise-ready MFT ecosystem.

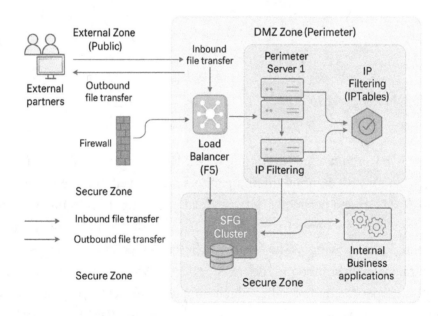

2.11.2 Global File Transfer Architecture

Global File Transfer (GFT) is a centralized, enterprise-grade Managed File Transfer (MFT) platform designed to enable secure, protocol-agnostic, and high-throughput data exchanges across a diverse IT ecosystem, including mainframes, UNIX environments, and external trading partners. The architecture of GFT reflects the standard capabilities of modern MFT solutions, while offering extended protocol support, deep system integrations, and centralized management features that make it a critical hub for enterprise file exchange operations.

Protocol Integration and Platform Connectivity

GFT is uniquely positioned to interface with heterogeneous systems by supporting a wide array of industry-standard and legacy file transfer protocols. For mainframe integration, GFT establishes native connectivity using Connect:Direct (NDM), PeSIT-HS, and PeSIT-PEL-S protocols, which are optimized for high-reliability, checkpoint restart, and secure host-to-host file transfers. These protocols enable seamless communication between the GFT application and critical transactional systems running on IBM z/OS mainframes, ensuring guaranteed delivery and job scheduling alignment with batch processing workloads.

In contrast, when interacting with UNIX-based systems, GFT supports widely adopted file transfer mechanisms such as SFTP (SSH File Transfer Protocol) and FTP/FTPS, which are utilized for scheduled and ad-hoc transfers involving middleware platforms, enterprise data warehouses, application servers, and internal business units. GFT's flexible protocol adapter framework allows it to dynamically route, encrypt, and log these transfers according to pre-configured business process rules.

Inbound and Outbound File Flow – Security and Routing

GFT handles both inbound and outbound file flows from external partners and internal business units (BUs). When files are received from external trading partners, connections are first established through a hardened network DMZ layer, protected by external firewalls, Web Application Firewalls (WAF), intrusion detection/prevention systems (IDS/IPS), and reverse proxies. These security layers validate the source, protocol, and port before the data is allowed into the perimeter. Once approved, the files are staged onto the GFT-controlled file system within the secure network zone, where they are processed, audited, and distributed to internal endpoints or applications as per routing definitions.

Similarly, for outbound transmissions, internal systems initiate transfers through an internal Load Balancer (LB), routing the traffic to the appropriate GFT node. These files land on the internal GFT file system, where policy-driven logic including encryption, protocol negotiation, compliance tagging, and partner resolution is applied. The GFT system then routes the payload to external recipients via secure channels while ensuring that transfer events are fully logged and visible through centralized dashboards.

Operational Monitoring and Partner Management

GFT provides a graphical web-based User Interface (UI) for real-time transmission monitoring, error alerting, and transfer lifecycle visibility. This enables operational teams to monitor the status of all inbound and outbound flows across environments, with features such as searchable audit trails, automated retries, transfer latency insights, and failure notifications integrated with email or incident management tools (e.g., ServiceNow).

In addition, a dedicated Configuration Manager component is included for managing partner onboarding, protocol configurations, key/certificate updates, and routing rules. Partner profiles can be defined with fine-grained control over IP allowlists, authentication credentials, protocol versions, encryption requirements (e.g., PGP, TLS), and delivery instructions, ensuring every transfer complies with enterprise security policies and regulatory obligations.

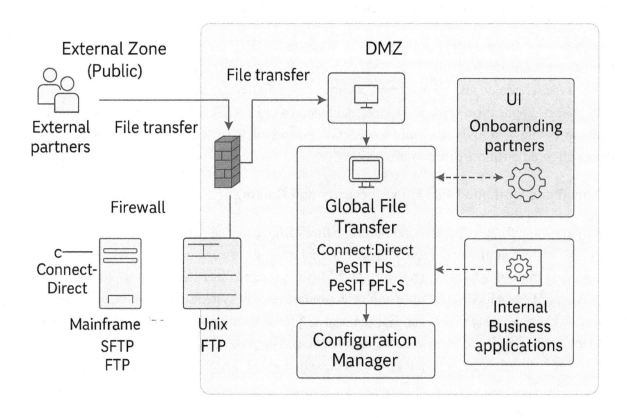

2.11.3 ThornSFTP Gateway Architecture for Cloud

Thorn SFTP Gateway for Google Cloud Platform (GCP) is a robust, cloud-native managed file transfer solution designed to facilitate secure, scalable, and compliant file exchanges between external SFTP clients and cloud storage systems. It acts as a protocol-bridging gateway, allowing traditional SFTP clients to interact seamlessly with cloud object storage, specifically Google

Cloud Storage (GCS) while maintaining compatibility with legacy systems. One of its most powerful features is its multi-cloud transfer capability, enabling cross-cloud file routing between Google Cloud, AWS S3, and Azure Blob Storage, which is particularly valuable in hybrid cloud and multi-cloud environments where data needs to be exchanged across different cloud providers with minimal operational overhead.

Deployed as a Compute Engine virtual machine inside a Google VPC, Thorn SFTP Gateway integrates tightly with GCP's native services for networking, IAM, and storage. The application supports deployment behind Google Cloud Load Balancers, enabling high availability and session distribution across multiple SFTP Gateway nodes. At its core, the application leverages a PostgreSQL database (either bundled locally or managed externally) to persist critical metadata such as SFTP user configurations, virtual folder mappings, encryption settings, audit logs, SSH keys, and transfer job status. This backend database ensures operational consistency across instances and plays a central role in maintaining the integrity of the gateway's multi-tenant architecture.

When a file is uploaded via SFTP, it is first temporarily cached in a local staging directory before being automatically pushed to the designated cloud storage target be it GCS, AWS S3, or Azure Blob based on user-specific routing rules. For downloads, a reverse process is used: files are pulled from the cloud bucket, cached locally, and streamed securely to the requesting SFTP client. Each SFTP user is isolated with chroot-style virtual directories mapped to cloud buckets or subdirectories, ensuring strong data segregation and access control. Authentication is supported via passwords or SSH keys, and user provisioning is managed through a web-based administration portal, which interfaces with the PostgreSQL backend to dynamically apply updates without downtime.

Security is embedded at multiple layers: SFTP traffic is encrypted in transit using SSH over TLS, data at rest is secured through Google-managed encryption keys (SSE-S3 or SSE-KMS) or customer-managed keys (CMEK) via Google Cloud Key Management Service (KMS). Role-Based Access Control (RBAC) and IP allowlisting can be enforced to restrict access to approved clients, and firewall rules within the VPC tightly control ingress and egress traffic. Audit logs including login events, file access history, and background job results can be streamed to Cloud Logging, forwarded to SIEM solutions, or exported for compliance and reporting.

Thorn SFTP Gateway's multi-cloud routing logic allows administrators to create user profiles that send files to different cloud destinations based on business rules, partner location, or compliance region. This is particularly useful for multinational organizations that need to meet data residency requirements or ensure low-latency transfers across globally distributed cloud infrastructures. It also supports automated cloud lifecycle operations, such as applying storage class transitions, object versioning, and deletion policies via native APIs after file ingestion.

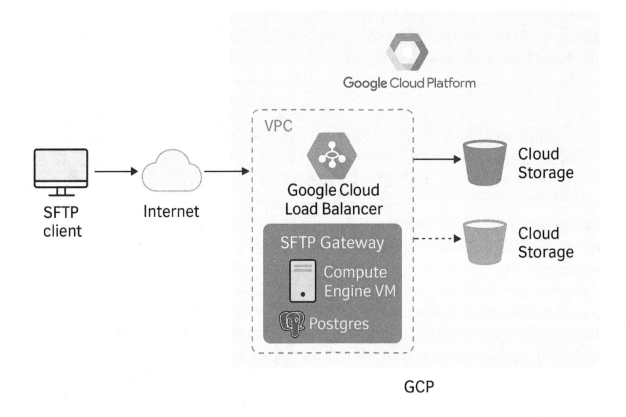

GCP

2.11.4 IBM Connect:Direct High Speed Add-On Architecture for Cloud

In a robust enterprise Managed File Transfer (MFT) architecture utilizing IBM Connect:Direct with High-Speed Add-On (HSAO), organizations can achieve secure, high-throughput, and protocol-optimized file movement even at multi-terabyte scale. This architecture integrates a hardened network perimeter with firewalls, F5 load balancing, IPTables-based IP filtering, and deep infrastructure tuning to support both internal and external file flows. At its core lies a two-node Connect:Direct cluster deployed in the Secure Zone, which acts as the high-performance transfer engine. Leveraging HSAO, Connect:Direct significantly reduces transfer times over WAN and high-latency links through mechanisms such as multi-threaded streaming, data segmentation, on-the-fly compression, and critically, the use of UDP-based data channels for transfer acceleration.

Unlike standard Connect:Direct sessions which operate over TCP, HSAO opens dedicated UDP ports to transfer file blocks in parallel, enabling far greater throughput than what a single TCP stream can provide. For this to function correctly, organizations must ensure that UDP port ranges used by HSAO are explicitly opened on internal firewalls, external perimeter devices, and across the Secure Proxy Server (SSP) infrastructure. These ports allow high-speed packet delivery with minimized overhead, ensuring performance while preserving reliability via checkpoint and restart capabilities native to Connect:Direct.

To optimize throughput and prevent bandwidth saturation, administrators must configure the bandwidth parameter in the initparm.cfg file within Connect:Direct. This setting controls the maximum transfer rate available to HSAO and should align with both network capacity and Quality of Service (QoS) policies. In tandem, the IBM Secure Proxy Server (SSP) which sits in the DMZ and brokers secure sessions must also be tuned to accommodate UDP-based high-speed transfer sessions, including configuration of corresponding bandwidth policies and UDP port access rules. Proper alignment between Connect:Direct and SSP ensures end-to-end optimization and security of accelerated transfers.

In a typical inbound scenario, external trading partners initiate Connect:Direct sessions that pass through internet-facing firewalls and are load-balanced by an F5 device across two DMZ-based Perimeter Servers (Linux VM1 and VM2), each enforcing IP-based whitelisting and protocol validation. The session is then forwarded to the Connect:Direct nodes in the Secure Zone, where UDP-based HSAO transfers are executed efficiently with high-speed acceleration. For outbound flows, internal systems push files to Connect:Direct, which applies performance policies and routes traffic back through the DMZ Perimeter Servers, using UDP channels to deliver files to external partners at scale.

Throughout the entire transfer process, data-in-transit is encrypted using TLS 1.2/1.3 and session-level authentication, while access logs and transfer events are captured for audit, compliance, and monitoring. With high-speed optimization enabled via HSAO, UDP-based parallel streaming, and precisely tuned bandwidth settings across both Connect:Direct and SSP, this architecture offers enterprise-class scalability, security, and performance making it well-suited for financial institutions, supply chain platforms, and any environment requiring fast, large-volume, and secure file movement.

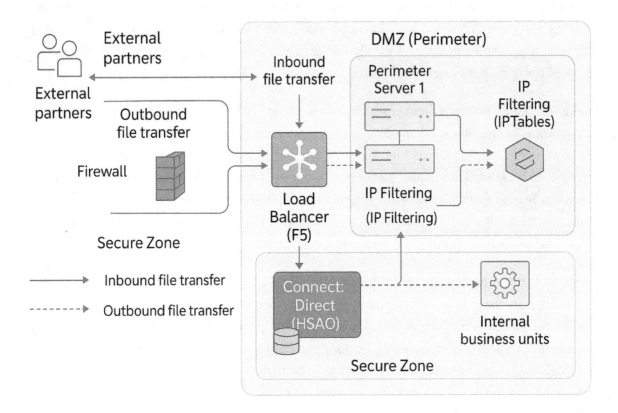

2.11.5 TibcoMFT Architecture

TIBCO Managed File Transfer (MFT) Internet Server 8.6.0 is a secure, protocol-agnostic gateway designed to facilitate reliable file exchanges between external trading partners and internal enterprise systems. It supports a wide range of protocols, including SFTP, FTPS, HTTPS, AS2, and TIBCO's proprietary protocols, ensuring compatibility across diverse environments.

The architecture typically employs a two-tier DMZ setup:

- DMZ1: Hosts the MFT Internet Server, acting as the initial point of contact for external connections. It handles protocol negotiation, authentication, and preliminary security checks

- DMZ2: Contains the Connection Manager Agent (CMA), which brokers secure connections between the Internet Server and internal systems. This separation enhances security by preventing direct access to internal networks from external sources.

Within the internal network, the MFT Platform Server manages automated file transfers, scheduling, and routing. The MFT Command Center provides centralized administration, monitoring, and reporting, offering a comprehensive view of all file transfer activities.

This layered architecture ensures that sensitive data remains protected throughout the transfer process, aligning with enterprise security policies and compliance requirements.

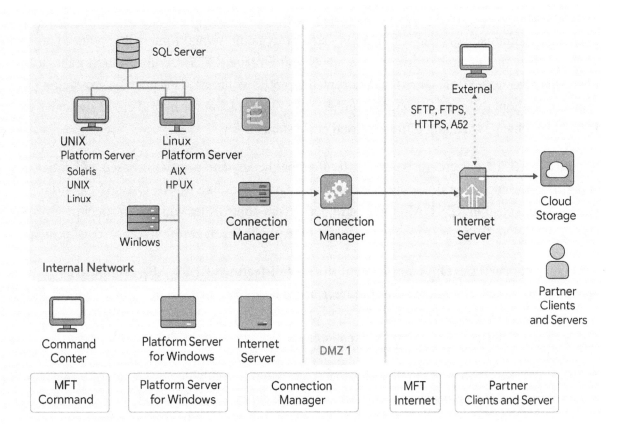

2.11.6 Open-source MFT SFTPGo Architecture

SFTPGo is a powerful, production-ready Managed File Transfer (MFT) platform built for modern enterprises. It supports a wide range of secure file transfer protocols including SFTP, FTPS, WebDAV, HTTPS, and SCP providing interoperability across legacy and modern systems. Its architecture is designed for high availability, flexibility, and extensibility, making it suitable for both on-premises and multi-cloud deployments.

At its core, SFTPGo utilizes a PostgreSQL database (as well as MySQL or SQLite alternatives) to store critical configuration data such as user definitions, permissions, file metadata, transfer logs, and virtual folder mappings. The PostgreSQL backend ensures transactional integrity, advanced query capabilities, and scalability for large, enterprise-grade installations. SFTPGo's integration with SQL databases also enables seamless synchronization with identity providers and policy engines.

A major differentiator of SFTPGo is its native support for multi-cloud and hybrid storage backends. Administrators can configure isolated or dynamic virtual folders that point to multiple storage layers including Amazon S3, Google Cloud Storage (GCS), Azure Blob Storage, local filesystems, remote SFTP servers, or encrypted CryptFS volumes. This enables cross-cloud file transfers without the need for external orchestration layers ideal for hybrid cloud strategies or B2B file exchange spanning different cloud ecosystems.

Security in SFTPGo is enterprise-grade. It offers public key and password-based authentication, supports 2FA, and integrates with external identity providers like LDAP, OAuth2/OpenID Connect, and custom REST APIs. Fine-grained access controls let you assign specific read/write/delete/list permissions at the folder or even file level, enforcing Zero Trust principles.

Administrators and DevOps teams benefit from a full-featured REST API, event-driven automation framework, and WebAdmin interface. These tools make it possible to build dynamic workflows triggered by events (e.g., file upload/download), which can execute shell commands, notify external systems via webhooks, send emails, or interact with cloud service buses.

Additionally, SFTPGo supports load-balanced, horizontally scalable deployments, with shared configuration and event orchestration enabled via the central SQL backend. This ensures it can support high-throughput, mission-critical file transfers in regulated industries like finance, healthcare, and logistics.

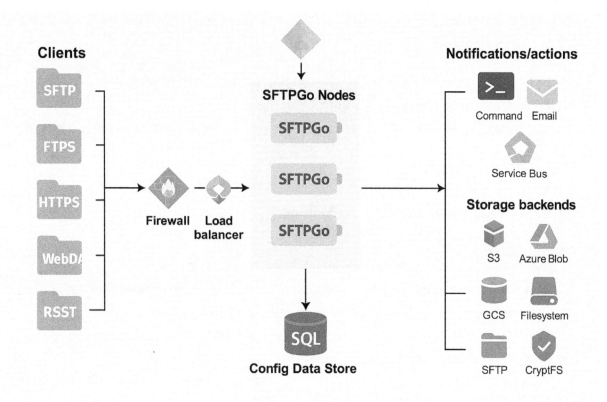

PART 3: The Role of AI in Modern MFT

3 Why AI in Managed File Transfer (MFT)

As businesses handle more data, more partners, and more regulatory pressure, traditional Managed File Transfer (MFT) systems, while secure and robust, are increasingly expected to do more than just move files. They need to be smart, adaptive, and proactive.

That's where Artificial Intelligence (AI) steps in.

By embedding AI into MFT platforms, organizations can automate decision-making, predict issues before they happen, and optimize performance continuously transforming file transfer from a static process into a dynamic, intelligent ecosystem.

3.1 Key Reasons to Integrate AI with MFT

3.1.1 Proactive Issue Detection and Resolution

Traditional MFT systems rely on reactive monitoring errors that are detected only after they occur. AI changes this by:

- Detecting anomalies and potential failures based on historical patterns
- Predicting transfer delays or SLA breaches
- Triggering automated remediation (e.g., retrying transfers, rerouting files, or notifying admins)

3.1.2 Smarter Automation and Decision Making

AI enables context-aware automation:

- Automatically prioritizes critical transfers (e.g., real-time transactions over batch jobs)
- Decides when to scale resources based on current demand
- Suggests optimal transfer routes, partners, or protocols based on past performance and network conditions

3.1.3 Improved Security through Behavioral Analysis

AI adds a layer of intelligent security:

- Monitors file access and transfer behavior to spot suspicious activity
- Flags anomalies like unexpected file sizes, transfer frequencies, or unauthorized access
- Supports adaptive access controls and intelligent policy enforcement

3.1.4 Operational Efficiency and Cost Savings

With AI:

- System loads are better managed (avoiding over-provisioning)
- Manual intervention is reduced (fewer support tickets and escalations)
- Human error is minimized through intelligent workflows

This leads to leaner IT operations and reduced downtime, especially in high-volume environments.

3.1.5 Compliance and Audit Intelligence

AI-powered MFT platforms:

- Automatically generate smart compliance reports

- Identify policy violations or risky behaviors
- Use natural language processing (NLP) to scan file metadata or content for compliance-sensitive terms (e.g., PII, financial data)

3.1.6 Continuous Learning and Optimization

Unlike rule-based systems, AI learns and evolves:

- Adapts to changes in partner behavior, network loads, or user habits
- Improves accuracy over time (e.g., predicting peak hours or high-risk files)
- Recommends performance and architecture optimizations

3.2 Challenges with Traditional Managed File Transfer (MFT) Systems

While traditional Managed File Transfer (MFT) systems were revolutionary at the time of their emergence bringing structure, automation, and security to enterprise file transfers they were primarily designed for static, predictable, and infrastructure-heavy environments. As businesses have evolved, embracing cloud technologies, API-first architectures, AI-driven automation, and globally distributed teams, these legacy MFT systems have begun to show their limitations.

Below are the key challenges organizations face when relying on traditional MFT systems in today's dynamic and fast-paced digital landscape:

3.2.1 Lack of Real-Time Intelligence

Traditional MFT platforms typically function as reactive systems. They:

- Execute file transfers based on predefined schedules or event-based triggers
- Log transfer results passively, without real-time analytics or dynamic response mechanisms
- Generate basic success/failure reports, offering limited operational insight
- Require high ongoing operational maintenance, including monitoring, troubleshooting, and manual interventions
- Incur significant licensing and infrastructure costs, especially at scale
- Often result in suboptimal resource utilization, due to lack of intelligent load balancing and automation

However, they lack real-time analytics and intelligent decision-making. There is no predictive insight into failures, bottlenecks, or anomalies, which makes it difficult to proactively manage risks or optimize performance.

As a result, issues are often detected *after the fact*, increasing downtime, support workload, and mainly business disruption.

3.2.2 Limited Scalability and Elasticity

Traditional Managed File Transfer (MFT) systems were designed for predictable, centralized data exchange in on-premises environments. While effective for basic scheduled transfers, they often fall short when faced with modern demands for flexibility, scale, and responsiveness.

Here's a breakdown of the challenges:

- **Fixed Infrastructure Constraints**

  Traditional MFT platforms are typically hosted on dedicated on-premises servers or static virtual machines. This setup imposes rigid boundaries on compute power, memory, and storage. As data volume or user load increases, these systems cannot dynamically scale up or down leading to bottlenecks, performance issues, or the need for manual infrastructure upgrades.

- **Lack of Auto-Scaling Capabilities**

  Modern cloud-native systems can scale horizontally (adding more instances) or vertically (adding more resources) based on real-time load. Traditional MFT lacks this elasticity. When transfer volumes spike such as during quarter-end reporting, system migrations, or bulk file submissions the system may slow down or fail unless over-provisioned in advance.

- **Monolithic Architectures**

  Older MFT platforms are often monolithic in design, meaning all components (transfer engine, scheduler, monitor, logging, etc.) are tightly coupled. This makes it difficult to isolate, scale, or optimize specific services independently unlike microservices-based architectures that enable targeted scaling and high availability.

- **Manual Load Balancing**

  Load distribution in traditional MFT often relies on static routing or manual configuration. There's no intelligent, dynamic way to balance workloads across multiple nodes or prioritize critical transfers. This leads to inefficient resource usage, queuing delays, and increased risk of failed transfers during peak times.

- **Difficulty Adapting to Hybrid and Multi-Cloud Environments**

Modern enterprises are shifting to hybrid or multi-cloud strategies. Traditional MFT systems, built for on-prem deployment, struggle to extend into cloud-native ecosystems or integrate smoothly with containerized, serverless, or edge-based architectures. This limits their ability to scale globally or support distributed teams and systems.

3.2.3 Weak Integration Capabilities

Traditional MFT tools often come with:

- Limited or outdated APIs
- Rigid integration frameworks
- Dependency on custom scripts or middleware

As organizations adopt modern applications (e.g., Salesforce, SAP S/4HANA, cloud data lakes), MFT solutions must integrate seamlessly with APIs, cloud platforms, and event-driven architectures. Legacy MFT platforms lack this plug-and-play flexibility, leading to manual workarounds and integration silos.

3.2.4 Minimal Automation and Smart Workflow Design

While traditional MFT offers basic automation (e.g., scheduled transfers), it lacks:

- Context-aware workflow execution
- Dynamic routing decisions
- Conditional logic based on file content, size, or metadata
- Self-healing capabilities

There is no **automation intelligence** such as automatically rerouting failed transfers, adjusting transfer priorities, or optimizing protocols based on performance trends.

Manual intervention is still heavily required to manage exceptions and optimize operations.

3.2.5 Limited Visibility and Monitoring

Traditional MFT systems typically provide:

- Text-based logs
- Basic dashboards with little to no real-time insight
- Weak anomaly detection or alerting capabilities

In modern enterprises, especially those with compliance needs (e.g., HIPAA, GDPR, SOX), visibility into who sent what, when, where, and how is critical.

Teams are blind to performance issues, security risks, or compliance breaches until too late.

3.2.6 Inadequate Security Posture

Older MFT systems may lack:

- Support for modern encryption standards (e.g., TLS 1.3)
- Behavioral anomaly detection (AI-driven security)
- Role-based access control (RBAC) with fine-grained permissions

They may also store logs or files in unencrypted formats, or transmit data over outdated, vulnerable protocols. There is a possibility for higher vulnerability to data breaches, compliance failures, and reputational damage.

3.2.7 Rigid Deployment and Maintenance

Traditional MFT platforms are often tied to:

- On-premises infrastructure
- Lengthy setup/configuration cycles
- Manual patching and software updates
- Static licensing models (based on partners or connections)

In contrast, modern businesses demand cloud-first, containerized, and DevOps-ready solutions with Artificial Intelligence that can be updated and scaled effortlessly. Hence, traditional MFT demands higher maintenance burden, reduced agility, and slower time-to-market.

3.2.8 High Total Cost of Ownership (TCO)

Maintaining a traditional MFT system typically involves:

- Dedicated infrastructure
- Manual monitoring and troubleshooting
- Custom integrations
- Licensing and support fees
- Security and compliance overhead

Without AI or automation, the operational cost of managing file transfer increases exponentially with system growth. Traditional MFT accumulates hidden costs and reduces ROI over time.

3.2.9 Poor User Experience and Limited Self-Service

Many legacy MFT systems were designed for administrators and lack:

- User-friendly portals
- Self-service options for business users or partners
- Customizable dashboards or no-code workflow builders

This leads to constant IT intervention for even basic tasks like setting up a new transfer or checking file status. Traditional MFT reduces business agility and increases IT burden.

3.2.10 Lack of AI and Predictive Capabilities

Perhaps the most significant limitation is the **absence of Artificial Intelligence**:

- No predictive analytics for transfer trends
- No machine learning for anomaly detection
- No automation intelligence for error resolution or optimization
- No adaptive scaling based on usage patterns

In the face of increasing data complexity and cyber threats, legacy MFT platforms become a **liability**, rather than an asset.

Organizations miss out on the benefits of intelligent automation and proactive operations.

4. AI as a tool for prediction, automation, and anomaly detection

As organizations scale, the complexity of data exchange, partner ecosystems, compliance obligations, and security risks multiplies. Managed File Transfer (MFT) systems are no longer just file movers they are critical to the digital nervous system of the enterprise. To meet modern demands, these systems must become intelligent, proactive, and adaptive. This is precisely where Artificial Intelligence (AI) transforms the MFT landscape.

AI acts as a force multiplier by enabling MFT systems to predict issues before they occur, automate operational tasks, and detect anomalies in real time dramatically improving performance, reliability, and security.

4.1 AI for Prediction in MFT

AI's predictive capabilities enable MFT platforms to foresee patterns and potential issues by analyzing historical data, behavioral trends, and system usage. This proactive insight gives organizations the edge in planning, scaling, and avoiding disruptions.

Key Predictive Capabilities:

- **Transfer Volume Forecasting**:
  AI models analyze past transfer loads and seasonal trends to forecast upcoming spikes (e.g., end-of-quarter reporting, holiday sales cycles).

- **Failure Prediction**:
  Machine learning algorithms detect early signals of potential transfer failures such as slowdowns, unstable endpoints, or format mismatches before they occur.

- **SLA Breach Anticipation**:
  Based on real-time processing speed, file size, and network health, AI can project whether a transfer might miss a service-level agreement (SLA) deadline and suggest preemptive action.

- **Capacity Planning**:
  Predicts infrastructure needs for compute, storage, and bandwidth based on transfer behavior, helping organizations optimize resource allocation.

Benefits:

- Reduced downtime and last-minute firefighting
- Better resource utilization and scaling
- Improved SLA compliance and planning accuracy

4.2 AI for Automation in MFT

Traditional MFT automation is rule-based and reactive. AI upgrades this by enabling context-aware, intelligent automation that adapts to changing conditions in real time.

Intelligent Automation Use Cases:

- **Self-Healing Transfers**:
  If a file fails to reach its destination due to a network error or malformed content, AI can:

    - Retry with alternative protocols
    - Clean or reformat the file
    - Reroute the transfer to a backup endpoint

- **Dynamic Workflow Execution**:
  AI can trigger workflows based on file content, metadata, user behavior, or external business events (e.g., large invoice files trigger immediate compliance checks and approvals).

- **Priority Optimization**:
  During high-load periods, AI can prioritize high-value or time-sensitive transfers while delaying non-critical ones automatically adjusting queue behavior.

- **Auto-Scaling and Load Balancing**:
  In cloud-native environments, AI can dynamically scale MFT instances up or down based on predicted load, while balancing traffic for optimal performance.

Benefits:

- Reduced need for manual oversight

- Faster and smarter responses to operational events

- Greater operational efficiency and reliability

4.3 AI for Anomaly Detection in MFT

Anomaly detection is one of the most powerful security and performance benefits AI brings to MFT. It helps detect unusual behavior, potential breaches, and misconfigurations early, often before traditional rule-based systems would notice.

Anomaly Detection Capabilities:

- **Behavioral Profiling**:
  AI builds behavioral baselines for users, endpoints, file types, and protocols. When behavior deviates (e.g., a user uploads 10x their usual file size at midnight), the system flags it as anomalous.

- **Security Threat Identification**:
  AI can detect:
  - Suspicious access patterns (e.g., repeated failed login attempts)
  - Data exfiltration attempts (e.g., large outbound transfers to unknown IPs)
  - Insider threats (e.g., unusual downloads by privileged users)

- **Integrity Monitoring**:
  Files modified or tampered with unexpectedly based on hash checks or embedded metadata can trigger alerts or automatic quarantining.

- **Content-Based Anomaly Detection**:
  Natural Language Processing (NLP) can be used to scan file content for sensitive or unexpected data (e.g., PII in non-compliant files) and stop the transfer.

Benefits:

- Early detection of threats and compliance risks
- Minimized false positives compared to rule-based alerts
- Improved incident response time and risk mitigation

5 AI-Powered Automation in MFT

As digital transformation accelerates across industries, data exchange workflows are no longer peripheral; they're central to business continuity and competitiveness. In this context, Managed File Transfer (MFT) has evolved from a background IT utility to a mission-critical infrastructure that supports everything from financial transactions and customer onboarding to supply chain coordination and regulatory reporting.

However, with this elevated importance comes greater complexity. Organizations are managing higher volumes of data, facing stricter compliance requirements, and needing to support faster delivery cycles across increasingly heterogeneous environments on-prem, cloud, hybrid, and multi-tenant.

Amid this growing demand, the shortcomings of traditional automation within legacy MFT systems become starkly apparent. These systems are often built around rigid configurations, rule-based logic, and batch processing. While these worked well in the past, today's digital environments demand far greater agility, resilience, and intelligence. Traditional automation is static; it reacts only when predefined rules are triggered. It cannot adjust in real time to changes in network health, user behavior, file attributes, or security conditions.

This is where Artificial Intelligence (AI) steps in to revolutionize MFT automation.

AI-powered automation redefines how MFT systems operate. Rather than simply following pre-set rules, AI learns from data, identifies trends, detects anomalies, and makes decisions on the fly. It transforms MFT from a reactive engine into a proactive and adaptive system. The result is not just better file delivery performance but a fundamental shift in how organizations govern, secure, and scale their data transfers.

With AI embedded at the core of automation, MFT platforms can now:

- Adapt dynamically to real-time workloads
- Reroute transfers based on context
- Prioritize high-value data flows
- Predict failures before they happen
- Resolve issues autonomously
- Optimize performance continuously

Instead of hardcoding workflows for every possible scenario, AI builds **intelligent models** that evolve over time. These models understand patterns such as peak load hours, typical transfer sizes for each user, or preferred routes for specific partners and apply that knowledge to improve future operations.

Imagine a scenario where a file transfer fails due to an unexpected endpoint outage. In a traditional system, the transfer would retry blindly or trigger a manual alert. With AI, the system analyzes the failure in real-time, identifies the root cause, reroutes the transfer via a backup protocol, and completes the delivery all without human intervention.

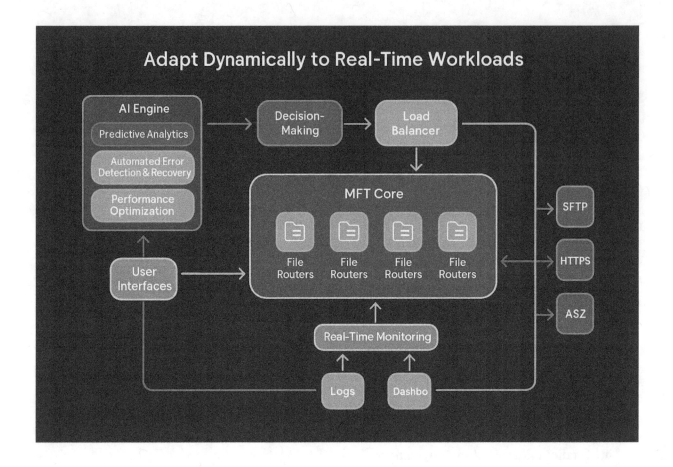

Similarly, AI can monitor network traffic, transfer frequencies, and data types to make informed routing decisions. For instance, it may determine that large financial reports transfer faster via AS2 during off-peak hours, while marketing assets are better routed via HTTPS with CDN support.

This level of automation is not static, it's learning-based. Every successful transfer, failed attempt, or latency spike adds to the AI model's understanding of how the system behaves. Over time, this results in smarter decisions, fewer failures, faster resolution, and higher system efficiency.

Moreover, AI-powered automation extends beyond operations into governance and compliance. Intelligent engines can detect non-compliant file formats, personally identifiable information (PII) in unauthorized transfers, or access attempts from unusual IP addresses and take preventive action automatically. This is especially valuable for organizations in regulated industries such as healthcare, finance, and logistics, where data integrity and confidentiality are paramount.

AI also supports context-aware file handling. For example, if a large, encrypted file is received from a trusted partner but lacks an expected metadata tag, the AI engine can flag the issue, initiate a metadata validation step, or automatically tag the file based on historical patterns.

In multi-cloud or hybrid environments, AI plays a critical role in workload distribution and resource optimization. It can:

- Predict transfer surges based on business events or seasonality

- Scale up processing nodes in advance

- Distribute tasks across geographically distributed nodes

- Ensure data sovereignty rules are followed by routing transfers through compliant regions

These benefits culminate in reduced downtime, lower operational costs, and greater reliability without compromising security or control.

What's more, AI-powered MFT automation enables self-service capabilities for business users. Instead of relying on IT for every change, users can initiate workflows that adapt intelligently to their data needs. The system handles the complexity under the hood, offering a simplified, yet powerful interface for non-technical teams.

The transition from traditional automation to AI-driven automation is not just a technical upgrade, it's a strategic shift. It aligns file transfer operations with the broader goals of digital agility, cyber resilience, and customer-centric delivery models.

In essence, AI turns MFT into a thinking system, one that doesn't just move data but understands and optimizes every transfer, every time.

As we delve deeper into this chapter, we'll explore specific use cases where AI transforms automation in MFT, including:

- Smart file routing based on real-time conditions

- Predictive load balancing to prevent system strain

- Intelligent retry and self-healing mechanisms for failed transfers

These intelligent automation components are not just enhancements, they are the foundation of the **next-generation MFT platforms** that will power data movement in the AI-driven enterprise.

5.1 Smart Routing of Files

Smart routing in a modern Managed File Transfer (MFT) environment refers to the intelligent, policy-driven, and dynamic selection of file delivery paths based on contextual metadata, operational conditions, and business logic. Unlike traditional static routing where files are transferred to predefined endpoints regardless of network or business state, smart routing leverages real-time decision-making to optimize delivery across hybrid, multi-cloud, and on-premise infrastructures.

At the core of smart routing is a combination of rules engines, metadata analysis, and increasingly, AI/ML-driven inference models. When a file enters the MFT system whether inbound from an external partner or outbound from an internal application it is tagged with metadata such as file type, priority, sensitivity level, partner ID, region, SLA requirements, and even content characteristics (e.g., EDI type, encryption format, file size, etc.). This metadata is then evaluated against a centralized routing policy engine, which determines the most appropriate delivery path.

For example, a high-priority file destined for a financial regulator in a specific region may be routed through a low-latency, encrypted tunnel that complies with regional data sovereignty laws. Meanwhile, large, non-time-critical files may be routed through cost-optimized cloud storage tiers or delayed queues. Routing decisions can also be made based on network performance metrics, system load, compliance constraints, or partner availability. Some advanced MFT platforms integrate real-time monitoring APIs, allowing routing logic to adapt to live telemetry such as link congestion, node failures, or SLA breaches.

From a technical perspective, smart routing in MFT platforms may involve:

- Dynamic partner resolution using directory services or external APIs

- Workflow branching using conditional logic in business process definitions (e.g., IBM Sterling BPs, Cleo Integration Studio flows)

- Load-balanced path selection across geographically distributed nodes

- AI-enhanced prediction models that suggest optimal routes based on historical trends and traffic patterns

- Fallback and failover routing in response to transmission errors or unavailable endpoints

Additionally, smart routing supports protocol abstraction, allowing the MFT engine to dynamically select between SFTP, AS2, HTTPS, or proprietary transport methods depending on partner configuration, file type, and compliance requirements. For instance, the same file may be routed via AS2 for a retail partner while an SFTP path is used for a bank, based on trading partner profiles stored in the system.

By implementing smart routing, enterprises can achieve greater efficiency, enhanced security, reduced transmission costs, and higher SLA adherence, especially in complex environments involving thousands of partners, multiple file types, and regulatory mandates. It also lays the groundwork for self-healing file flows, where AI agents can autonomously reroute or retry failed transfers based on contextual learning pushing MFT closer to true intelligent automation.

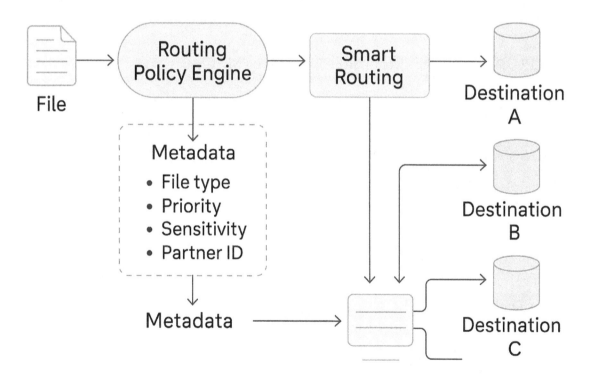

5.2 Predictive Load Balancing in MFT

Predictive load balancing in a modern Managed File Transfer (MFT) environment refers to the intelligent, proactive distribution of file transfer workloads across multiple nodes, gateways, or processing engines based on real-time analytics, historical patterns, and AI-driven forecasts. It moves beyond traditional round-robin or static rule-based load distribution by incorporating machine learning models, system telemetry, and behavioral heuristics to predict traffic surges, identify potential bottlenecks, and preemptively optimize transfer flows.

In traditional MFT systems, load balancing is typically reactive and follows deterministic logic spreading jobs based on node availability or transfer size at the moment of execution. However, in high-volume, latency-sensitive, or compliance-critical environments, this static approach often fails to adapt to dynamic workloads, especially during peak hours, month-end batch runs, or seasonal data bursts. Predictive load balancing addresses this limitation by analyzing multiple data points such as:

- Historical transfer volume patterns by time of day/week

- CPU, memory, and network utilization trends on MFT nodes

- Partner-specific throughput behavior

- Transfer failure/retry frequencies

- SLA violations and escalation histories

- External signals like forecasted transaction spikes (e.g., from ERP or trading systems)

Using this intelligence, the MFT system can forecast imminent resource contention or network saturation and preemptively shift file transfer jobs to underutilized nodes, reroute traffic through alternative paths, or throttle non-critical transfers. This ensures optimal performance, reduces latency, and prevents overload scenarios before they occur.

Technically, predictive load balancing can be implemented through an orchestration layer that integrates with:

- Monitoring and observability platforms (e.g., Prometheus, Datadog, GCP Operations)

- Machine learning models trained on historical transfer metadata

- Dynamic routing engines capable of redirecting flows mid-transit

- Queue prioritization and shaping policies for staging high-value or time-sensitive jobs

- Auto-scaling MFT clusters in cloud environments (e.g., AWS, Azure, GCP)

In hybrid architectures, predictive load balancing becomes even more critical. For example, if an on-premise MFT node is predicted to reach saturation due to an upcoming batch window, the orchestrator can proactively redirect traffic to a cloud-based MFT gateway, provided bandwidth and compliance constraints are satisfied.

Additionally, predictive algorithms can use reinforcement learning techniques to continuously improve their routing logic. By measuring the success rate, throughput, and SLA compliance of past decisions, the models refine future predictions creating a self-optimizing, adaptive transfer layer.

The benefits of predictive load balancing in MFT are substantial:

- Improved SLA adherence through preemptive workload smoothing

- Higher system uptime by avoiding node-level overload and cascading failures

- Better resource utilization, especially in distributed or multi-cloud deployments

- Scalability and resilience during data spikes without manual intervention

In summary, predictive load balancing transforms MFT into a resilient, intelligent, and future-ready system capable of dynamically adapting to fluctuating demands while ensuring business-critical file transfers remain secure, efficient, and on schedule.

5.3 Intelligent Retry and Recovery Mechanisms in MFT

In a high-availability Managed File Transfer (MFT) environment, intelligent retry and recovery mechanisms are essential for ensuring the resilience, reliability, and continuity of file-based workflows especially when dealing with fluctuating network conditions, external partner dependencies, and large-scale distributed infrastructures. Unlike traditional retry logic that operates with rigid intervals or fixed thresholds, intelligent mechanisms leverage real-time feedback, contextual awareness, and AI-driven decision-making to handle failures more gracefully and efficiently.

In conventional MFT systems, when a file transfer fails (e.g., due to a dropped connection, partner unavailability, or protocol mismatch), the system typically retries the transmission after a predetermined delay, often with a fixed number of attempts. This approach is inefficient, particularly in dynamic environments, because it lacks insight into why the failure occurred, whether the endpoint is still down, or if retrying immediately is even appropriate.

Modern MFT platforms overcome this limitation through contextual retry logic integrated with adaptive learning and diagnostic intelligence. Here's how it works:

1. **Failure Classification and Root Cause Analysis:**
   When a failure is detected, the system performs rapid classification distinguishing between transient errors (e.g., timeouts, network congestion), systemic issues (e.g., destination server offline), or configuration faults (e.g., certificate mismatch, incorrect directory path). This classification is crucial to determine if, when, and how to retry.

2. **Dynamic Backoff Algorithms:**
   Instead of static retry intervals, intelligent MFT engines use exponential backoff or predictive backoff algorithms, adjusting retry timing based on partner behavior history, recent success/failure rates, and current system load. This avoids overloading either the sender or receiver during recovery attempts.

3. **Alternate Path or Node Failover:**
   In clustered or multi-zone deployments, the system can reroute the file to a healthy node or alternate endpoint if the original destination is unreachable. This requires integration with smart routing engines, geo-awareness, and session state replication between nodes.

4. **Partial Transfer Recovery & Checkpoint Restart:**
   For large files or critical data transfers, intelligent recovery mechanisms support checkpointing allowing the transfer to resume from the last successful byte rather than restarting from scratch. This is particularly effective in Connect:Direct with HSAO, TIBCO MFT, or IBM Sterling Integrator, where restart markers and transactional logging are built in.

5. **Time-Based Retry Suppression & SLA Awareness:**
   If retries consistently fail or if the window for SLA compliance is exceeded, the system can suppress further retries and escalate the issue to operational teams or send notifications to trading partners, reducing unnecessary resource consumption.

6. **Self-Healing Automation via AI:**
   Some advanced MFT systems integrate AI/ML-based anomaly detectors to learn from historical retry patterns and auto-tune retry behaviors. For instance, the system might learn that Partner X's server often becomes unavailable between 2–3 AM and automatically delays retries during that period to reduce failure rates and unnecessary logs.

7. **Visibility and Auditing:**
   Every retry and recovery action is logged, tagged with failure metadata, and made visible in dashboards or SIEM platforms. This enables operations teams to audit what failed, what recovered, and what required manual intervention.

6 Anomaly Detection and Threat Prevention

In modern Managed File Transfer (MFT) environments, anomaly detection and threat prevention play a critical role in safeguarding sensitive data flows against misuse, exfiltration, and cyber threats. One of the most effective ways to implement proactive security is by detecting unusual transfer patterns, specifically deviations in transfer time, file size, frequency, or endpoint behavior which may signal either operational anomalies or malicious activity.

Traditional MFT platforms focus primarily on protocol security (e.g., TLS, SSH, authentication), but these measures alone do not protect against insider threats, credential misuse, or zero-day exploitation. AI-driven anomaly detection fills this gap by continuously analyzing behavioral baselines for users, partners, and systems. For instance, the system learns typical patterns such as:

- Partner A usually sends files between 2–3 AM and only on weekdays

- User B typically uploads files under 5 GB and never on weekends

- Internal application X sends files every 15 minutes to a fixed destination

These behavioral models are built using historical telemetry and enriched with contextual metadata like file type, protocol used, transfer route, latency, and success rates. When the system observes a deviation from the norm such as a file that's 10x larger than usual, a transfer occurring during non-business hours, or a sudden spike in transmission frequency an anomaly score is computed using statistical thresholds or unsupervised machine learning models like Isolation Forests, k-Means clustering, or Autoencoders.

Based on configurable severity levels, the system can take real-time actions such as:

- Flagging the transfer for manual review

- Blocking the transmission pending investigation

- Quarantining the file for further inspection

- Triggering an automated incident workflow in a SOAR or SIEM platform

For example, if an employee's compromised credentials are used to initiate a large outbound transfer to an unfamiliar destination during a national holiday, the anomaly detection engine may score this event as high risk and automatically prevent the file from leaving the network. Additionally, anomaly detection systems integrate with Threat Intelligence feeds to enrich detections for instance, identifying that the destination IP belongs to a flagged malicious ASN or a high-risk geographic region.

To enhance precision and reduce false positives, modern systems apply behavioral baselining per entity (user, partner, application), employ adaptive thresholds, and support feedback loops where analysts can mark events as true or false positives thereby training the detection engine over time. Logs and anomaly events are indexed for compliance audits, and are exportable to platforms like Splunk, Elastic, or Chronicle Security.

In essence, anomaly detection in MFT transforms the system from being a transactional conduit into a proactive sentinel capable of detecting insider threats, misconfigurations, accidental leaks, and advanced persistent threats (APTs) before they cause harm. It's a foundational pillar in building a zero-trust MFT architecture, where every action is monitored, scored, and evaluated in context.

Anomaly Detection and Threat Prevention

Detecting unusual transfer patterns (e.g., time, size, frequency)

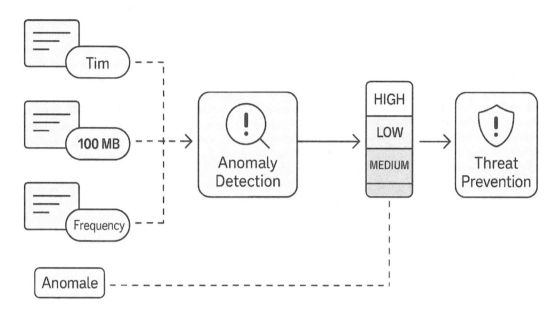

6.1 AI Models for Intrusion and Exfiltration Detection in MFT

As cyber threats become increasingly sophisticated, traditional rule-based security systems are often inadequate to detect subtle or evolving attack patterns especially in the context of file transfer systems that handle high-volume, sensitive, and often regulated data flows. Artificial Intelligence (AI) models, particularly those rooted in machine learning (ML) and behavioral analytics, are now central to the defense strategy in next-generation Managed File Transfer (MFT) platforms. They enable real-time detection of intrusions, data exfiltration attempts, and insider misuse by modeling expected behavior and flagging deviations that indicate potential compromise.

These AI models function by ingesting vast amounts of historical telemetry, including metadata such as transfer time, file type, size, frequency, sender/receiver profiles, authentication patterns, endpoint behaviors, and geographic origin. Once sufficient baseline data is established, AI algorithms such as unsupervised anomaly detection models (e.g., Isolation Forests, One-Class SVMs), statistical outlier detectors, and time-series forecasting models (e.g., ARIMA, LSTM networks) are used to create behavioral profiles for every user, application, or integration endpoint.

When live traffic deviates from these established baselines such as:

- An internal user transferring an abnormally large set of files to a new external IP

- A known partner account initiating file requests at unusual times or frequencies

- Transfers occurring to geo-locations that violate corporate data residency policies

- Sessions exhibiting signs of lateral movement (indicative of attacker pivoting)

The system assigns a risk score to the event. High-risk scores may trigger immediate containment actions, such as:

- Blocking or quarantining the file in transit

- Revoking the active session token

- Isolating the impacted user or system

- Escalating the alert to a Security Operations Center (SOC) via SIEM/SOAR platforms

Furthermore, advanced AI-based MFT systems utilize Natural Language Processing (NLP) models to scan file contents for sensitive data patterns (e.g., PII, PCI, HIPAA-protected data), which when matched with high-risk behavioral signals can indicate a data exfiltration attempt rather than a legitimate business transaction.

Some platforms also use graph-based ML to model relationships between users, endpoints, and transfer paths. These models detect unusual traversal patterns across the MFT topology that may indicate intrusion campaigns, such as privilege escalation or command-and-control beaconing behavior.

An important feature of AI-driven intrusion detection is its adaptive learning capability. The models improve over time by incorporating feedback from security analysts on true vs. false positives, allowing the system to continuously evolve, reduce alert fatigue, and increase detection accuracy. This approach is particularly effective in identifying low-and-slow exfiltration attempts and credential misuse, which would otherwise go undetected by threshold-based security policies.

By integrating these AI models directly into the MFT workflow, enterprises are equipped with a zero-trust file transfer environment where every action is verified, contextualized, and risk-scored. This not only ensures compliance with industry standards (e.g., NIST 800-53, ISO 27001, PCI-DSS) but also elevates MFT to a proactive security control in the organization's broader cyber defense strategy.

AI Models for Intrusion and Exfiltràtion Detection

File Transfers

- User Behavior
- File Characteristics
- Transfer Activity

AI Models

Detection

- Anomalous Activity
- Exfiltration Attempts
- Malicious Behavior

7. Natural Language Interfaces (AI Agents)

As enterprise IT environments become more complex and time-sensitive, there is a growing need to democratize access to Managed File Transfer (MFT) systems and streamline operational workflows. Natural Language Interfaces (NLIs) powered by advanced AI agents and large language models (LLMs) are emerging as transformative tools in next-generation MFT platforms. These interfaces allow users, administrators, and even non-technical stakeholders to interact with the MFT system through natural, conversational commands rather than traditional command-line inputs or graphical workflows.

A Natural Language Interface in MFT enables human users to initiate, monitor, troubleshoot, and even configure file transfer processes by typing or speaking intuitive queries such as:

- "Transfer the latest invoice batch to Partner A via SFTP."

- "Show me failed transfers from the last 24 hours."

- "Pause all outbound transfers to the EU region."

- "Add a new trading partner with endpoint IP 10.20.1.5 and AS2 credentials."

Behind the scenes, these natural language inputs are parsed and interpreted by an AI agent, which uses Natural Language Understanding (NLU) models to map the intent to specific system actions or API calls. The system then executes the necessary workflow whether it's triggering a predefined job, querying transfer logs, modifying routing rules, or initiating a secure handshake with a new partner.

To ensure accuracy and safety, the NLI is typically backed by:

- Intent classification models (e.g., BERT, T5) to determine what action is being requested

- Named Entity Recognition (NER) to extract key attributes like partner names, file paths, or protocol types

- Role-based access control (RBAC) and policy enforcement layers to verify user permissions before execution

- Audit logging and confirmation loops to track every action and require verification for sensitive operations

In more advanced implementations, the AI agent can act as an autonomous assistant proactively alerting users of anomalies ("There were 3 failed file transfers to Partner B overnight"), suggesting optimizations ("Would you like to enable compression for these large files?"), or initiating recovery actions based on pre-trained logic.

Natural Language Interfaces can also integrate with collaboration tools like Slack, Microsoft Teams, or ServiceNow, enabling MFT administrators to interact with the system directly from their existing workspaces. For instance, an admin could type "List all files pending delivery to external vendors" in a chat window and receive a structured response pulled from the MFT engine.

From a technical perspective, these interfaces leverage:

- LLMs or fine-tuned models hosted via APIs or on-prem deployments (e.g., OpenAI, Google Vertex AI, HuggingFace models)

- Secure webhooks and REST APIs to bridge the NLI with backend MFT logic

- Stateful memory for context-aware dialogue, allowing users to refine or follow up queries seamlessly

The result is a more accessible, intelligent, and responsive MFT environment reducing operational overhead, shortening incident response time, and enabling cross-functional collaboration. It also lowers the barrier for new team members or business users to safely engage with complex file transfer workflows without requiring deep system knowledge.

In the long term, the integration of AI agents and Natural Language Interfaces in MFT platforms not only enhances usability but also lays the foundation for fully autonomous file movement orchestration, where conversations drive automation, and intelligent agents manage security, compliance, and performance end-to-end.

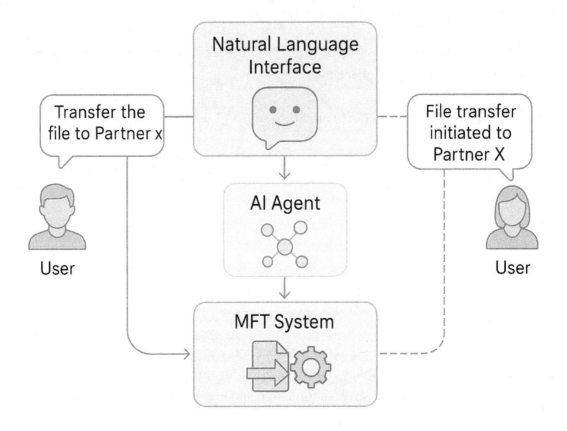

7.1 Using Chatbots and AI Agents for Managing File Transfers

In the era of intelligent automation and conversational interfaces, chatbots and AI agents are revolutionizing how Managed File Transfer (MFT) systems are operated, monitored, and maintained. Traditionally, managing file transfers required interaction through complex UIs, command-line interfaces, or tightly scoped APIs. However, with the emergence of conversational AI, organizations can now manage end-to-end MFT operations through interactive, natural language-based chat interfaces integrated into everyday platforms like Slack, Microsoft Teams, or web portals.

These intelligent agents are built upon Natural Language Processing (NLP) and Natural Language Understanding (NLU) frameworks that can interpret user intent, extract relevant parameters, and execute corresponding MFT actions via secure backend integrations. For instance, an MFT administrator can instruct a chatbot with simple commands like:

- "Pause transfers to Partner B for the next 2 hours"

- "Send yesterday's reconciliation file to the finance team"

- "Create a new AS2 partner with endpoint xyz.company.com"

- "List failed SFTP deliveries in the past 24 hours"

These commands are interpreted by the AI agent using intent classification models (e.g., BERT, DistilBERT, or fine-tuned LLMs) and entity extraction algorithms to identify parameters such as partner names, protocols, or time ranges. The agent then maps the request to predefined MFT system APIs, enforces role-based access control (RBAC) policies, and executes the workflow often with an optional confirmation step for critical tasks.

From a technical architecture standpoint, chatbots and agents for MFT are typically built with the following layers:

- Frontend Chat Interface (Slack, Teams, custom web UI)

- Conversational Middleware that handles session context, multi-turn conversations, and fallback handling

- NLU/NLP Engine powered by open-source or commercial models (e.g., Rasa, Dialog Flow, OpenAI GPT, Azure Bot Framework)

- MFT Orchestration Layer, which securely connects the agent to underlying file transfer engines (like IBM Sterling, Cleo, TIBCO, or custom systems) via REST APIs, message queues, or service meshes

- Security & Governance Layer, enforcing audit logging, encryption, multi-factor authentication, and role validation

- Feedback Loop to continuously learn from usage patterns and improve the agent's accuracy and responsiveness

Advanced agents can go beyond reactive commands to offer proactive insights and alerts. For example, the chatbot might automatically notify a user that "File transfers to Partner Z are experiencing high latency" or suggest, "Would you like to reroute through the backup gateway?"

These interactions are powered by telemetry data, system health metrics, and AI-based predictive analytics integrated into the MFT environment.

Benefits of chatbot-driven file transfer management include:

- Faster operational response time without logging into complex UIs

- Lower technical barrier for business users to initiate and monitor transfers

- Increased visibility and control through real-time conversational logging

- Greater automation of common admin tasks like partner onboarding, certificate updates, and job restarts

- Seamless integration into IT workflows through ticketing systems, notifications, and approval chains

In regulated environments, chatbot interactions are fully auditable, with every action logged and traceable ensuring compliance with standards such as ISO 27001, HIPAA, and SOX. Moreover, organizations can define guardrails to limit which users can execute high-impact commands or require secondary approvals for sensitive actions.

Ultimately, integrating chatbots and AI agents into MFT platforms represents a paradigm shift transforming file transfer operations from a reactive, manual process into a responsive, intelligent, and user-friendly experience. It empowers both technical and non-technical stakeholders to manage secure file movement confidently, efficiently, and in real time.

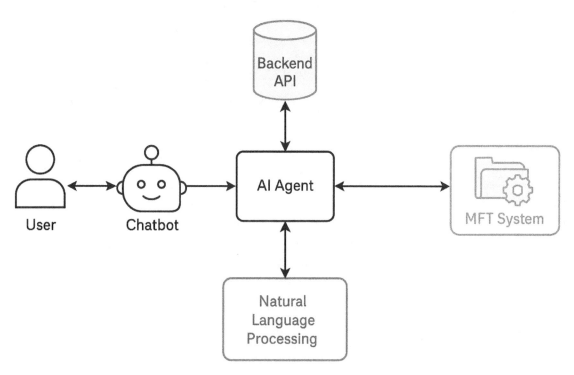

Natural Language Interfaces

7.2 Conversational Interfaces for Operations in MFT

As enterprise IT environments grow in complexity, the demand for more intuitive, responsive, and user-friendly interfaces is accelerating particularly in the realm of Managed File Transfer (MFT) operations. Conversational interfaces, powered by natural language processing (NLP) and AI-driven orchestration layers, are redefining how operational teams interact with MFT systems. These interfaces enable administrators, support engineers, and business users to engage with MFT platforms through dialogue-driven commands, replacing traditional graphical dashboards or command-line tools with interactive, context-aware, and conversational experiences.

A conversational interface allows users to execute operational tasks via plain English prompts such as:

- "List all active file transfer sessions right now."

- "Retry the failed AS2 delivery to Partner B."

- "Add a new SFTP endpoint for the legal department."

- "When was the last successful transfer to AWS S3?"

Behind the scenes, the interface leverages a multi-layered architecture:

1. **Natural Language Understanding (NLU) Layer**
   This layer interprets user input, determines intent (e.g., 'list', 'retry', 'create'), and extracts parameters such as partner names, time windows, protocols, or statuses. It is typically powered by transformer-based models like BERT, GPT, or T5, often fine-tuned for domain-specific MFT vocabulary.

2. **Conversational Orchestration Engine**
   Once the intent is parsed, the orchestration engine maps it to a predefined set of workflows, decision trees, or API calls within the MFT system. This may involve querying real-time logs, modifying partner configurations, or invoking job schedules. Context retention is also supported, allowing users to follow up with commands like "retry the last one" or "show details for that."

3. **Backend Integration Layer**
   This layer connects the conversational interface to the actual MFT engines (e.g., IBM Sterling, TIBCO MFT, GoAnywhere, Cleo Integration Cloud) via RESTful APIs, gRPC, message queues, or command execution shells. It handles secure execution, error handling, and structured data retrieval.

4. **Security and Governance Framework**
   Every action initiated through the interface is gated by role-based access control (RBAC), multi-factor authentication (MFA), and audit logging. Sensitive operations may require confirmation, additional approvals, or automated policy validation before execution.

5. **Multi-Channel Deployment**
   Conversational interfaces are often deployed within enterprise collaboration tools like Slack, Microsoft Teams, Webex, or custom portals. This enables MFT operations to be managed within the tools that teams already use, enhancing responsiveness and reducing context-switching.

From a technical standpoint, conversational interfaces can be stateless (each command is processed independently) or stateful, retaining context across interactions to support multi-step workflows. For example:

- User: "Send the month-end report to Finance."

- System: "Which partner should receive the file?"

- User: "Use Partner ID 8043."

- System: "Transfer scheduled. Would you like confirmation when complete?"

AI agents can also proactively notify users of anomalies e.g., "Five transfers to Partner Z failed due to timeout. Would you like to reroute or retry?" enabling real-time operational decision-making without logging into the core platform.

Benefits of Conversational Interfaces in MFT Operations:

- Reduced cognitive load and learning curve for users

- Faster incident response and task execution

- Enhanced collaboration across technical and non-technical teams

- Minimized reliance on manual scripts or deep UI navigation

- Improved accessibility and availability across devices and locations

In regulated industries, conversational operations are fully auditable, with interaction logs exportable to SIEM or compliance tools. In AI-enhanced environments, the interface itself may learn over time recommending actions, pre-populating parameters, or optimizing queries based on past behavior.

Ultimately, conversational interfaces shift the operational paradigm from system-driven to user-centric MFT, empowering teams to manage secure, compliant, and high-volume file transfers with speed, precision, and intelligence.

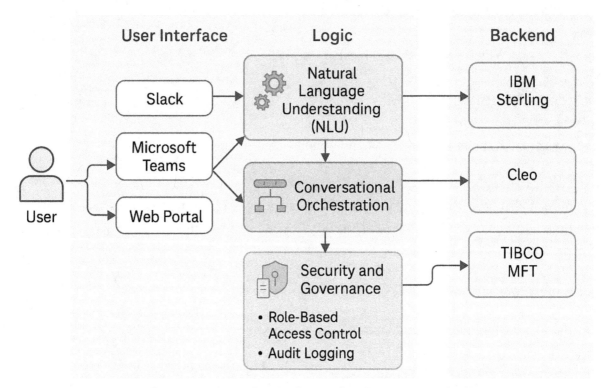

Conversational Interfaces for Operations 'MFT

8. Forecasting and Resource Optimization

In modern Managed File Transfer (MFT) environments, forecasting and resource optimization are essential capabilities for achieving performance efficiency, cost control, and SLA adherence particularly in large-scale, hybrid, and multi-tenant deployments. Traditional MFT systems often rely on static provisioning and reactive scaling, which leads to underutilized infrastructure during low-load periods or degraded performance during peak activity. In contrast, next-generation MFT platforms integrate predictive analytics, machine learning (ML), and telemetry-based insights to forecast demand and dynamically optimize resource allocation in real-time.

At the core of this capability is the collection and modeling of historical file transfer data. This includes time-series metrics such as:

- File volume and size per hour/day/week

- Transfer initiation timestamps and completion durations

- System CPU, memory, and I/O load during transfer windows

- Partner-specific traffic patterns

- Frequency of protocol usage (e.g., SFTP vs. AS2)

Using this data, time-series forecasting models such as ARIMA, Prophet, or deep learning models like LSTM (Long Short-Term Memory) networks are applied to predict future system load, transfer frequency, and bandwidth consumption. These forecasts feed into automated orchestration systems, enabling proactive decisions such as:

- Auto-scaling cloud-based MFT nodes during predicted peak periods

- Dynamic adjustment of thread pools, buffer sizes, or connection limits

- Rebalancing workloads across MFT clusters, regions, or data centers

- Pre-fetching or staging files in advance for expected batch transfers

For example, if the system predicts that the last three days of every month show a 5x increase in outbound invoice transfers to financial institutions, it can pre-allocate additional compute resources, widen bandwidth pipes, or distribute load across secondary MFT gateways. Similarly, forecasted drops in activity (e.g., public holidays or weekends) allow idle resources to be decommissioned or put into standby reducing infrastructure cost in cloud-hosted models.

Forecasting models also support capacity planning for long-term infrastructure growth. They provide insight into storage utilization trends, licensing thresholds (e.g., partner count limits), or protocol saturation (e.g., SFTP sessions per minute), allowing IT and DevOps teams to plan upgrades, migrations, or cloudburst configurations with high confidence.

Beyond compute and bandwidth optimization, forecasting is also applied to job prioritization and scheduling. If the MFT system predicts resource contention during certain hours, it can:

- Reorder non-critical jobs to off-peak windows

- Throttle bulk file transfers to preserve bandwidth for priority payloads

- Alert administrators about impending SLA risks for specific partners

Integration with cost management systems (e.g., GCP Billing, AWS Cost Explorer) also enables cost-aware optimization, where the MFT platform considers transfer urgency, protocol choice, and destination location when routing files for example, preferring intra-region S3 buckets during peak egress periods to reduce cross-region data transfer costs.

Security and compliance considerations are also embedded into forecasting engines. For instance, when anticipating a spike in transfers involving sensitive data, the system may pre-enable deeper logging, increase file-level encryption throughput, or schedule regulatory audit trail exports.

In summary, forecasting and resource optimization transform MFT platforms from reactive transfer agents into intelligent, self-tuning systems. They allow enterprises to reduce operational overhead, improve performance, and maximize cost-efficiency while ensuring SLA integrity and transfer security particularly in AI-enhanced, cloud-integrated, and compliance-sensitive environments.

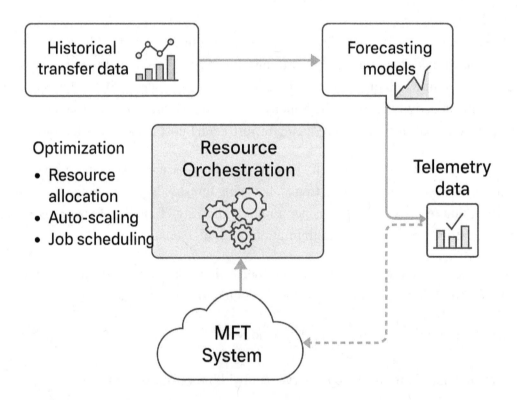

8.1 Predicting Transfer Peaks in MFT Systems

One of the most critical capabilities in next-generation Managed File Transfer (MFT) platforms is the ability to predict transfer peaks periods of exceptionally high data movement volume before they occur. These peaks can arise from scheduled batch jobs, end-of-month processing, partner-specific data dumps, or even unexpected surges due to downstream application activity. Left unmanaged, transfer spikes can lead to resource saturation, missed SLAs, delayed processing, and potential system outages. By leveraging AI-driven forecasting, MFT systems can anticipate these peaks and proactively scale infrastructure, reallocate workloads, or reprioritize job execution to maintain performance and reliability.

The prediction process starts with the collection of time-series telemetry across multiple dimensions: number of file transfers, file sizes, protocol usage, network bandwidth, system load (CPU, IOPS, memory), user access patterns, and partner-specific behavior. This data is fed into forecasting algorithms such as ARIMA, Facebook Prophet, or deep learning models like LSTM (Long Short-Term Memory) networks, which excel in modeling temporal dependencies. These models analyze historical trends and seasonal patterns such as spikes occurring every Friday at 6 PM, or during end-of-quarter reporting cycles and produce transfer volume projections with associated confidence intervals.

These predictions are then utilized by the MFT orchestration engine in several ways:

- Auto-scaling compute and network resources (e.g., provisioning additional transfer nodes or bandwidth capacity)

- Pre-staging critical files for faster access or preprocessing

- Dynamically rerouting low-priority transfers to alternate paths or off-peak windows

- Throttle-based control to prevent non-essential jobs from consuming peak-period bandwidth

- Early alerting to operations teams via dashboards or chatbots for proactive monitoring

For example, if a forecast model indicates that Monday mornings typically experience a 4x load increase due to overnight partner submissions, the system can automatically increase thread pool size, open additional ports, or shift internal batch jobs to avoid congestion. In cloud-native deployments, these predictions can also drive horizontal auto-scaling policies, spinning up additional MFT container instances ahead of time and gracefully spinning them down post-peak to optimize cost.

More advanced models integrate external signals such as ERP schedules, order volumes, or trading activity from APIs or upstream systems to refine their predictions and better correlate business events with data transfer patterns. In highly regulated environments, forecasted peaks involving sensitive or compliance-bound transfers can trigger temporary logging level escalation, additional encryption enforcement, or policy revalidation to ensure governance during high-risk transfer windows.

The ability to predict transfer peaks enables organizations to move from reactive to proactive MFT operations, reducing the likelihood of failure, optimizing resource utilization, and ensuring end-to-end service reliability even during critical business cycles. It forms a foundational capability in intelligent MFT ecosystems, especially when paired with predictive load balancing, automated routing, and smart retry frameworks.

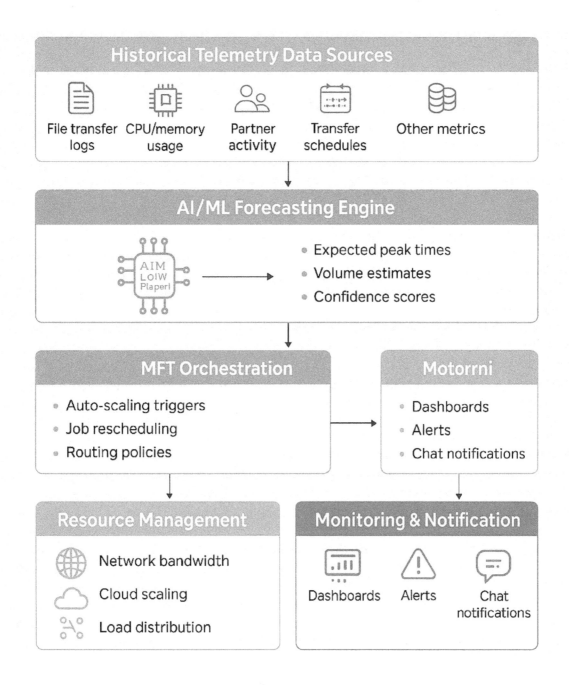

8.2 Resource Allocation Based on Predictive Analytics in MFT

In high-throughput, enterprise-scale Managed File Transfer (MFT) environments, predictive analytics-driven resource allocation represents a critical leap forward in ensuring efficiency, uptime, and cost-optimization. Rather than statically assigning compute, memory, or network resources to transfer engines, predictive analytics enables data-driven, anticipatory scaling and orchestration aligning system capacity with actual workload forecasts derived from historical patterns and real-time telemetry.

This approach begins with the continuous collection of operational metrics across the MFT ecosystem, including:

- Transfer volume trends (files/hour, bytes/day)

- Protocol usage distribution (e.g., SFTP vs. AS2)

- File size patterns and growth rates

- Partner-specific activity schedules

- System resource utilization (CPU, RAM, IOPS, bandwidth)

- Error rates, retries, and latency anomalies

Using this historical dataset, advanced machine learning models such as time-series predictors (ARIMA, Prophet, LSTM) and classification/regression models (Random Forests, Gradient Boosting Machines) forecast upcoming demand spikes, idle periods, and resource consumption curves. These forecasts are then integrated into MFT orchestration engines or infrastructure-as-code systems, enabling real-time resource tuning.

Key optimization strategies driven by predictive analytics include:

- **Dynamic Thread Pool Adjustment**: Transfer engine thread pools (used to handle concurrent file transfers) are automatically resized based on expected traffic, preventing over-threading during peaks and conserving memory during lulls.

- **Elastic Compute Scaling:** In containerized or cloud-native deployments (e.g., Kubernetes, AWS ECS), predicted high-load intervals trigger horizontal pod autoscaling, provisioning additional MFT nodes ahead of anticipated demand and deallocating them post-peak to avoid waste.

- **Adaptive Storage Provisioning**: Forecasts related to file size growth or aggregation trends are used to pre-expand local staging areas, cloud buckets, or buffer queues, preventing transfer failures due to insufficient disk space.

- **Bandwidth Reservation & Throttling**: If high-volume transfers are predicted to coincide with other critical workloads, bandwidth can be pre-reserved, and non-critical jobs throttled to preserve QoS and SLA compliance.

- **Load-Aware Routing**: Predictive analytics informs routing policies, directing transfers to underutilized MFT nodes, edge proxies, or regional gateways to avoid congestion.

- **Cost-Aware Resource Control**: In cloud environments, forecast models drive cost optimization, shifting workloads to low-cost storage tiers, intra-region zones, or off-peak windows balancing performance with economic efficiency.

In environments where MFT systems serve multiple business units, resource allocation can be tenant-aware, assigning resource quotas and priority tiers dynamically based on expected departmental usage. This allows for predictive multi-tenancy orchestration, where compute is intelligently redistributed across clients or projects to maximize utilization while preserving SLAs.

Importantly, this predictive model operates in closed-loop orchestration, where real-time monitoring continuously feeds back into the analytics engine, allowing for recalibration and self-correction. This ensures that if forecasted patterns deviate due to network outages, partner-side issues, or emergent business events the system can autonomously adapt, reschedule, or scale accordingly.

By leveraging predictive analytics for resource allocation, modern MFT platforms evolve into self-aware, self-adjusting infrastructures that deliver consistently high performance, optimized operational costs, and resilient, SLA-bound file movement whether on-premises, in the cloud, or across hybrid networks

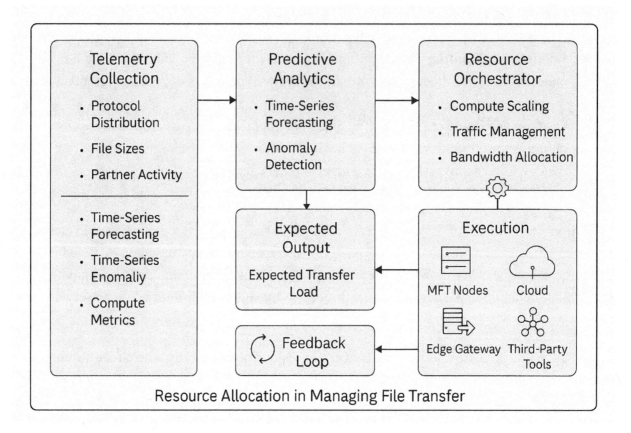

Resource Allocation in Managing File Transfer

9 AI + MFT for Data Classification

In the evolving landscape of secure data exchange, AI-powered data classification within Managed File Transfer (MFT) systems has become a critical enabler of precision, compliance, and automation. Traditional MFT solutions have long relied on static metadata tags, file naming conventions, and manual classification rules to determine how files should be routed, encrypted, and audited. However, as file volumes grow and compliance requirements become more stringent, these conventional methods fall short in providing granular control and real-time adaptability. Artificial Intelligence (AI) specifically machine learning (ML) and natural language processing (NLP) augments MFT platforms with the ability to automatically detect, classify, and tag file contents based on their sensitivity, context, and regulatory profile.

At the core of AI-driven data classification is a pipeline that performs deep inspection of file contents during or immediately after ingestion into the MFT system. This inspection is no longer limited to file extensions or metadata. Instead, AI models are applied to analyze the actual content of documents (structured or unstructured), identify entities, and classify data according to predefined sensitivity levels such as Public, Confidential, Restricted, Personally Identifiable Information (PII), Protected Health Information (PHI), Payment Card Industry (PCI) data, and more.

These classification models typically use:

- Supervised learning algorithms (e.g., Support Vector Machines, Random Forests) trained on labeled datasets to categorize known document types.

- NLP models (e.g., BERT, RoBERTa, GPT-based classifiers) that understand language patterns and context to flag sensitive keywords, phrases, or entities.

- Regular expression and pattern detection modules for structured data recognition (e.g., credit card numbers, Social Security Numbers, IBANs).

- Computer vision models for scanning images and PDFs for watermarking, signatures, or embedded sensitive data.

Once classified, each file is tagged with an associated security label, which directly influences how the MFT system handles it:

- High-sensitivity files can trigger automatic PGP encryption, enforced dual-authenticated delivery, or restricted routing to compliance-cleared endpoints.

- Public or low-risk data may be routed through cost-effective storage tiers or less stringent delivery channels.

- Files containing regulated data types (e.g., GDPR, HIPAA, PCI) may be logged at higher granularity, have access controls reinforced, or require legal hold retention.

These intelligent classification outcomes are not just operational they feed directly into:

- Dynamic routing decisions

- Policy-based encryption enforcement

- Automated compliance reporting

- Access control decisions and audit log enrichment

Moreover, by using continuous learning models, AI-enhanced MFT systems improve classification accuracy over time. They adapt to new document templates, changing business lexicons, and evolving regulatory patterns. Integration with data loss prevention (DLP) and cloud access security broker (CASB) solutions ensures that data is consistently monitored and controlled throughout its lifecycle, not just at the point of transfer.

For example, if a legal team uploads a confidential merger document via an MFT portal, the AI agent detects sensitive legal terminology, tags the file as "Highly Restricted," and automatically routes it through encrypted channels, logs the transfer for audit, and restricts download permissions to authorized recipients only.

Ultimately, AI-powered data classification transforms MFT systems from simple conduits of file movement into intelligent gatekeepers of data governance ensuring that every file is treated with the appropriate level of scrutiny, security, and compliance based on what it contains, not just where it's going.

9.1 Auto-Tagging and Classifying Sensitive Files in MFT

In the domain of secure file transfer, auto-tagging and classification of sensitive files represents a critical evolution in how enterprises protect and govern data-in-motion. Traditional MFT systems rely heavily on manual configuration or static policies such as file extensions, directory paths, or user-defined metadata to determine how files should be handled. However, in environments where the volume, velocity, and variability of file content are constantly increasing, these static models are error-prone, inconsistent, and unscalable. AI-powered auto-tagging introduces an intelligent, automated layer that dynamically identifies and classifies sensitive content in real time, ensuring that MFT platforms make informed, policy-driven decisions at the moment of transfer.

Auto-tagging begins at the pre-processing or ingestion layer of the MFT workflow. As a file is uploaded whether via SFTP, HTTPS, AS2, or a web portal its content is immediately scanned using a combination of machine learning classifiers, pattern recognition algorithms, and natural language processing (NLP) engines. These components work together to inspect the semantic structure, entity types, and contextual indicators embedded in the file's content.

Key AI models and techniques used in this process include:

- **Named Entity Recognition (NER)** to detect structured identifiers such as Social Security Numbers, credit card numbers, health insurance codes, etc.

- **Contextual NLP models** (e.g., BERT, GPT) to interpret sentences and paragraphs for sensitive phrases such as "non-disclosure agreement", "patient record", or "internal audit".

- **Image recognition** (OCR and vision AI) to extract sensitive text from scanned documents or embedded images within files (e.g., scanned passports, medical forms).

- **Pre-trained classification models** trained on labeled datasets to determine whether a file belongs to categories such as "PII", "PHI", "Confidential", "Public", or "Export-Controlled".

Once identified, the file is **auto-tagged** with metadata labels indicating its sensitivity level. For example:

- "classification=PII"

- "data-type=Financial_Record"

- "compliance=HIPAA"

- "security-level=Restricted"

These tags are then consumed by downstream components of the MFT system to enforce a wide array of **security and governance policies**:

- **Dynamic encryption enforcement**: Files tagged as "Confidential" are automatically encrypted using PGP, S/MIME, or TLS at rest and in transit.

- **Routing decisions**: Files containing export-controlled data may be restricted from cross-border transmission based on the file's tags.

- **Audit and logging granularity**: Highly sensitive files may trigger deep logging, SIEM integration, or retention policies based on regulatory frameworks (e.g., SOX, GDPR).

- **Access control**: Role-based access restrictions are applied to sensitive files to prevent unauthorized downloads or uploads.

- **Automated quarantine or review**: Files that meet certain high-risk thresholds may be automatically held for manual approval before release.

A critical advantage of AI-based auto-tagging is its **adaptability**. These models can learn from new content types, evolving regulatory taxonomies, or organizational classification schemas. Feedback loops (e.g., user overrides, review audits) are used to retrain classifiers, minimizing false positives and continuously improving detection accuracy.

In enterprise environments, these capabilities are often integrated with external data classification engines, Data Loss Prevention (DLP) tools, or CASB platforms, creating a consistent data security posture across endpoints, networks, and the cloud.

Ultimately, auto-tagging and classification empower MFT systems to treat every file based on what it contains, not just who sent it or where it's going, resulting in a more secure, compliant, and intelligent file exchange infrastructure.

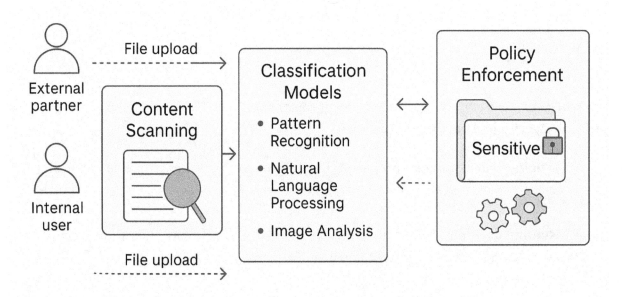

Auto-Tagging and Classifying Sensitive Files

9.2 Integrating AI with DLP (Data Loss Prevention)

In modern enterprise environments where vast amounts of sensitive data are exchanged through Managed File Transfer (MFT) systems, the risk of inadvertent or malicious data leakage is higher than ever. While traditional Data Loss Prevention (DLP) solutions are designed to detect and prevent unauthorized transmission of sensitive data, they often rely on static rules, manual policy updates, and pattern-based inspection, which limits their effectiveness against evolving threats and unstructured content. The integration of Artificial Intelligence (AI) with DLP in the MFT context significantly enhances detection accuracy, enables adaptive policy enforcement, and automates sensitive data governance.

AI-augmented DLP within MFT pipelines operates by introducing machine learning and natural language processing (NLP) capabilities to inspect, classify, and score data flows in real time. Rather than relying solely on keyword matching or regular expressions, AI models are trained to understand semantic context, file structure, and behavioral patterns of data movement.

For example, an AI-enhanced DLP engine can:

- Detecting contextually embedded PII or PHI even when obfuscated or embedded in complex formats like scanned PDFs, spreadsheets, or email text.

- Recognize industry-specific terms and taxonomies using NLP models trained on domain corpora (e.g., financial, legal, healthcare).

- Apply entity recognition and classification algorithms (like BERT or transformer-based models) to flag suspicious payloads that mimic high-risk documents such as invoices, tax records, or internal audit reports.

- Correlate behavioral telemetry such as unusual timing, destination, or volume to enhance decision-making on whether a file poses a potential exfiltration threat.

These AI-powered engines are integrated directly into the MFT workflow, acting as inline content inspectors. As files are ingested (inbound or outbound), the system performs:

- Pre-transfer deep content inspection, tagging files with sensitivity classifications (e.g., Confidential, Export-Controlled, PCI, etc.)

- Dynamic risk scoring based on content, context, and user history

- Automated policy enforcement, such as:

  - Blocking or quarantining high-risk transfers

  - Requiring secondary approvals or encryption

  - Triggering alerts to security teams

  - Logging metadata to centralized SIEM platforms

Advanced integration enables cross-system intelligence sharing between MFT, DLP, and CASB (Cloud Access Security Broker) solutions. For instance, if a DLP engine flags a file transfer from an MFT system to a personal cloud storage account (e.g., Dropbox or Google Drive), the CASB can immediately revoke access or block the endpoint. This creates a zero-trust enforcement model, where every data movement is evaluated in real time.

Moreover, AI integration introduces self-learning feedback loops. Security analysts can label false positives or undetected leaks, which are then used to retrain the underlying ML models, improving future detection rates and reducing alert fatigue. Some platforms also leverage federated learning to aggregate learning across environments without compromising data privacy.

The result is a context-aware, adaptive, and intelligent DLP framework embedded within the MFT ecosystem capable of:

- Protecting sensitive data in structured and unstructured forms

- Understanding contextual intent, not just static patterns

- Dynamically evolving with the threat landscape and organizational data trends

In essence, AI-integrated DLP transforms traditional file transfer security from rule-based control into cognitive governance, making MFT platforms not only secure but intelligently responsive to real-world risk.

9.2.1 AI-Driven Content Inspection Pipeline

When a file is received by the Managed File Transfer (MFT) system whether through secure protocols such as SFTP, AS2, RESTful APIs, or via a web-based user interface upload it is immediately routed to an AI-driven Content Inspection Layer. This layer is commonly deployed either as a sidecar microservice alongside the MFT application or as an inline processing module tightly integrated into the transfer pipeline. Its primary purpose is to perform deep content analysis before any routing, storage, or distribution action takes place, ensuring that all files are intelligently classified and policy-compliant.

The inspection process begins with a Text Extraction Layer, which is responsible for handling a wide variety of complex and unstructured formats. For example, if the incoming file is a PDF, scanned image, ZIP archive, or a nested document format, the system employs Optical Character Recognition (OCR) along with robust content extraction frameworks such as Apache Tika or Amazon Textract. These tools parse the document contents to extract human-readable text, embedded metadata, and structural elements such as tables or headers, regardless of file type or encoding.

Next, the pipeline moves to the Structured Parsing Stage, where data stored in structured formats such as CSV, Excel spreadsheets, JSON, or XML is parsed and normalized. This includes flattening hierarchical structures and mapping data into a unified schema suitable for downstream machine learning analysis. The goal is to ensure consistency in data representation so that all content types whether raw text or structured tables can be analyzed uniformly.

Following this, the extracted content enters the Tokenization and Preprocessing Phase. Here, Natural Language Processing (NLP) techniques are applied to prepare the data for classification and semantic analysis. This includes steps such as stop word removal, lemmatization (reducing words to their root form), tokenization (splitting text into meaningful units), and vectorization using word embeddings or transformer-based encoders. These transformations convert raw textual content into numerical representations that machine learning models can understand, enabling the system to perform highly accurate and context-aware content classification.

This multi-layered approach allows the AI-powered inspection pipeline to detect sensitive data, enforce compliance rules, and block or reroute high-risk transfers in real-time, while ensuring scalability and adaptability across diverse file formats and business use cases.

9.2.2 AI Classification and Detection Models

Once the content has been extracted, parsed, and preprocessed, it is passed into the AI classification and detection engine, which serves as the analytical core of the content inspection pipeline. This engine leverages a combination of pre-trained Natural Language Processing (NLP) models, named entity recognition (NER) systems, and machine learning classifiers to derive semantic insights from the file's content and assess its sensitivity.

At the forefront are transformer-based NLP models such as BERT, RoBERTa, or domain-adapted versions (e.g., ClinicalBERT for healthcare), which are employed to perform semantic classification. Unlike traditional pattern-matching approaches, these models analyze the context and relationships between terms, enabling them to differentiate between phrases like "invoice number" and "social security number" even when they appear within similar document formats. This contextual understanding is crucial for reducing false positives and accurately identifying regulated content in legal, financial, or medical documents.

In parallel, Named Entity Recognition (NER) pipelines are executed to extract and tag predefined sensitive entities. These include Personally Identifiable Information (PII) such as full names, phone numbers, email addresses, and social security numbers; Protected Health Information (PHI) like patient IDs or ICD codes; and Payment Card Industry (PCI) data, such as credit card numbers or CVVs. These NER models are either trained on domain-specific corpora or fine-tuned using enterprise datasets to ensure high precision in real-world deployments.

To quantify the sensitivity of the content, the system uses ML-based risk scoring algorithms. Models such as XGBoost or regularized logistic regression aggregate multiple feature sets including metadata (e.g., file origin, ownership, destination), behavioral context (e.g., frequency of access, recent anomalies), and semantic risk indicators to output a sensitivity score. This score helps determine whether the content should be routed, encrypted, quarantined, or escalated for manual review.

For previously unseen or unclassified documents, the engine employs zero-day detection techniques. These models use cosine similarity metrics on vectorized embeddings to perform fuzzy matching against a repository of known sensitive document profiles. This allows the system to flag novel file types or content structures that share semantic similarity with classified materials, even if no explicit policy rule exists. Such capabilities are essential for detecting obfuscated data exfiltration attempts or emerging compliance risks.

Together, these AI-driven models ensure a comprehensive, adaptive, and intelligent approach to content classification, going far beyond conventional static rules to deliver real-time sensitivity assessment and decision-making within MFT environments.

9.2.3 Auto-Tagging and Policy Binding

Once the sensitivity level and classification of a file have been determined through AI inference, the next step in the content inspection pipeline is Auto-Tagging and Policy Binding. This stage translates analytical insights into actionable metadata that governs how the file is handled throughout the MFT lifecycle. The system automatically generates a set of security labels, compliance tags, and transfer control metadata, which are embedded into the file's metadata layer for enforcement and auditability.

Security labels are created to define the content's classification and associated risk. For example, a document containing medical records may be tagged as classification=PHI and risk=High. These labels are critical for downstream components such as routing logic, encryption modules, and secure access controls. They inform the system whether a file needs to be stored in an encrypted vault, routed through a hardened channel, or escalated to a compliance officer.

In parallel, the system assigns compliance tags based on the identified regulatory obligations. These tags are derived using contextual interpretation and pattern recognition from the content. For instance, if the document contains European customer data, the system may set GDPR=true; if it contains healthcare information from U.S. residents, it may add HIPAA=true. These tags enable the MFT system to enforce jurisdiction-specific data handling policies dynamically such as restricting cross-border transfers or applying mandated encryption schemes.

The final outcome of this stage is the injection of transfer metadata into the MFT system's metadata repository. This metadata includes classification labels, compliance annotations, risk scores, and any routing constraints associated with the file. It becomes part of the file's transfer profile, which travels with it across the pipeline, allowing MFT orchestration engines, security proxies, and storage targets to make policy-driven decisions. Additionally, all auto-generated metadata is logged for traceability and audit, feeding into centralized logging systems and SIEM platforms for compliance reporting and security analytics.

This intelligent tagging and binding mechanism ensures that content-aware decisions are made at every step of the file's journey, automating governance, enhancing operational efficiency, and reinforcing enterprise-wide data protection policies.

9.2.4 Policy Enforcement Layer

The Policy Enforcement Layer serves as the operational gatekeeper of the AI-driven content inspection pipeline, executing real-time decisions based on the classification, risk scoring, and compliance tags previously generated. This layer is tightly integrated with the MFT orchestration engine, enabling dynamic, content-aware actions to be applied to each file as it moves through the transfer lifecycle. One of the primary enforcement capabilities is encryption enforcement, where files marked with high sensitivity (e.g., PII, PHI, trade secrets) are automatically encrypted using strong cryptographic standards such as AES-256 or PGP. The encryption keys are securely sourced either from enterprise Hardware Security Modules (HSMs) or cloud-based Key Management Services (KMS) such as AWS KMS, Azure Key Vault, or Google Cloud KMS ensuring tamper-proof confidentiality.

Additionally, the layer implements geo-fencing and intelligent routing, particularly crucial for regulated industries and multinational organizations. For instance, files subject to ITAR, GDPR, or similar data residency laws are validated against destination geolocation using IP intelligence and classification tags. If a transfer is detected to be targeting a non-compliant or restricted region, it is automatically blocked, and a policy violation log is recorded. This ensures that cross-border data transfers remain compliant with regional legal frameworks.

For files that are either high-risk, anomalously structured, or contain unknown classification types, the system enforces transfer quarantine. Such files are moved to a secure, isolated zone where they are held pending further inspection. A manual or supervisory approval process is triggered, which may involve security teams or compliance officers reviewing the flagged content through an integrated user interface before final disposition.

Furthermore, for more active threat responses, the enforcement layer can initiate session termination and real-time alerting. If a file transfer exhibits suspicious behavior such as protocol anomalies, inconsistent classification tags, or violation of content routing policies the session can be aborted mid-stream. Simultaneously, alerts are dispatched to the Security Operations Center (SOC) through channels like syslog, webhooks, or direct integration with SIEM platforms such as Splunk, IBM QRadar, or Elastic Stack. This real-time feedback loop enhances visibility and incident response capabilities.

In borderline or ambiguous cases, the system also supports a consent and acknowledgment flow. This feature prompts the user (or a designated operator) to provide justification for the transfer, review the content classification, and formally acknowledge the applicable policies. This step ensures accountability and creates a defensible audit trail for sensitive transfers that fall into gray areas of compliance or risk scoring.

Together, these enforcement mechanisms make the Policy Enforcement Layer a vital component of next-generation MFT systems enabling automated, intelligent control over sensitive data flows while ensuring regulatory compliance and enterprise-grade security posture.

9.2.5 Behavioral Correlation

An advanced and optional component of the AI-driven content inspection pipeline is the Behavioral Correlation Layer, which adds contextual intelligence to traditional DLP operations by analyzing user and system behavior patterns over time. While earlier stages of the pipeline focus on what is inside the file, this layer examines how, when, and where the transfer is taking place offering an additional dimension of dynamic risk assessment. The primary objective is to determine whether the current transfer behavior aligns with historical norms for a given user, system, or partner profile.

To achieve this, the system employs time-series analytics and unsupervised learning models such as Isolation Forest, DBSCAN, or K-Means clustering. These algorithms are trained on historical logs of file transfers, building behavioral baselines across multiple features such as typical file sizes, content types, destination endpoints, transfer frequency, and temporal patterns (e.g., business hours vs. late-night activity). When a new transfer event is initiated, its metadata and behavioral signature are evaluated against these learned baselines.

For example, the system may flag a transfer as anomalous if a user who typically sends 5 MB financial spreadsheets to a domestic server suddenly attempts to transmit a 500 MB compressed archive to an unfamiliar external partner. Similarly, the system can detect irregularities such as file types uncommon to a user's profile (e.g., an HR employee attempting to send source code) or deviations from typical destination geographies. These insights are used to correlate behavioral context with content classification, thereby enriching the overall risk posture of the transfer.

Crucially, this behavioral intelligence is not just observational, it actively contributes to dynamic risk scoring. If a transfer exhibits behavioral anomalies, the system can escalate the risk score, override previous policy decisions, or trigger enhanced enforcement actions such as multi-party approval, delayed release, or real-time alerts to the Security Operations Center (SOC). By integrating behavioral analytics with AI-driven content inspection, this layer empowers organizations to detect sophisticated threats such as insider data leakage, account compromise, or policy circumvention scenarios where static rules and keyword matching would likely fail.

While optional, the Behavioral Correlation Layer significantly strengthens the system's ability to identify high-risk transfers in complex and evolving environments, making it a powerful addition to next-generation Managed File Transfer (MFT) architectures that prioritize proactive and adaptive security.

9.2.6 Feedback Loop & Model Optimization

The final and most critical stage in the AI-driven content inspection pipeline is the Feedback Loop & Model Optimization Layer, which transforms the system from a static rule executor into a continuously learning, adaptive security engine. All classification outcomes, enforcement actions, user decisions, and system-generated alerts are comprehensively logged and optionally routed to an Active Learning Engine. This engine serves as the intelligence backbone for model refinement, policy evolution, and operational tuning.

At the heart of this feedback loop is the ability for security analysts, compliance officers, or system administrators to review flagged events and label them as true positives, false positives, or false negatives. For example, if a legitimate business document is incorrectly flagged as containing sensitive financial data, an analyst can label it as a false positive. These human-labeled instances are ingested into a continuously growing curated training dataset, which is periodically used to retrain the underlying machine learning models including content classifiers, risk scorers, and anomaly detectors. This process ensures the system evolves with changing data profiles, emerging content types, and organizational usage patterns.

Moreover, the system leverages automated threshold tuning mechanisms that adjust decision boundaries based on precision-recall trade-offs and performance metrics derived from real-world operation. For instance, if a particular model exhibits excessive false alarms, its sensitivity threshold can be recalibrated to strike a better balance between detection accuracy and operational noise. These adjustments can be made autonomously or based on predefined SLAs, using techniques such as Bayesian optimization or grid search tuning.

This closed-loop adaptive framework enables the MFT ecosystem to incrementally improve over time, becoming more context-aware, more accurate, and better aligned with business risk tolerance. It significantly reduces the burden of manual rule maintenance and ensures that AI models remain relevant even as organizational policies, regulatory requirements, or attack vectors evolve. In essence, the Feedback Loop & Model Optimization Layer transforms the content inspection pipeline into a living system one that learns from its environment, adapts to its mistakes, and continuously enhances its precision in securing enterprise data flows.

AI-Driven Content Inspection Pipeline

Content Inspection Layer

F- /Intem MFT system
- SFTP, AS2, REST API or UI upload

↓

Text Extraction Layer

- ORC extraction Layer
- Tokeniztion CSS, E XML, metada

↓

AI Classification and Detection Models

- Pre-trained NLP models (BERT, RoBoRTaa)
- Named Entiy Recognising (NER)
- Zero-day Detection

↓

Policy Enforcement Layer

- Encrryption-Geo-fencing
- Transfer Quarantine
- Session Termination and Alerting

↓

Behavioral Correlation (Optional Layer)

- False positives and negatives
- Logged: model retraining

↓

Feedback Loop & Model optimation

- Logged: False positives/negatives
- Model retraning gadel tretraining
- Thresholds auto-tuned

PART 4: Implementation Case Studies and Future Outlook

10. Real-World Use Cases for Next-Gen Managed File Transfer

1. Financial Services – Intelligent Routing for High-Value Transactions

A multinational bank processes over 3 million daily file exchanges related to trading, reporting, and interbank settlement. By integrating AI-powered smart routing in its MFT system, the bank dynamically prioritizes high-value transfers, reroutes during peak network usage, and ensures compliance with real-time audit trails. This drastically reduced SLA breaches and cut average latency during month-end cycles by 35%.

2. Healthcare – AI-Based Data Classification and HIPAA Compliance

A large healthcare provider uses AI-augmented MFT to scan and classify outbound files. NLP-based data classification ensures that PHI (Protected Health Information) is automatically tagged and encrypted. Files violating policy are quarantined. The solution integrates with DLP and EMR systems, ensuring that no unencrypted PHI is ever transferred to non-compliant endpoints achieving 100% HIPAA audit pass rate.

3. Government Agency – Cross-Border File Flow Governance

A government ministry responsible for international data exchange uses predictive analytics to forecast spikes in secure document transfers during global events (elections, policy rollouts, etc.). AI-assisted routing ensures data sovereignty by enforcing country-specific compliance rules and geo-fenced routing. The system dynamically allocates resources to handle sensitive diplomatic cables and embargoed documents across multiple jurisdictions.

4. Manufacturing – Predictive Load Balancing in Global Supply Chain

A global automotive manufacturer uses MFT to exchange engineering blueprints, IoT logs, and shipping documentation with over 500 suppliers. The system uses machine learning models to anticipate traffic surges (e.g., during procurement spikes), and predictive load balancing routes file flows through multiple regional hubs. This eliminated downtime caused by node congestion and reduced costs through elastic cloud scaling.

5. Retail – Intelligent Retry Mechanism for eCommerce Data Integration

A major eCommerce platform relies on file transfers for syncing pricing, promotions, and order fulfillment data with third-party vendors. Using intelligent retry logic, failed transfers due to partner outages are automatically rescheduled during maintenance windows, with checkpoint resume enabled. The platform observed a 42% drop in manual ticket resolution and improved synchronization integrity across channels.

6. Pharmaceutical – AI-Powered Anomaly Detection in Clinical Trial Data

A pharma company running global clinical trials leverages AI-powered MFT with embedded anomaly detection. The system flags unusual transfers of patient data (e.g., spikes in file size or unusual timing) for manual review. Integrated with GxP compliance controls and audit logging, this prevents unauthorized data movement and safeguards research integrity.

7. Insurance – Chatbot-Enabled Partner Onboarding

An insurer with hundreds of brokers and agents uses a conversational AI agent to onboard partners into their MFT environment. The chatbot automates certificate exchange, endpoint configuration, and partner provisioning. What used to take 2–3 days per onboarding is now completed within minutes enabling real-time business scaling and reducing IT overhead.

8. Media & Entertainment – Auto-Tagging and Secure Content Delivery

A digital content production studio sends daily video assets to streaming partners worldwide. Their MFT system uses AI models to auto-tag content based on genre, sensitivity, and licensing terms. Based on tags, content is routed through DRM-enforced channels or delayed until embargoes lifted. This enabled zero data leak incidents across dozens of pre-release campaigns.

9. Logistics – Resource Optimization via Forecasting Models

A global logistics provider integrates predictive forecasting into its MFT platform to schedule large B2B EDI batch transfers based on seasonal shipping patterns. Forecasts drive bandwidth provisioning and node scaling, ensuring that EDI file processing meets strict SLA timelines even during Black Friday or Lunar New Year surges.

10. Energy – Secure File Movement Across Hybrid Infrastructure

An energy conglomerate operates across both on-premise data centers and multiple cloud providers. Its AI-powered MFT solution handles the secure transfer of seismic data, maintenance logs, and compliance documentation. Intelligent data classification ensures sensitive field data is encrypted and retained per compliance standards, while predictive routing ensures low-latency delivery to analysis clusters in Azure.

10.1 Case Study: AI Integration in Financial MFT Operations – Before and After

10.1.1 Healthcare Provider: Classification and Compliance

Before AI Integration:

The MFT platform processed large volumes of lab results and insurance forms. Classification relied solely on directory structures or file name patterns (e.g., "PHI_" prefix). Files were mistakenly routed to general cloud storage buckets without consistent encryption. Compliance audits revealed gaps in identifying and securing Protected Health Information (PHI). DLP tools flagged many transfers post-delivery, causing manual intervention and reputational risk.

After AI Integration:

An NLP-based AI engine now inspects the file contents in real time during transfer ingestion. Models trained to detect ICD codes, patient names, and policy numbers automatically tag files as PHI=TRUE, triggering FIPS 140-2 compliant encryption, HIPAA-specific routing rules, and audit trail logging. Integration with EHR systems improved context awareness. SLA breaches dropped by 80%, and policy violations were eliminated through automated enforcement.

10.1.2 Logistics & Supply Chain: Load Management

Before AI Integration:

A global logistics company transferred EDI files from warehouses to central systems every 15 minutes. During seasonal spikes (e.g., Black Friday), static provisioning of transfer threads caused backlogs. Batch failures overloaded retry queues, and IT teams had to manually re-run jobs during peak hours. Latency often exceeded 60 minutes per delivery.

After AI Integration:

The platform now uses LSTM-based time-series models trained on shipping and order volumes to **forecast load surges 12–24 hours in advance**. Transfer thread pools and bandwidth reservations are automatically scaled up using Kubernetes HPA (Horizontal Pod Autoscaler). Predictive load balancing re-routes files to regional hubs based on node health and network saturation. Delivery latency was reduced by 68%, and job re-runs dropped by 90%.

10.1.3 Banking Sector: Smart Routing and SLA Optimization

Before AI Integration:
All files were routed through static IP-to-endpoint maps configured in the MFT gateway. When a primary data center experienced downtime, failover relied on manual DNS updates. There was no concept of partner behavior-based routing or route optimization. Peak-hour SLAs were missed regularly, especially during market close times.

After AI Integration:
AI-enhanced smart routing now evaluates partner endpoint responsiveness, SLA priority, and network latency in real time. Reinforcement learning agents adapt routing decisions per partner profile. For example, high-value FX trades during the London market close are routed via low-latency paths with TLS offloading. Alternate paths are chosen automatically when response times degrade. SLA adherence improved by 93%, and fallback time dropped from 30 minutes to 2 seconds.

10.1.4 Retail eCommerce: Retry & Anomaly Detection

Before AI Integration:
When file deliveries failed due to SFTP server unavailability at partner systems, the MFT platform retried based on fixed schedules (e.g., 3 retries every 20 minutes). There was no context around partner maintenance windows or downtime patterns. Some files failed permanently despite servers being available shortly after.

After AI Integration:
The system now uses AI to **model partner availability windows** using historical retry success logs. A Bayesian probability model dynamically adjusts retry logic, delaying retries until windows of higher success likelihood. Additionally, anomaly detection models scan file transfer metadata (e.g., abnormal size/frequency) and flag suspicious spikes, preventing potential fraud. The platform achieved 100% reduction in unnecessary retries and proactively blocked 3 attempted data exfiltration.

10.1.5 Insurance Company: Partner Onboarding Automation

Before AI Integration:
Partner onboarding required manual configuration of endpoints, credentials, protocols, certificates, and folder mappings. It typically took 1–2 days of back-and-forth between IT and the external broker/agency. Errors in AS2 certificate exchange often caused production failures during go-live.

After AI Integration:
An AI-powered chatbot integrated into the MFT management console now guides onboarding

via conversational prompts. The agent auto-collects partner metadata, validates protocol compatibility, provisions test transfers, and confirms encryption and signature policies. Certificate mismatches are caught through pre-validation using AI-based OCR on uploaded credentials. Onboarding time was reduced from 2 days to 15 minutes, with zero go-live transfer failures.

11 Building Your Own AI-Enhanced MFT System

Designing a custom AI-enhanced MFT system requires a modular, microservices-based architecture that integrates traditional file transfer capabilities with modern AI-driven intelligence and automation. At the core is a secure file orchestration engine built using technologies like Java Spring Boot, Node.js, or Python-based services responsible for handling core protocols (SFTP, FTPS, AS2, HTTPS), scheduling transfers, and managing partner endpoints. Files flow through an ingestion layer where AI hooks are triggered. Here, a content inspection microservice powered by pre-trained NLP models (e.g., BERT, spaCy, or GPT-based classifiers) performs deep file classification, detecting sensitive content such as PII, PHI, or financial data. Metadata and classification outputs are passed to a policy enforcement engine, which determines encryption (e.g., PGP, AES-256), routing, and compliance rules. For operational intelligence, telemetry (CPU, I/O, transfer volume, protocol load) is continuously streamed into a time-series database (e.g., InfluxDB or Prometheus), and analyzed by forecasting models (e.g., Prophet, LSTM) to enable predictive load balancing and resource scaling. Smart retry logic is implemented using a rule engine (e.g., Drools) with ML-inferred partner availability patterns. An anomaly detection module using Isolation Forest or AutoEncoder models flags behavioral outliers such as unusual destinations or file sizes. Integration with SIEMs (e.g., Splunk, ELK Stack) ensures that all events are logged and auditable. Access and task automation is layered with a conversational AI interface (e.g., Rasa or Dialogflow), allowing users to initiate or monitor transfers via Slack or Teams. The system is deployed in a Kubernetes cluster with CI/CD pipelines for model updates and policy rollouts. All components are secured using TLS 1.3, JWT-based API gateways, and IAM policies, ensuring a resilient, scalable, and intelligent MFT platform that evolves in real time with business needs and threat landscapes.

11.1 Frameworks and Tools for Building AI-Enhanced MFT Systems

To build a scalable, secure, and intelligent AI-enhanced Managed File Transfer (MFT) system, a modern architecture must leverage a combination of cloud-native AI services, open-source machine learning libraries, and enterprise-grade integration frameworks. This layered ecosystem enables organizations to automate transfer orchestration, classify data in motion, predict system load, and secure sensitive information all while maintaining compliance and operational efficiency. Below is a breakdown of the most effective tools and frameworks by function:

11.1.2 AI & Machine Learning Platforms

Azure AI, which combines the capabilities of Microsoft Cognitive Services and Azure Machine Learning, offers a comprehensive suite of tools ideally suited for embedding intelligence into Managed File Transfer (MFT) workflows. Within this ecosystem, Azure Text Analytics plays a critical role in automating entity recognition by leveraging deep learning-based Natural Language Processing (NLP) models to extract and classify sensitive information such as Personally Identifiable Information (PII) and Protected Health Information (PHI) from unstructured content. These entities such as names, passport numbers, national IDs, patient references, or financial records can be detected across multiple languages and document types, enabling contextual risk classification within the MFT pipeline. For scanned or semi-structured inputs such as invoices, contracts, and shipping forms, Azure offers Custom Vision and Form Recognizer. Custom Vision allows users to train models to identify domain-specific visual features (e.g., seals, barcodes, compliance stamps), while Form Recognizer uses advanced layout analysis and OCR to convert scanned documents into structured data, extracting tables, key-value pairs, and semantic sections. These capabilities are vital for transforming image-based content into machine-readable formats for downstream classification and routing. Additionally, for predictive analytics and operational optimization, Azure AutoML and Azure Machine Learning Studio can be used to build and deploy time-series forecasting models such as LSTM (Long Short-Term Memory) or ARIMA to anticipate file transfer volume surges, detect seasonal patterns, and proactively manage bandwidth or server loads. These models can be auto-tuned and deployed as REST endpoints, integrating seamlessly into transfer orchestration engines. To unify all these AI capabilities within operational pipelines, Azure Data Factory and Logic Apps offer workflow automation and event-driven orchestration. For instance, upon detecting a new file upload in Azure Blob Storage or an SFTP endpoint, Logic Apps can trigger a cascade of AI services such as invoking the Text Analytics API for inspection, calling a classification model in Azure ML, and routing the file based on compliance outcomes. This integration transforms Azure AI into a dynamic and scalable intelligence layer that powers real-time decision-making, compliance enforcement, and predictive optimization within enterprise-grade MFT architectures.

Azure AI (Microsoft Cognitive Services + Azure Machine Learning)

Classification, Anomaly Detection, and NLP within MFT • Implementing claffication anomaly detection	**Azure Text Analytics** Use Azure Text Analytics for entity recognition (e.g., identifying PII, PHI in files)
Custom Vision and Form Recognizer Deploy Custom Vision and Form Recognizer to extract structured data from scanned documents (e.g. invoices, contracts)	**Azure AutoML or Azure Machine Learning Studio** Use Azure AutoML or Azure Machine Learning Studio to train time-series models (e.g.) LSTM) for forecasting transfer volume peaks

Integration with Azure Data Factory or Logic Apps helps embed these AI workflows into data movement pipelines

11.1.3 AWS AI & ML Services (SageMaker, Comprehend, Forecast, Macie)

AWS offers a broad suite of AI and machine learning services that are highly effective in augmenting MFT platforms with intelligent automation, predictive analytics, and real-time content inspection. At the core of this ecosystem is Amazon SageMaker, a fully managed machine learning service that allows organizations to build, train, and deploy custom models such as classifiers, anomaly detectors, or regression models for predictive file routing, content sensitivity classification, or anomaly detection in transfer patterns. These models can be exposed as RESTful endpoints and integrated directly into the MFT orchestration engine via Lambda functions or Step Functions for scalable and serverless deployment. Complementing this, Amazon Comprehend provides NLP-driven insights such as topic modeling, entity recognition, language detection, and document classification making it ideal for auto-tagging content based on semantic meaning rather than static rules. It supports custom entity recognition as well, allowing the MFT system to detect domain-specific metadata (e.g., contract types, healthcare terms, legal phrases) embedded within file content.

For automated data protection and compliance, AWS Macie is particularly powerful. Macie uses machine learning to identify PII and other sensitive data within objects stored in Amazon S3. It can scan newly uploaded files triggered via S3 events and return classification metadata or risk scores to the MFT engine, which can then quarantine, route, or redact files based on security policy. This is especially useful for real-time inspection of partner uploads, content vaults, or cloud-based drop zones.

On the predictive analytics front, Amazon Forecast enables the creation of time-series forecasting models for anticipating data transfer volumes, partner system downtime, or network congestion windows. By training models on historical MFT logs or telemetry data, Forecast helps optimize scheduling, resource provisioning, and SLA management. Like other AWS services, it can be orchestrated using AWS Lambda, Step Functions, and Simple Notification Service (SNS) or Simple Queue Service (SQS), allowing event-driven pipelines to be constructed with minimal operational overhead. Together, these AWS AI and ML capabilities provide a modular, scalable, and cost-efficient framework for transforming traditional MFT platforms into intelligent, context-aware, and proactive data movement systems.

11.1.4 Google Vertex AI

Vertex AI, Google Cloud's unified machine learning platform, offers a powerful and flexible environment for building, deploying, and managing end-to-end ML pipelines, particularly well-suited for enhancing Managed File Transfer (MFT) systems with intelligent automation. Vertex AI supports both AutoML (for low-code model development) and custom model training (using TensorFlow, PyTorch, or scikit-learn), enabling organizations to implement robust use cases such as content classification, anomaly detection, and time-series forecasting. One of its standout capabilities is support for explainable AI (XAI), which provides visibility into model decisions essential for regulated environments where transparency in content classification and risk scoring is mandatory. With built-in model monitoring, drift detection, and retraining workflows, Vertex AI ensures that deployed models remain accurate and aligned with evolving business needs.

In the context of MFT, Vertex AI can be tightly integrated with other Google Cloud services to enable real-time AI-enhanced transfer validation pipelines. For example, files uploaded to Cloud Storage can trigger Cloud Functions or Cloud Run services that invoke Vertex AI models for inspection performing content tagging, PII detection, or risk scoring within milliseconds. Using Pub/Sub, MFT systems can implement asynchronous processing workflows where large volumes of transfers are evaluated in parallel and routed dynamically based on AI-driven insights. These event-driven workflows are highly scalable, serverless, and latency-optimized, making them ideal for enterprise-grade, global MFT environments. Additionally, Vertex AI Pipelines, built on Kubeflow, allow organizations to orchestrate complex model training, evaluation, and deployment processes ensuring that MFT-integrated AI systems are not only intelligent but also maintainable, secure, and compliant.

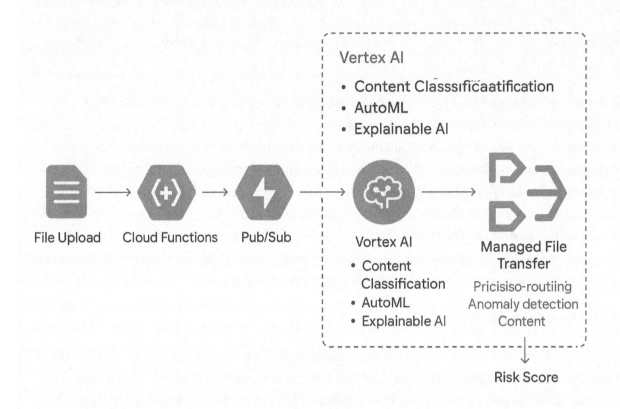

Vertex AI
- Content Classsificaatification
- AutoML
- Explainable AI

File Upload → Cloud Functions → Pub/Sub →

Vortex AI
- Content Classification
- AutoML
- Explainable AI

Managed File Transfer
Pricisiso-routiing
Anomaly detection
Content

↓

Risk Score

11.2 Core Programming & ML Frameworks (Open Source)

11.2.1 Python

Open-source programming frameworks form the technological backbone of AI-enhanced MFT systems, with Python emerging as the de facto language due to its expressive syntax, vast ecosystem, and mature libraries for machine learning, natural language processing, and data engineering. For classical machine learning, scikit-learn is widely adopted to build lightweight and highly interpretable models for classification, regression, and anomaly detection. Algorithms such as Isolation Forest, Random Forest, and Logistic Regression are frequently used to assess transfer behavior anomalies, classify content sensitivity, or score risk levels based on metadata. For more complex, deep learning-driven tasks, TensorFlow and its high-level API Keras provide a scalable platform for training neural networks especially models like LSTM (Long Short-Term Memory) for time-series forecasting (e.g., predicting transfer peaks) and CNNs (Convolutional Neural Networks) for parsing visual documents or embedded image content. Alternatively, PyTorch is preferred for custom model architectures and advanced research applications, particularly in NLP and transformer-based modeling. Its flexibility makes it ideal for fine-tuning pre-trained models like BERT or RoBERTa to handle domain-specific document classification or sensitive content detection in MFT files.

For natural language tasks that don't require heavy models, libraries like spaCy and NLTK are used for tokenization, lemmatization, part-of-speech tagging, and Named Entity Recognition (NER) crucial for identifying PII, PHI, and confidential business terms in unstructured text. On the data engineering front, Pandas and NumPy are indispensable tools for Extract, Transform, and Load (ETL) operations. They are used to cleanse and structure telemetry data, MFT logs, and content metadata before feeding into model pipelines, whether for training, validation, or real-time inference. Combined, these open-source tools offer a modular, transparent, and customizable foundation for building intelligent MFT systems that adapt to organizational needs, scale across infrastructure, and deliver explainable AI outcomes.

11.2.2 Workflow & MFT Integration

Seamlessly orchestrating AI-driven decisions within Managed File Transfer (MFT) systems requires robust workflow engines and integration frameworks. These components ensure that classification, policy enforcement, and file handling operate cohesively across distributed systems. Several open-source and enterprise-friendly tools have emerged as foundational pillars in this integration layer.

Apache NiFi / MiNiFi

Apache NiFi is a powerful data flow automation tool purpose-built for secure, scalable, and traceable data movement. Within the context of MFT, NiFi acts as a dynamic orchestration engine that can trigger AI modules at various points in the file lifecycle such as pre-ingestion, mid-transfer inspection, or post-delivery validation. NiFi's flow-based programming paradigm allows for conditional routing based on metadata or AI classification results. For instance, files tagged as "high-risk" by a classifier can be automatically routed to a quarantine flow or an encryption service. NiFi's Provenance Engine enables end-to-end traceability, offering detailed visualizations and logs for file movement, content transformations, and decision points. Its edge-friendly counterpart, MiNiFi, allows deployment of lightweight agents at perimeter nodes or DMZ zones, enabling edge-based inspection or forwarding logic before data even reaches the core MFT platform ideal for hybrid or distributed environments.

Apache Airflow / Prefect

For batch-oriented orchestration and AI lifecycle management, Apache Airflow and Prefect are well-suited tools. These workflow schedulers are particularly useful for managing ML pipelines, periodic model retraining, content classification, and auto-tagging tasks. MFT systems can emit event hooks (e.g., file received, transfer complete, policy violation) that are used to trigger

Directed Acyclic Graphs (DAGs) in Airflow or Prefect. These DAGs can define sequences such as: validate metadata → invoke content classification → apply policy tags → store audit logs. Both platforms allow fine-grained dependency management, error handling, alerting, and retry logic. Prefect, in particular, offers a Python-native approach and is easier to integrate with event-driven architectures, making it ideal for real-time or semi-streaming AI workflows.

Spring Boot (Java)

For organizations building custom MFT backends, Spring Boot offers a lightweight yet production-grade framework to create RESTful APIs, secure service layers, and policy enforcement gateways. MFT systems often need to expose or consume microservices for classification decisions, enforcement logic, or audit logging and Spring Boot is an excellent choice for implementing these interfaces. It supports seamless integration with Python-based ML microservices using JSON-over-HTTP or gRPC, allowing cross-language interoperability between the policy engine (in Java) and inference services (in Python). Additionally, Spring Boot can handle authentication, rate limiting, and logging, which are vital when integrating AI decisions into security-sensitive MFT workflows.

11.2.3 Observability, Forecasting & Analytics

In next-generation Managed File Transfer (MFT) environments, observability and real-time analytics are essential for ensuring operational transparency, proactive performance tuning, and security intelligence. AI-enhanced MFT systems generate a high volume of telemetry data ranging from file transfer statistics to classification decisions and enforcement actions. To harness this data for monitoring, alerting, and forecasting, modern observability stacks such as Prometheus + Grafana and the Elastic Stack (ELK) provide robust, scalable, and extensible solutions.

Prometheus + Grafana

Prometheus is a high-performance, open-source metrics collection and time-series database specifically designed for real-time monitoring. In the context of MFT, Prometheus can scrape and store fine-grained operational metrics such as:

- Protocol distribution (e.g., SFTP vs AS2 usage),

- Transfer throughput per node or partner,

- File queue depths and processing latencies,

- CPU/memory/network saturation levels across MFT nodes.

These metrics are made human-readable and actionable through Grafana, which offers rich, customizable dashboards. Grafana can visualize data as heatmaps, trendlines, or correlation plots, enabling MFT operators and SREs to identify bottlenecks, track SLA compliance, or monitor unusual spikes in data movement. Most importantly, this telemetry data can be exported or streamed into machine learning workflows, where time-series forecasting models such as Facebook Prophet, ARIMA, or LSTM (Long Short-Term Memory) are used to predict future events like transfer volume surges, downtime windows, or resource contention scenarios. These models can be hosted in cloud services (e.g., Azure ML, SageMaker, Vertex AI) or deployed locally in Python microservices, providing predictive insights that feed back into load balancing, auto-scaling, or alerting systems.

Elastic Stack (ELK)

The Elastic Stack, comprising Elasticsearch, Logstash, and Kibana, is a powerful toolkit for log aggregation, indexing, and visual analytics. Within an MFT context, it can be used to ingest and parse:

- Transfer logs, including timestamps, partner IDs, file metadata,

- AI-generated classification results and enforcement actions,

- Anomaly detection outputs, confidence scores, and policy violations.

Logstash acts as a data pipeline, enriching logs with AI-driven metadata or geolocation info before ingesting them into Elasticsearch, where they are stored in optimized indexes. Kibana then provides powerful visualization and dashboarding capabilities for exploring this data. For example, Kibana dashboards can be configured to show real-time alerts for classification errors, false positives flagged by analysts, or regions experiencing compliance violations. Furthermore, ELK integrates well with Security Information and Event Management (SIEM) platforms like Splunk, QRadar, or Microsoft Sentinel, enabling unified compliance monitoring and audit trail visibility.

By integrating Prometheus-Grafana for real-time performance monitoring and Elastic Stack for intelligent log analytics, MFT platforms gain full-stack observability. When paired with AI-driven forecasting and adaptive alerting, this observability layer ensures not only operational stability but also predictive resilience enabling the system to adapt to workload dynamics, detect threats early, and enforce governance at scale.

11.2.4 Security, Compliance, and Governance

As AI becomes embedded within Managed File Transfer (MFT) systems, ensuring secure, policy-driven, and auditable workflows is critical. Intelligent MFT platforms must not only classify and route sensitive content but also enforce access controls, encryption protocols, and audit mechanisms in alignment with enterprise governance standards. Open-source tools like Open Policy Agent (OPA) and Vault by HashiCorp, along with conversational chatbot frameworks, form the backbone of this AI-integrated governance layer.

Open Policy Agent (OPA)

OPA is a lightweight, open-source policy engine that allows for declarative, fine-grained access control and decision-making based on runtime context. In the context of AI-powered MFT, OPA can enforce conditional policies based on AI classification outcomes, metadata tags, or dynamic risk scores. For instance, a policy can declare: *"allow outbound transfers only if file.classification ≠ Restricted AND riskScore < 0.7"*. OPA is particularly effective when integrated into API gateways or MFT orchestration engines, where it acts as a gatekeeper that evaluates real-time transfer requests against AI-derived tags (e.g., PHI, ExportControlled, HighRisk) and approves or denies actions accordingly. These policies are written in Rego, a purpose-built language designed for policy as code, which supports version control and formal verification making it suitable for compliance-heavy industries like finance, healthcare, or defense.

Vault by HashiCorp

Vault serves as a secure, scalable secrets management and encryption-as-a-service platform. Within MFT pipelines, Vault can be dynamically invoked to provide encryption keys, access tokens, SSH credentials, or digital certificates with issuance and access governed by AI-informed sensitivity tags or risk scores. For example, if a file is flagged by the AI model as containing confidential trade secrets, Vault can be used to fetch an AES-256 key from a secure backend (e.g., HSM, KMS) and apply encryption before transfer. It also supports dynamic secrets, such as time-bound, usage-limited credentials that are generated on-demand only when the AI engine validates the context. Vault integrates with OPA and CI/CD pipelines, enabling full policy-governed control over sensitive data movement, identity brokering, and key lifecycle management.

Chatbot Frameworks: Rasa, Dialogflow, Microsoft Bot Framework

AI-enhanced MFT systems can greatly benefit from conversational interfaces that offer real-time visibility, control, and responsiveness. Tools like Rasa, Google Dialogflow, and Microsoft Bot Framework enable the development of intelligent chatbots or virtual agents that serve as operational frontends for interacting with the MFT system. These bots can be embedded in collaboration tools like Slack, Microsoft Teams, or custom web portals, allowing users to:

- Initiate file transfers via guided prompts,

- Query file status or policy violations,

- Respond to anomaly alerts triggered by AI models (e.g., "This transfer is flagged as unusual. Approve or deny?"),

- Troubleshoot errors or retrieve audit logs in natural language.

Advanced bots can also integrate with SIEM tools and incident response platforms, enabling SOC teams to triage and respond to transfer-related security events through chat interfaces. With multilingual NLP capabilities, contextual memory, and real-time decision integration, chatbot frameworks transform MFT from a static backend service into a conversational, transparent, and user-friendly platform.

12 Step-by-step implementation guidance

Implementing an AI-driven Managed File Transfer (MFT) system involves a multi-phase process that blends traditional secure data transfer mechanisms with modern artificial intelligence, orchestration, and observability frameworks. The first step is to define the architectural scope, identifying key data flows between internal systems, external partners, DMZ zones, and cloud storage locations. This includes choosing your deployment topology on-prem, cloud-native, or hybrid and establishing secure communication channels using protocols such as SFTP, HTTPS, AS2, and REST APIs. Next, architect the file ingestion pipeline to support interception points where AI services can be invoked. This involves integrating components like Apache NiFi, AWS Lambda, or Azure Logic Apps, which can trigger AI modules on pre-ingestion or mid-transfer events. At this point, incorporate content extraction services using tools like Apache Tika, Textract, or Form Recognizer to normalize content into structured formats. This enables AI models to analyze data regardless of whether it's coming from PDFs, images, or spreadsheets.

Once the content is extracted, build and integrate AI/ML models such as entity classifiers, anomaly detectors, and time-series forecasters using platforms like SageMaker, Vertex AI, or Azure Machine Learning Studio. You can start with pre-trained models (e.g., BERT, RoBERTa, or spaCy pipelines) and gradually fine-tune them using organization-specific datasets (e.g., MFT logs, file contents, and access metadata). To operationalize these models, expose them via REST or gRPC microservices and wire them into the MFT orchestration flow. These models should output classification labels, risk scores, and content tags which are then processed by a policy enforcement engine such as Open Policy Agent (OPA) to determine actions like encrypt, quarantine, route, or block. For encryption, integrate secure key management using Vault by HashiCorp, AWS KMS, or Azure Key Vault, with keys dynamically sourced based on classification outputs (e.g., AES-256 for PHI-tagged files).

After AI integration, configure observability and logging using Prometheus/Grafana for operational metrics and Elastic Stack (ELK) for detailed event logs, classification decisions, and enforcement outcomes. This enables real-time dashboards and predictive alerts for transfer anomalies or compliance breaches. For governance, enforce policy-as-code and automate compliance checks (e.g., HIPAA, GDPR) via tags generated during AI analysis. Introduce a feedback loop mechanism using human-in-the-loop (HITL) tools or active learning engines, allowing security analysts to label false positives/negatives. These insights should feed back into model retraining pipelines to improve precision, recall, and reduce alert fatigue over time.

Lastly, enhance usability by deploying conversational interfaces using chatbot frameworks like Rasa, Dialogflow, or Microsoft Bot Framework. These interfaces can integrate with collaboration platforms (e.g., Slack, Teams) to allow users to query transfer statuses, approve flagged files, or receive anomaly alerts conversationally. Throughout the implementation, adopt incremental delivery via CI/CD pipelines, ensuring each module whether it's model training, policy enforcement, or monitoring is independently deployable, versioned, and rollback-safe. A well-structured and modular rollout allows for continuous refinement, rapid incident response, and long-term scalability across evolving data landscapes and compliance regimes.

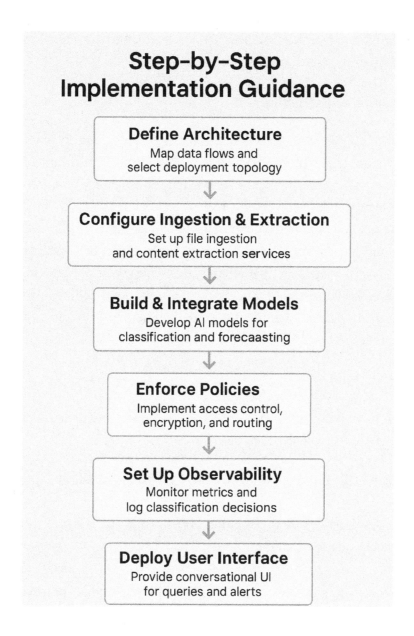

12.1 Define Architecture

This initial phase involves designing the end-to-end system blueprint for the MFT environment. It requires mapping all data flows including external partner connections, internal applications, cloud storage endpoints, and DMZ-based edge services. Key architectural decisions must cover deployment topology (on-premises, cloud-native, or hybrid), security perimeter, protocols to support (e.g., SFTP, AS2, REST), and network zoning (e.g., firewalls, load balancers, interconnects). Defining architecture also includes evaluating scalability needs, integration points with existing systems (ERP, DLP, SIEM), and identifying strategic points where AI models will be embedded (e.g., pre-ingestion inspection, mid-transfer validation, post-delivery classification).

The goal is to build a modular, secure, and extensible architecture that supports real-time AI inference without disrupting core transfer workflows.

12.2 Configure Ingestion & Extraction

This step focuses on setting up robust mechanisms to ingest files securely and extract their content for AI processing. Ingestion can be handled using event-driven frameworks like Apache NiFi, AWS Lambda, or Azure Logic Apps, which listen for file uploads via SFTP servers, APIs, or cloud buckets. For content extraction, tools like Apache Tika, Amazon Textract, or Azure Form Recognizer are integrated to parse documents in diverse formats PDFs, DOCX, CSV, XML, JSON, ZIP archives, or scanned images. These tools extract both structured (e.g., tables, key-value pairs) and unstructured (e.g., paragraphs, metadata) data, normalizing it into a consistent format ready for downstream AI classification. Proper tokenization, OCR (for image-based content), and schema alignment are essential here to maintain content fidelity and enable accurate semantic analysis.

12.3 Build & Integrate Models

At this stage, AI/ML models are developed or adapted to power intelligent decisions across the MFT pipeline. These models typically include:

- Classification models for tagging files as PII, PHI, confidential, or export-controlled;

- Anomaly detection models (e.g., Isolation Forest, AutoEncoder, or clustering models) to identify unusual transfer behavior;

- Time-series forecasting models (e.g., LSTM, ARIMA, Prophet) to predict transfer peaks, load surges, or downtime risks.

Tools such as Azure ML Studio, AWS SageMaker, or Vertex AI are used for model training, hyperparameter tuning, and deployment. Once trained, models are containerized and deployed as REST/gRPC microservices. These services are then called during file processing, either inline (synchronous) or asynchronously, providing real-time outputs like sensitivity classification, risk scores, and suggested actions. Model retraining pipelines, version control, and performance monitoring should also be established to support continuous learning and adaptation.

12.4 Enforce Policies

Once files are classified, this layer applies automated, rule-based actions aligned with enterprise security and compliance policies. Using Open Policy Agent (OPA), declarative access policies can be enforced based on AI outcomes. For example, policies can block a file from leaving the network if it's classified as "Restricted" or require encryption if a file contains PII. Integrations with HashiCorp Vault, AWS KMS, or Azure Key Vault enable dynamic key generation and encryption based on classification tags. This step ensures that MFT operations are context-aware, auditable, and automatically compliant with regulations like GDPR, HIPAA, and ITAR. Policies can also route files to specific destinations, request manual approval for borderline cases, or send alerts for policy violations all governed by AI-driven metadata and classification results.

12.5 Set Up Observability

In this phase, full **observability tooling** is implemented to monitor system health, analyze AI decisions, and detect operational anomalies. Tools like **Prometheus** are configured to collect metrics such as file transfer throughput, protocol usage patterns, classification frequency, and latency across MFT nodes. These metrics are visualized in **Grafana dashboards** to provide real-time situational awareness. Concurrently, the **Elastic Stack (ELK)** is used to ingest logs containing classification results, access decisions, and anomaly detection outputs. These logs support forensic analysis, policy auditing, and compliance reporting. Integrating observability with **SIEM tools** (e.g., Splunk, QRadar) allows security teams to correlate MFT events with broader threat intelligence signals, making the AI-enhanced MFT system more resilient, transparent, and responsive.

12.6 Deploy User Interface

The final step introduces user-facing interfaces for interacting with the AI-enhanced MFT platform. These interfaces may include web dashboards or conversational UIs powered by chatbot frameworks like Rasa, Dialogflow, or Microsoft Bot Framework. Users can initiate file transfers, view transfer history, acknowledge or override flagged anomalies, and respond to policy prompts all via natural language interactions in Slack, Microsoft Teams, or web portals. These interfaces enhance usability, traceability, and human-in-the-loop governance by ensuring that security analysts and operations teams can engage with AI insights without deep technical expertise. Additionally, these interfaces may display AI confidence scores, justifications (explainability), and escalation paths to improve user trust and operational responsiveness.

13 Key Considerations and Challenges in AI-Enhanced MFT Implementation

Implementing an AI-powered MFT solution requires an intricate balance of data engineering, infrastructure design, compliance frameworks, and operational maturity. While the integration of artificial intelligence introduces powerful capabilities such as intelligent content classification, predictive risk scoring, and anomaly detection it also creates several layers of complexity that must be systematically addressed to ensure scalability, trust, and regulatory alignment.

13.1 Data Quality, Consistency & Preprocessing Pipelines

In any AI-augmented Managed File Transfer (MFT) environment, data quality is the linchpin of accurate and reliable model behavior. The effectiveness of AI-driven decisions whether to block, route, quarantine, or encrypt a file depends entirely on the fidelity of the underlying training data. However, MFT systems generate heterogeneous, semi-structured telemetry, composed of protocol metadata, payload information, operational logs, and partner interaction history. This raw data is often riddled with inconsistencies, duplication, missing fields, and loosely structured textual content that cannot be used directly in modeling. Hence, building a robust data preprocessing and transformation pipeline is foundational to any AI deployment within MFT.

At the core of preprocessing is a multi-stage ETL (Extract, Transform, Load) pipeline, typically constructed using scalable frameworks such as Apache Beam (for stream/batch abstraction), Apache Spark (for distributed processing), or Python libraries like Pandas, PyArrow, and Dask for localized development. The initial extraction stage interfaces with MFT backends (e.g., IBM Sterling, Cleo, GoAnywhere) to ingest logs from audit trails, protocol-layer events (SFTP handshake metadata, AS2 headers), partner configurations, and file metadata (file names, timestamps, MIME types, sizes, transmission direction, and destinations).

During the transformation phase, multiple technical operations are performed:

- Schema Normalization: Logs are often unstructured or vary by protocol. All records are mapped into a canonical event schema using consistent column formats (e.g., ISO-8601 for timestamps, unified protocol enums, standardized status codes). Event streaming platforms like Kafka may be used to publish enriched records to downstream consumers.

- Entity Standardization: Partner names, geographic zones, department codes, and endpoint URIs are standardized using lookup tables and regular expression-based mappings. This ensures that Partner_A, PARTNERA, and partner.a.local are all treated as the same logical entity in model training.

- Label Engineering & Feature Enrichment: Supervised models require ground-truth labels. Auto-labeling pipelines assign tags like sensitive, normal, or policy_violation based on DLP rules, historical audit findings, or external compliance dictionaries. Files may also be tagged based on transfer outcome (retry, delayed, quarantined, etc.). These labels are used to train classifiers or feed reinforcement learning agents.

- Text Vectorization & Embedding: For models dealing with raw content (e.g., text documents or filenames), textual data must be converted into dense numerical vectors.

Techniques include:

- TF-IDF for sparse frequency-based representation.

- Word2Vec or FastText for capturing word semantics in metadata fields.

- Transformer-based embeddings (e.g., BERT, RoBERTa) for full content analysis, particularly effective in identifying file categories, intent, or sensitivity based on file content.

- Noise Reduction and Cleansing: Low-quality or irrelevant data such as test transfers, malformed logs, or empty payloads are filtered out. Statistical outlier detection is used to discard rows with abnormal values (e.g., file sizes in petabytes, null partner IDs). Log stitching logic merges multi-part transactions (e.g., multi-chunk uploads) into single atomic records for proper modeling.

- Temporal Feature Engineering: Transfer timestamps are converted into cyclical features (hour of day, day of week, fiscal calendar mapping), allowing time-aware models (like LSTM or Prophet) to learn patterns tied to business hours, holidays, or seasonal peaks.

Once processed, the clean dataset is versioned and stored in a feature store (e.g., Feast, Tecton) or directly loaded into ML pipelines via feature engineering frameworks like dbt, or model training services like SageMaker, Vertex AI, or Azure ML. For supervised learning, semi-automated labeling pipelines powered by active learning loops allow humans to validate uncertain classifications. Platforms like Label Studio, Amazon SageMaker Ground Truth, or custom labeling UIs help operationalize this step. These platforms integrate with model confidence thresholds to identify samples where human-in-the-loop labeling is most impactful, ensuring that model training data is both representative and high precision.

Finally, metadata lineage tracking (e.g., with OpenLineage or Great Expectations) ensures that every transformation is traceable and audit-ready a critical requirement for AI explainability in regulated MFT environments.

13.2 Real-Time Inference and SLA-Aware Deployment in MFT

Integrating AI inference into real-time MFT pipelines introduces a delicate trade-off between model intelligence and system latency, especially when files must be scanned, classified, or scored inline before transfer completion. In modern deployments, MFT systems may embed AI models to perform tasks like sensitivity classification, PII detection, anomaly scoring, or intent-based routing, but these operations must occur within strict SLA windows. For example, in financial services or supply chain networks, a delay of even a few hundred milliseconds per file can lead to cascading backlogs, failed SLA commitments, or missed regulatory deadlines. This is particularly challenging when using transformer-based models like BERT, RoBERTa, or DistilBERT, which even with CPU-optimized inference can introduce latency ranging from 300–700 ms per document, depending on input length and model depth.

To make real-time inference viable in production-grade MFT environments, multiple performance engineering strategies must be employed:

Model Optimization Techniques

- **Quantization and Graph Optimization**: Leveraging tools like TensorRT, ONNX Runtime, or OpenVINO, pre-trained models are converted from floating-point (FP32) to lower precision formats (e.g., INT8, FP16), significantly reducing memory footprint and compute cost while preserving acceptable accuracy. Static and dynamic quantization also removes redundant layers and fuses operations.

- **Model Pruning and Distillation**: Rather than running full-sized transformer models, lightweight variants such as MobileBERT, TinyBERT, or DistilBERT are used. These are either distilled from larger models or structurally pruned to retain the most salient layers. Such models can reduce inference time by up to 70%, while maintaining sufficient classification and tagging accuracy for MFT use cases.

High-Performance Serving Infrastructure

- **GPU-Accelerated Inference Servers**: To meet sub-100 ms latency targets, AI inference workloads should be offloaded to GPU-powered microservices using platforms such as:

  - **NVIDIA Triton Inference Server**: Supports dynamic batching, model ensemble pipelines, and concurrent model serving.

  - **TorchServe**: Tailored for PyTorch models with native REST and gRPC endpoints.

  - **TensorFlow Serving**: Production-grade for TensorFlow models with automatic model versioning.

- These servers are typically containerized and deployed in Kubernetes clusters with horizontal pod autoscaling based on metrics like QPS (queries per second), GPU memory utilization, or input queue depth.

Asynchronous and Parallel Inference Patterns

- In extremely latency-sensitive environments, AI inference is decoupled from the main transfer pipeline using message queues or task orchestration frameworks like:

  - Redis Streams, Kafka, RabbitMQ for event queuing

  - Celery or Prefect for task execution orchestration

- When a file is ingested, it is temporarily cached (e.g., in-memory blob store or secure staging area), and its metadata/content is dispatched to the AI classifier asynchronously. The transfer is paused or marked pending until the inference result is returned or a timeout threshold is hit.

- To prevent bottlenecks, queues are partitioned by priority, file size, or transfer class, and inference workers are scaled accordingly.

SLA-Aware Model Routing and Resilience

- AI inference endpoints are deployed in multi-node, active-active clusters across high-availability zones (HAZ). Traffic is routed via intelligent load balancers or service meshes (e.g., Istio, Linkerd) based on node health, model latency, or SLA profiles.

- Fallback mechanisms are defined: If inference latency exceeds thresholds, the system can switch to:

  - A cached classification from previous runs (if available)

  - A simpler rules-based backup model (e.g., regex + dictionary-based)

  - A "safe default" policy such as forcing encryption or triggering manual review

- All inference decisions, latencies, and confidence scores are logged for SLA audits, root cause analysis, and model drift detection.

13.3 Compliance, Explainability, and Auditability in AI-Driven MFT

In regulated industries such as healthcare, finance, defense, and critical infrastructure the deployment of AI within Managed File Transfer (MFT) systems must adhere to stringent standards for explainability, accountability, and auditability. Regulations like GDPR Article 22, HIPAA Security Rule, SOX, and ITAR explicitly prohibit opaque automated decision-making without transparent justification and traceable human override. When AI models are used to classify files, route sensitive data, or block non-compliant transfers, every decision must be provable, reviewable, and aligned with policy governance frameworks. This requires a comprehensive technical strategy that spans from AI interpretability to log integrity and policy enforcement.

Explainable AI (XAI) Integration

To provide reasoning behind AI-based classifications (e.g., tagging a document as containing PII or export-controlled content), the system must incorporate post-hoc model interpretability frameworks, such as:

- **SHAP (SHapley Additive Explanations):** Calculates feature contributions to a model's prediction on a per-file basis. For example, SHAP values might indicate that the presence of a Social Security Number and a personal name in the document header led to a "High Risk" tag.

- **LIME (Local Interpretable Model-Agnostic Explanations):** Used to explain black-box predictions for individual files by perturbing the input and observing output changes.

- **Integrated Gradients (for deep learning models):** Helps explain neural network-based classification by quantifying input feature importance.

These explanations are serialized as part of the transfer metadata and stored alongside the transaction log, enabling auditors, security teams, or compliance officers to review not just what decision was made but *why*.

Tamper-Proof Audit Trails

In environments where audit integrity is critical, digitally signed and immutable logging mechanisms must be used. Techniques include:

- Blockchain-backed ledgers using platforms like Hyperledger Fabric or AWS QLDB (Quantum Ledger Database) to maintain cryptographically verifiable, append-only logs of

AI decisions.

- Every AI action (e.g., classification label assignment, policy enforcement trigger, confidence score, override event) is logged with a unique hash, digital signature, and timestamp.

- This ensures that audit records can be independently verified and have not been tampered with fulfilling regulatory expectations for data integrity and non-repudiation.

Standardized Metadata Tagging & Retention Policies

To enforce long-term governance, file-level metadata must conform to industry-standard tagging and access control vocabularies, such as:

- XACML (eXtensible Access Control Markup Language): Used to encode access policies based on classification outcomes e.g., only users with "Compliance_Officer" role can access files tagged as "PII".

- ISO/IEC 27001 Classification Labels: Apply sensitivity levels (e.g., Confidential, Restricted, Internal Use) that inform routing, encryption, and deletion policies.

- These labels must persist through the file lifecycle and be enforceable by policy engines and searchable by compliance tools.

SIEM Integration and Threat Correlation

AI-based classification and anomaly detection decisions must be integrated with enterprise security monitoring infrastructure, such as:

- Splunk, IBM QRadar, Microsoft Sentinel, or Elastic SIEM platforms, via syslog, Kafka, or RESTful connectors.

- For example, a sudden increase in files classified as "Export-Controlled" from a partner in a non-compliant region can trigger an automated security incident and initiate a forensic workflow.

- AI decision context (confidence score, model version, source file, triggering features) is attached to the SIEM event to enhance triage fidelity.

Policy Engines for Enforcement and Auditing

Systems like Open Policy Agent (OPA) serve as the runtime bridge between AI classification results and enforcement logic:

- OPA receives classification tags and decisions via input context, evaluates them against a defined Rego policy bundle, and returns a Boolean decision (e.g., "allow", "block", "quarantine").

- All policy evaluations are recorded with decision traces, which can be exported for audit or submitted for retrospective policy validation.

- This ensures that decisions are not only AI-driven but policy-bound, and that every automated enforcement step is independently traceable and reversible.

13.4 Integration Complexity & Cross-Platform Interoperability

One of the most intricate challenges in modernizing a Managed File Transfer (MFT) platform with AI is managing the integration complexity between heterogeneous technology stacks. Traditional MFT systems are often built on enterprise-grade frameworks such as Java (Spring Boot) or .NET Core, while AI workloads typically leverage Python-based ecosystems due to the rich availability of machine learning libraries like TensorFlow, PyTorch, and scikit-learn. Achieving cross-platform interoperability between these components requires a carefully orchestrated architecture that embraces language-agnostic, loosely coupled communication protocols. The most effective design pattern involves exposing AI services as stateless RESTful or gRPC microservices, using standardized data serialization formats such as JSON (for simplicity and readability) or Protocol Buffers (Protobuf) (for performance and type safety). These endpoints serve as dedicated AI inference APIs that accept file metadata, vectorized content, or encoded payloads and return classification scores, policy tags, or routing decisions in a consistent schema.

To reduce coupling and ensure security, AI models are often deployed as sidecar containers alongside the MFT core service in the same pod or node leveraging service meshes such as Istio, Linkerd, or Envoy Proxy to enforce mutual TLS (mTLS), observability, circuit breaking, and routing policies. This pattern ensures that ML services can be scaled, updated, or replaced independently of the core MFT logic. For event-driven coordination, workflow orchestration frameworks such as Apache NiFi, Apache Airflow, Prefect, or AWS Step Functions are used to sequence file ingestion events through preprocessing, model inference, decision enforcement, and post-transfer actions. These orchestrators allow for asynchronous execution, retry strategies, branching logic, and failover handling crucial for maintaining SLA guarantees in real-time MFT systems.

To support model lifecycle management, integration with model registries such as MLflow, Amazon SageMaker Model Registry, or Vertex AI Model Registry is critical. Each deployed model version is tracked with metadata including training data lineage, hyperparameters, performance metrics (F1, AUC, latency), and approval status. This enables version-controlled deployment, blue/green rollout, and rollback on drift or degradation. MFT systems querying the inference API include the model version or ID in their request logs, ensuring that every file transfer decision can be traced back to the exact model instance responsible supporting both compliance and incident resolution.

Ultimately, enabling seamless AI integration in an MFT ecosystem is not just about exposing endpoints, it's about architecting for modularity, resilience, auditability, and extensibility across polyglot services and dynamic workloads.

13.5. Scalability, Resource Management & Model Lifecycle Automation in AI-Driven MFT

At enterprise scale where thousands of business partners and internal systems generate millions of daily file transfers, AI integration into MFT systems must be engineered for elastic scalability, intelligent resource management, and automated lifecycle control. Unlike static rule-based MFT systems, AI models embedded within transfer pipelines are subject to concept drift, traffic volatility, and regulatory evolution, necessitating dynamic adaptation of both infrastructure and model behavior. To detect model drift the degradation in prediction accuracy due to shifts in data distribution or emerging compliance requirements tools like Evidently AI, WhyLabs, or Fiddler AI are deployed alongside model inference services. These tools continuously track statistical indicators such as input feature distribution, confidence score divergence, and decision variance over time, triggering retraining pipelines when drift thresholds are breached.

End-to-end ML lifecycle automation is achieved through MLOps pipelines implemented using platforms such as Kubeflow Pipelines, Argo Workflows, GitHub Actions, or Jenkins. These workflows automate model retraining, validation, approval, and deployment, often integrating steps like data versioning (via DVC or LakeFS), feature engineering, hyperparameter tuning, and canary promotion. Each model version is tagged with performance metrics (e.g., F1 score, latency, drift score) and registered in a model registry for rollback and traceability.

To support unpredictable load patterns in file classification and routing, infrastructure scalability is managed via container orchestration tools such as Kubernetes Horizontal Pod Autoscaler (HPA), KEDA (Kubernetes Event-Driven Autoscaling), or AWS Fargate, which dynamically adjust AI inference resources based on metrics like CPU utilization, inference queue depth, or QPS. For example, during month-end transfer spikes, the number of classification pods may scale from 3 to 30 within minutes to prevent SLA degradation.

Crucially, AI workloads must be logically segregated between real-time inference (used for inline policy decisions and file blocking) and batch inference (used for historical forecasting, partner scoring, and retraining). This separation ensures that latency-sensitive operations are not impacted by background model updates or long-running batch analytics jobs. Resource isolation can be achieved through dedicated namespaces, GPU node pools, or separate autoscaling groups.

Robust AI systems also incorporate production-safe deployment strategies such as:

- Shadow mode (inference occurs silently without impacting decisions) to test models in live environments;

- Canary rollouts (serving a small percentage of production traffic to new model versions) with rollback triggers;

- A/B testing across model variants to evaluate performance under live traffic conditions.

All of these components are instrumented with observability tools like Prometheus, Grafana, ELK Stack, or OpenTelemetry, ensuring that system performance, model health, and operational SLAs are continuously monitored and enforceable. This architecture enables AI to scale with the evolving needs of enterprise-grade MFT environments delivering not just intelligence, but sustained resilience, reliability, and regulatory assurance.

13.6 Organizational Readiness and Governance Alignment

While the architecture and algorithms underpinning AI-enhanced MFT systems are critical, organizational readiness and governance alignment ultimately determine their long-term success, adoption, and trustworthiness. Even the most sophisticated AI pipeline will fail to deliver impact if its decisions are not properly understood, embraced, or regulated by the enterprise. Ensuring readiness requires building a cross-functional governance and operational culture where AI is not just a black-box automation tool but a collaborative decision-support layer integrated into people, process, and policy.

The first step is establishing a cross-disciplinary onboarding process that includes key stakeholders from Information Security, Compliance, Legal, Data Science, MFT Operations, and Infrastructure teams. Together, they define shared SLAs for AI inference timing (e.g., ≤100 ms per decision), set override workflows for when human review must supersede model outputs (e.g., auto-quarantine exemptions), and codify exception-handling procedures for classification errors or ambiguous outcomes. These agreements form the baseline of AI assurance contracts and must be encoded in service-level documentation and operational playbooks.

To maintain accountability and transparency, enterprises must also establish AI governance committees or steering bodies that oversee:

- Model change approvals, including risk analysis and compliance impact.

- Review of fairness and bias metrics (e.g., disparate false positive rates across partners or regions).

- Periodic alignment with evolving regulatory frameworks (e.g., GDPR, DORA, or NIST AI RMF). These bodies also validate that retrained models reflect organizational priorities and that deployment strategies (canary, rollback, shadow) are risk-mitigated.

From an operational visibility standpoint, it's essential to design role-specific interfaces tailored to stakeholder needs:

- Compliance officers require dashboards that surface explainable AI (XAI) insights, such as SHAP attributions showing why a file was flagged for PII.

- MFT administrators and DevOps teams need real-time telemetry on inference latency, error rates, retry events, and auto-scaling triggers.

- Security analysts may focus on audit trails of classification history, override frequency, and correlation with SIEM incidents.

Organizational maturity is further enhanced by conducting AI trust workshops, tabletop simulations, and incident response dry runs. These exercises evaluate whether staff can correctly interpret AI-driven decisions, react to classification anomalies, or challenge incorrect outcomes using override protocols. For example, a simulation may involve an AI system misclassifying a partner's monthly payroll file as export-controlled data testing how well compliance, MFT ops, and legal teams collaborate to resolve the false positive and retrain the model accordingly.

Finally, embedding a human-in-the-loop (HITL) validation culture ensures continuous improvement of AI performance. By integrating active learning loops, analysts can flag incorrect predictions in production (e.g., mislabeled files), which are then queued for retraining or model calibration. These feedback signals are critical for reducing drift, improving recall on edge cases, and aligning model behavior with business context. Annotation tools such as Label Studio, SageMaker Ground Truth, or in-house review portals support this loop with built-in auditability and feedback scoring.

In essence, organizational readiness is not just about permissions or policies, it's about cultivating a collaborative AI-operational ecosystem where human oversight, explainability, and governance reinforce the reliability, safety, and compliance of every AI-enhanced transfer decision.

14. The Future of MFT

The future of Managed File Transfer (MFT) is being redefined by the convergence of AI, cloud-native architectures, zero-trust security, and autonomous orchestration. As data ecosystems become increasingly distributed, real-time, and compliance-intensive, traditional MFT systems must evolve from static, rule-based engines into intelligent data exchange platforms that are context-aware, self-optimizing, and deeply integrated into enterprise digital fabrics. In this next generation, MFT platforms will no longer just move files they will make dynamic, real-time decisions about *how*, *when*, *where*, and *if* files should be moved, based on a combination of predictive analytics, semantic inspection, behavioral profiling, and policy-as-code logic.

At the core of this transformation is the full-stack infusion of AI/ML, enabling MFT systems to autonomously classify content (e.g., PII, PHI, trade secrets), detect and respond to anomalies (e.g., atypical partner behavior, transfer velocity spikes), and proactively forecast load surges or potential failures using LSTM, ARIMA, or reinforcement learning models. These insights feed into real-time enforcement engines, where micro-policies written in languages like Rego (for OPA) or Kyverno dynamically adapt file routing, encryption, or quarantine strategies based on sensitivity levels, jurisdictional compliance, or partner risk profiles.

Moreover, future MFT platforms will be inherently cloud-native, deployed on containerized microservices (via Kubernetes) with autoscaling and self-healing capabilities. They'll support multi-cloud transfer routing, geo-aware compliance enforcement, and edge MFT agents via lightweight components like MiNiFi or WASM-based runtimes. Integration with event-driven architectures using Kafka, Pub/Sub, or EventBridge will allow MFT workflows to become reactive and tightly coupled with business processes, security events, and real-time data triggers.

Security and compliance will evolve through zero-trust principles and policy-driven governance. MFT will integrate with confidential computing environments, runtime attestation frameworks, and hardware-backed key management (e.g., HSMs, TPMs). Files will be encrypted at rest and in transit, but also in-use, with secure enclaves inspecting content while preserving confidentiality. Auditability will become immutable and cryptographically verifiable through blockchain-based provenance chains or zero-knowledge proofs that validate policy conformance without revealing sensitive context.

Finally, the user experience will shift toward conversational and autonomous interfaces intelligent assistants embedded into Slack, Teams, or enterprise portals will provide contextual insights, alert users to potential policy violations, and allow approvals or overrides through natural language interfaces. Combined with continuous learning from operational feedback loops and human-in-the-loop corrections, the MFT of the future will be self-adaptive, transparent, and capable of operating at machine speed without compromising on control, compliance, or trust.

14.1 MFT and Edge Computing: Bringing Intelligence to the Periphery

As enterprises move toward highly distributed digital infrastructures, the integration of Managed File Transfer (MFT) with Edge Computing is rapidly becoming a foundational architectural pattern especially in data-intensive, real-time industries such as manufacturing, healthcare, energy, logistics, and autonomous transportation. These sectors are characterized by massive data generation at the edge from IoT sensors, industrial control systems (ICS), medical imaging devices, video surveillance systems, and smart robotics operating in environments with limited bandwidth, intermittent connectivity, or low-latency processing requirements. In such conditions, traditional MFT systems designed for centralized, hub-and-spoke data aggregation and post-processing introduce operational inefficiencies, latency bottlenecks, and security gaps.

To address these limitations, organizations are now deploying lightweight, containerized MFT agents directly at the edge, enabling autonomous, intelligent file processing at or near the data source. These agents can be built using technologies such as Apache MiNiFi (a lightweight version of Apache NiFi for data routing and transformation), K3s-based Kubernetes microservices, or custom agents compiled for ARM, x86, or RISC-V architectures, optimized for edge computing platforms like Raspberry Pi, Jetson Nano, or Intel NUC. These MFT edge nodes act as self-contained units capable of:

- Monitoring edge devices for new data files or streaming payloads,

- Performing pre-ingestion inspection, protocol normalization, and content validation,

- Enforcing data governance policies at the point of origin.

For instance, an MFT edge node deployed in an industrial manufacturing plant might collect sensor data and system telemetry from programmable logic controllers (PLCs), SCADA units, or robotic automation cells. Using embedded AI inference engines such as TensorFlow Lite, ONNX Runtime, or Triton Inference Server, the edge agent can perform content classification (e.g., detect operational anomalies), apply data sensitivity tags, and then conditionally compress, encrypt, redact, or quarantine files. These actions are performed prior to file transfer, significantly reducing data egress costs, minimizing cloud backhaul, and enabling faster incident response, particularly for use cases like predictive maintenance, equipment failure detection, or safety event logging.

From a security and compliance perspective, edge MFT agents are hardened with mutual TLS (mTLS) authentication, secure boot mechanisms, TPM-backed key storage, and runtime attestation. For encryption, secrets such as PGP keys, TLS certificates, and API tokens are dynamically retrieved from centralized key management systems including HashiCorp Vault, AWS Secrets Manager, or Azure Key Vault based on contextual AI risk scores and role-based access controls. These agents enforce geo-fencing and jurisdiction-aware routing logic, ensuring that content marked as "export-restricted," "region-sensitive," or "confidential" is not transmitted beyond legally permissible boundaries, in compliance with regulations such as GDPR, ITAR, and HIPAA.

To maintain centralized visibility and compliance reporting, all edge-generated logs, file classification decisions, audit trails, and execution metadata are synchronized back to the core MFT platform or SIEM tools using delta-based sync strategies, compressed bundles, or asynchronous event-driven messaging systems (e.g., MQTT, Kafka, Google Pub/Sub, or AWS IoT Core). This architecture allows for eventual consistency, ensuring that intermittent network outages at the edge do not disrupt global policy enforcement, visibility, or forensic traceability.

Looking forward, the fusion of AI and zero-trust principles will elevate MFT edge nodes into self-defending micro gateways. These will not only handle encrypted file delivery, but also in-situ decryption, contextual inspection, and re-encryption, while applying policy-aware filters and generating verifiable audit signatures (e.g., Merkle trees, blockchain hashes) for compliance. These nodes will support autonomous decision-making such as triggering quarantine actions, rerouting sensitive content, or issuing remediation instructions to local systems all within milliseconds, without requiring round-trips to a central controller.

In essence, the convergence of MFT with edge computing enables a shift from centralized, passive data relay to distributed, intelligent, and policy-enforced data handling, a critical leap for industries demanding resilience, real-time actionability, and regulatory assurance in geographically dispersed, security-sensitive environments.

14.2 MFT in the Era of Data Mesh and Data Fabric

As enterprises move toward **decentralized, scalable, and domain-driven data architectures**, the role of **Managed File Transfer (MFT)** is being redefined through its integration with modern paradigms like **Data Mesh** and **Data Fabric**. In this context, MFT is no longer just a back-office utility for moving files across systems; it becomes a **governed, intelligent, and policy-enforced data delivery mechanism** embedded into enterprise-wide data ecosystems that span cloud, on-prem, and edge environments.

14.2.1 MFT in a Data Mesh Architecture – A Federated Transport Backbone

As organizations shift from centralized data lakes to Data Mesh architectures, Managed File Transfer (MFT) systems must evolve from monolithic, hub-and-spoke pipelines to become federated, domain-aligned transport backbones. In a Data Mesh, each domain such as finance, logistics, HR, or supply chain is responsible for producing, curating, and exposing data as a product, complete with contracts, SLAs, and documentation. These domains often operate across heterogeneous systems, including on-prem databases, cloud storage, and legacy infrastructure. Here, MFT plays a pivotal role by enabling secure, auditable, and interoperable file-based data movement between decentralized data product teams.

Rather than centralizing transfers through a global ETL framework, modern MFT nodes are deployed per domain, either as standalone services or embedded into CI/CD-enabled data pipelines. Each node is configured to apply domain-specific governance rules such as:

- Field-level masking or redaction (e.g., PII obfuscation for outbound HR datasets),

- Policy-driven encryption-at-rest and in-transit, based on classification (e.g., AES-256 for confidential exports),

- Audit logging and digital signature stamping for immutable lineage and chain-of-custody.

These policies are enforced locally but coordinated globally through shared metadata contracts and governance frameworks. MFT transfers are packaged using interoperable data product formats such as Avro, Parquet, CSV, and JSON and enriched with version-controlled metadata (e.g., schema version, data sensitivity level, originating domain, SLA timestamp). These artifacts are automatically published to enterprise data catalogs like Collibra, Alation, or Amundsen, enabling downstream consumers to discover, request, and subscribe to datasets with full visibility into access constraints and data provenance.

From a systems design perspective, MFT in a Data Mesh must support:

- Self-service APIs that allow domain teams to expose or consume data feeds without centralized dependency. APIs expose endpoints for configuring transfers, setting validation schemas, and attaching access policies.

- RBAC and multitenancy, where domain producers and consumers operate within isolated execution environments, governed by organizational IAM policies and enforced via namespace isolation or policy engines like OPA (Open Policy Agent).

- Data Contracts, enforced through schema validation frameworks such as JSON Schema or Apache Avro. This ensures that producers publish data that structurally and semantically aligns with what consumers expect thereby reducing integration friction.

- Event-driven orchestration, powered by messaging backbones like Apache Kafka, Apache Pulsar, or cloud-native equivalents (e.g., Google Pub/Sub, AWS EventBridge). MFT nodes emit and subscribe to events representing data readiness, contract violations, SLA breaches, or lineage updates allowing transfers to be decoupled from upstream job completion.

Additionally, operational MFT telemetry such as transfer completion times, retries, schema validation results, and access pattern metadata can be exported to centralized observability tools or governance dashboards. This provides real-time insights into domain-level data product performance, compliance posture, and SLA adherence.

MFT in a Data Mesh Architecture

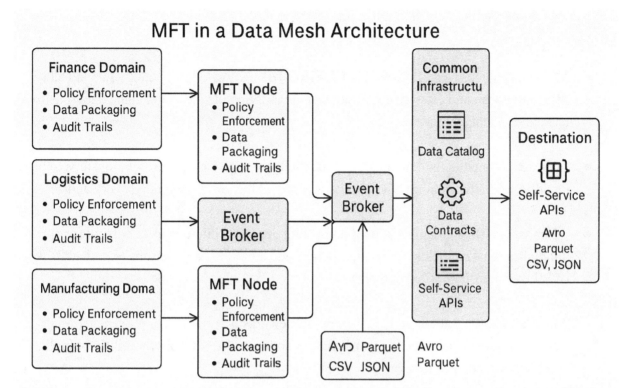

MFT in a Data Mesh Architecture

14.2.2 MFT within a Data Fabric Architecture – Enabling Secure, Metadata-Aware Ingress and Egress

In the context of a Data Fabric architecture, Managed File Transfer (MFT) is reimagined as a secure, policy-driven ingress and egress layer that integrates file-based systems with a unified, metadata-aware data ecosystem. Unlike the federated model of a Data Mesh, a Data Fabric offers centralized orchestration and intelligent abstraction of distributed data assets across hybrid and multi-cloud infrastructures. It leverages technologies such as AI/ML-driven metadata extraction, semantic graph modeling, and virtualization layers to deliver real-time access and governance over structured and unstructured datasets, regardless of their physical location or storage medium.

Within this fabric, MFT functions as the bridge between legacy or non-API-native systems and the modern data virtualization layer. Many external partners, regulated systems (e.g., healthcare, finance), or industrial edge devices (e.g., IoT sensors, SCADA logs) still produce data in file-based formats, often without native support for APIs or data streaming protocols. MFT nodes act as data on-ramps receiving, validating, encrypting, and tagging incoming files and as off-ramps, exporting governed datasets to external consumers while applying strict compliance rules.

MFT nodes in this architecture are tightly integrated with the Data Fabric's semantic and governance layers:

- Metadata engines (e.g., Informatica CLAIRE, IBM Knowledge Catalog, Talend Data Inventory) scan and classify files at ingestion, applying business metadata, data sensitivity tags, and schema definitions.

- Files are automatically registered in a knowledge graph, where their relationships to other datasets, domains, policies, and users are modeled for downstream discovery and access.

- AI-enhanced Data Quality (DQ) engines often deployed inline inspect content for anomalies, missing fields, formatting issues, and compliance violations (e.g., data leakage of PII or export-controlled content).

- All MFT activities are traced via lineage frameworks that track data provenance, transformation history, and usage metrics, enabling end-to-end observability for audit, compliance, and optimization.

The architecture also incorporates Edge MFT agents, especially in industrial and field environments. These lightweight agents ingest local files (e.g., IoT sensor dumps, facility compliance logs, shop floor batch exports), perform local schema validation, apply regulatory tagging (e.g., GDPR/CCPA), and securely stream the enriched payloads into the central fabric. This ensures schema fidelity, lossless ingestion, and decentralized enforcement of data classification policies, even before data reaches the core systems.

From an infrastructure standpoint, MFT nodes must support:

- Real-time integration with metadata lakes and virtualization engines (e.g., Denodo, Starburst, Dremio) to expose ingested files as virtual tables or assets without duplication.

- API connectors and event hooks for DataOps pipelines, enabling automation of downstream tasks like transformation, indexing, or semantic linking.

- Integration with access control layers (e.g., OAuth2, SAML, LDAP, fine-grained ABAC policies) to ensure that access to ingested files adheres to role- and policy-based governance models.

- Event-driven routing and enrichment using message queues or event buses (e.g., Kafka, EventBridge), which decouple file arrival from business logic execution.

In this model, MFT no longer acts as a simple point-to-point delivery mechanism; it becomes an intelligent gateway into the Data Fabric's dynamic, metadata-driven information architecture. It ensures that every ingested or exported file is not only secure and policy-compliant but also discoverable, lineage-tracked, and enriched for federated access ultimately enabling real-time, governed, and context-rich file-based data movement across the entire enterprise ecosystem.

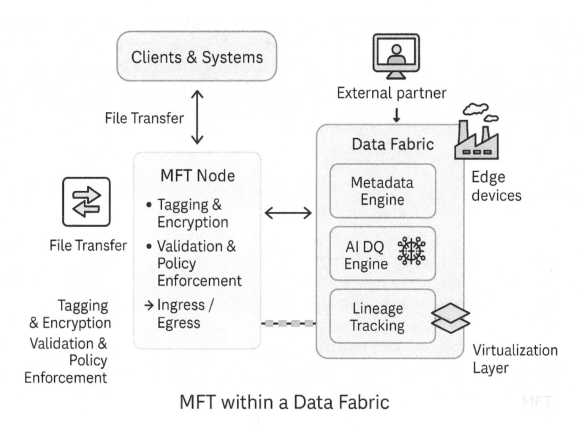

MFT within a Data Fabric

14.3 MFT with Blockchain and Decentralized Systems: Enabling Immutable, Trustless, and Auditable File Exchange

As enterprises and industries adopt blockchain technology and decentralized systems to achieve trust minimization, data integrity, and auditability, the role of Managed File Transfer (MFT) is rapidly evolving to support these emerging paradigms. Traditionally, MFT platforms have been designed to securely transfer files between known endpoints, relying on centralized infrastructure, access control lists, and backend audit logging. However, in decentralized ecosystems such as supply chain consortiums, decentralized finance (DeFi), inter-organizational healthcare, or Web3 marketplaces these assumptions no longer hold. Trust is distributed, identities are federated or anonymous, and tamper-proof auditability is mandatory. This introduces a powerful synergy between blockchain technologies and MFT, where decentralized ledgers, smart contracts, and distributed identity frameworks are leveraged to elevate the reliability, traceability, and compliance of file exchanges.

14.3.1 Immutable Audit Trails via Blockchain Integration in MFT

In the era of zero-trust architectures, heightened regulatory scrutiny, and cross-border data sharing, immutability of audit trails has become a cornerstone of trustworthy Managed File Transfer (MFT) systems. One of the most transformative ways to achieve this is through the integration of blockchain technology which provides tamper-evident, cryptographically verifiable records that can be independently audited without relying on centralized logs or traditional database integrity controls.

In a blockchain-enhanced MFT system, every file transfer operation becomes a traceable and immutable transaction, stored on a distributed ledger. This includes granular stages of the transfer lifecycle such as:

- File initiation (who, when, from where),

- Classification (tags applied by AI or DLP engines),

- Policy enforcement decisions (e.g., encryption, quarantine, routing),

- Transfer completion acknowledgments, and

- Receipts or digital confirmations from endpoints.

Each of these events is recorded as a structured transaction containing:

- A cryptographic hash of the file or its metadata (using SHA-256, BLAKE3, or Merkle root structures) to ensure content integrity without exposing actual data.

- Timestamps, sender and recipient identities, and transfer context (protocol used, SLA class, encryption status).

- The output of policy engines (e.g., "Blocked: PCI-DSS Violation" or "Encrypted with PGP Key X").

- Digital signatures from both the MFT service and the authenticated end entities to provide non-repudiation.

This metadata is then committed to a blockchain ledger. Enterprises may use:

- Permissioned blockchains like Hyperledger Fabric, Quorum, or R3 Corda when dealing with B2B transfers requiring private consortium governance, role-based access control, and deterministic consensus (e.g., Raft or PBFT).

- Public or hybrid blockchains like Ethereum, Algorand, or Polygon when universal auditability is required, such as for compliance with cross-border financial transfers, digital forensics, or long-term archival evidence.

Once the transaction is committed, it becomes immutable and cryptographically verifiable. No system administrator, vendor, or insider can retroactively alter, delete, or spoof entries making audit trails tamper-proof by design. More importantly, because only hashes and metadata are published, the raw file contents confidentiality is preserved while retaining audit fidelity.

This immutable ledger acts as a verifiable chain of custody across the file's lifecycle. Third-party regulators, auditors, or legal authorities can independently verify:

- That a particular file was transferred at a specific time,

- That the file met the necessary compliance standards,

- That policy decisions were consistently enforced,

- And that all actors involved were cryptographically authenticated.

Blockchain nodes can also be integrated with existing SIEMs, GRC platforms, and compliance dashboards, enabling real-time correlation between on-chain events and enterprise risk monitoring. Furthermore, smart contracts can be layered on top of these audit entries to automate SLA enforcement, dispute resolution workflows, or compliance checkpoints e.g., "release file only if the sender is accredited and the file was classified as 'internal' within the last 24 hours."

In sum, by integrating blockchain into MFT infrastructure, organizations can build zero-trust, fully auditable, and tamper-evident transfer ecosystems providing not only technical assurance but also legal-grade evidence for compliance, forensic investigation, and partner accountability in regulated data exchanges.

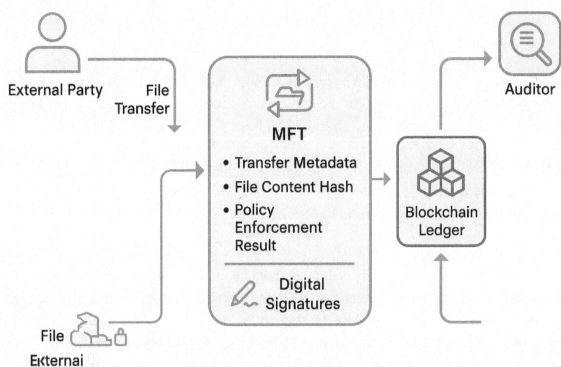

Immutable Audit Trail via Blockchain Integration

14.3.2 Decentralized Identity and Access Management in Blockchain-Enabled MFT

Traditional MFT platforms rely on centralized identity and access management (IAM) systems such as LDAP, Active Directory (AD), or static API tokens to authenticate users and authorize file transfer operations. While effective in controlled enterprise environments, these models break down in decentralized, multi-party ecosystems where organizations span legal jurisdictions, cloud providers, or regulatory frameworks. In such scenarios, Decentralized Identity (DID) and Verifiable Credentials (VCs), as defined by the W3C, provide a more scalable, secure, and federated alternative. By shifting identity management from siloed systems to cryptographically anchored, blockchain-resolved identifiers, MFT systems can now operate in trustless, cross-domain environments without compromising security or auditability.

Under this model, every participating entity whether a sender, recipient, or intermediary is represented by a Decentralized Identifier (DID). A DID is a globally unique string (e.g., did:example:123456abcdef) that resolves to a DID Document stored either on-chain or in a decentralized registry (e.g., ION, Sovrin, or Ethereum). This document contains the public keys, authentication mechanisms, service endpoints, and supported credential schemas for the entity. During a file transfer operation, the MFT system authenticates participants by verifying their cryptographic key pairs against their registered DID documents eliminating the need for password-based authentication or pre-shared credentials.

Access control decisions are driven by Verifiable Credentials, which are digitally signed, machine-readable claims issued by trusted authorities and held by the entity. For example, a hospital may possess a VC asserting that it is certified for HIPAA-compliant data handling until December 2026, signed by a national healthcare authority. When initiating a transfer, this VC is presented alongside the file request and validated either on-chain via smart contracts, or off-chain via a policy enforcement engine that checks issuer signatures, expiration, and revocation status. Policies can be encoded in Rego (OPA) or as on-chain smart contract logic, allowing conditions like:

> "Only allow outbound transfer of PHI if the recipient presents a valid VC from a HIPAA certifying body and the signature is less than 90 days old."

One of the key benefits of decentralized IAM is privacy-preserving authentication. Because credentials are cryptographically verifiable but do not require direct identity disclosure, MFT systems can support anonymous yet auditable transfers. For instance, two research institutions may exchange genomic data under a shared policy without knowing each other's full legal identities, yet both transactions are immutably recorded, policy-verified, and cryptographically traceable via blockchain. This is particularly valuable for use cases in cross-border compliance, zero-knowledge proofs of trust, and B2B data marketplaces where traditional federated identity models (e.g., SAML, OAuth) cannot span trust boundaries.

To enforce this model in practice, the MFT platform must include:

- DID resolver services that can query DID documents from a blockchain or decentralized storage layer (e.g., IPFS, Ceramic).

- VC verifiers that validate credential structure, signature, revocation status (via Revocation Registries), and issuer trustworthiness.

- Smart contract-based access control deployed on chains like Ethereum, Polygon, or Hyperledger Fabric, which encode and evaluate policies in real-time during transfer execution.

- Key rotation and delegation mechanisms, allowing DID controllers to manage key lifecycles and delegate transfer authority to automation agents or subprocesses.

By integrating Decentralized Identity into the fabric of MFT, organizations can build zero-trust, self-sovereign data exchange frameworks that are secure by default, globally interoperable, and inherently auditable without the fragility of centralized IAM systems.

14.3.3 Smart Contracts for Policy Automation and Dispute Resolution in MFT

As Managed File Transfer (MFT) systems extend beyond enterprise boundaries to support decentralized, cross-organizational data exchange, the need for automated, transparent, and enforceable governance becomes paramount. Smart contracts self-executing programs stored on blockchain platforms offer a powerful mechanism to embed policy logic, conditional workflows, and dispute resolution protocols directly into the MFT transaction lifecycle. By removing the need for intermediaries or post-facto enforcement, smart contracts transform MFT from a passive delivery mechanism into a proactive, protocol-aware participant in decentralized governance ecosystems.

At a foundational level, smart contracts can be deployed on permissioned blockchains (e.g., Hyperledger Fabric, Corda, Quorum) or public chains (e.g., Ethereum, Polygon, Avalanche) to act as programmable gatekeepers for file transfers. For example, a smart contract can:

- Validate transfer eligibility based on on-chain attributes such as Verifiable Credentials, partner certification status, or inclusion in regulatory allowlists.

- Dynamically approve or reject transfer requests based on real-time inputs such as classification tags, geolocation constraints, or transfer history.
  Example: "Reject outbound transfer if the recipient is not certified for GDPR-compliant data handling and the file is tagged as 'Contains PII'."

- Trigger metadata-driven routing logic, e.g., "If file metadata contains 'EAR-controlled', only allow routing through sovereign infrastructure located within specific jurisdictions."

Smart contracts can also facilitate conditional access workflows. In high-assurance environments such as legal discovery, finance, or defense contracting MFT systems can interface with smart contracts that:

- Lock decryption keys in escrow, only releasing them once predefined conditions are met:

    - Delivery confirmation from the recipient node.

    - Signature from multiple stakeholders (e.g., sender, receiver, auditor).

    - On-chain proof of payment or digital contract acceptance.

- Log non-compliance events (e.g., transfer SLA violations, policy breaches) and trigger compensating actions such as penalties, alerts, or automated arbitration processes.

For use cases involving dispute-prone environments, such as legal data sharing or multi-party financial settlements, smart contracts enable escrow-based conditional file release. The file or access credentials are held in a secure repository or encrypted vault. The smart contract ensures that:

- Only after multi-party consensus (e.g., legal teams, court-appointed agents) is recorded on-chain does the file become accessible.

- All actions are immutably logged, timestamped, and cryptographically verifiable creating a tamper-proof audit trail for post-event dispute resolution.

From a technical implementation standpoint, MFT systems must integrate with:

- Smart contract interfaces (ABIs) via client-side logic or middleware (e.g., Web3.js, ethers.js, Hyperledger SDKs).

- Event listeners that monitor blockchain state (e.g., using The Graph, Chainlink, or native event subscriptions) and trigger transfer logic upon contract fulfillment.

- Secure key vaults (e.g., HashiCorp Vault, AWS KMS, GCP Secret Manager) that interface with the smart contract to release encryption keys based on signed transactions.

- Off-chain computation engines (e.g., Chainlink Functions, Oracle scripts) for policy evaluation that requires real-world inputs, such as time-of-day, regulatory databases, or ML-driven classifications.

In this paradigm, MFT becomes more than a transport layer; it acts as a compliant execution agent in a larger decentralized application (dApp), bound by smart contracts that govern when, where, and how data is exchanged. This introduces code-based trust, minimizes human error, and enables verifiable policy compliance at scale, without reliance on centralized authorities or manual enforcement.

14.3.4 Decentralized Storage Integration (IPFS, Filecoin, Arweave) in MFT

As organizations evolve toward decentralized and sovereign data architectures, the need to decouple file storage from centralized infrastructure becomes increasingly critical. Traditional MFT systems rely on internal file systems, S3 buckets, or on-prem archives each vulnerable to central authority control, censorship, or data tampering. To mitigate these risks and embrace Web3-native design patterns, modern MFT platforms are being architected to interface directly with decentralized storage networks such as IPFS, Filecoin, and Arweave. In these ecosystems, file contents are stored off-chain, while cryptographic proofs, metadata, and access control logic are maintained on-chain for trustless governance and immutable auditability.

At the core of this integration is IPFS (InterPlanetary File System) a peer-to-peer, content-addressable file protocol. When an MFT system uploads a file to IPFS, it returns a Content Identifier (CID) , a SHA-256-like hash of the file's content. This CID acts as a permanent, verifiable reference to that specific file version, irrespective of storage location or replication path. Once uploaded:

- The file is optionally encrypted using recipient-specific public keys, ensuring that only authorized parties can decrypt and view it even if the raw bytes are publicly accessible on the network.

- The CID, classification metadata, sender DID, recipient policy, and expiration are then recorded on-chain via a smart contract or blockchain registry.

For long-term durability and permanence, IPFS is often paired with Filecoin or Arweave:

- Filecoin incentivizes decentralized nodes to store IPFS-hosted files through cryptographically verified proofs (e.g., Proof-of-Replication), ensuring that files are resiliently stored over defined durations.

- Arweave, on the other hand, offers permanent, one-time-payment archival by embedding file data into a chain of blocks called the blockweave, making it ideal for immutable storage of regulatory documents, legal contracts, or audit logs.

In operational terms, an MFT platform leveraging decentralized storage would perform the following workflow:

1. Encrypt and upload the file to IPFS or Arweave.

2. Capture the CID and link it to an on-chain transaction containing:

    o   The file's classification (e.g., PHI, PCI-DSS, Export-Controlled),

    o   Sender and receiver DIDs,

    o   Associated access control logic or credential checks.

3. Smart contracts or oracles validate recipient credentials or business policy (e.g., HIPAA compliance, jurisdictional access).

4. If conditions are met, the system resolves the CID, retrieves the file from IPFS/Filecoin, and decrypts it using the recipient's private key.

5. The download and access event is logged immutably on-chain, creating a full verifiable audit trail.

This architecture yields several benefits:

*   Resilience: Files remain available across replicated IPFS/Filecoin/Arweave nodes, avoiding single points of failure.

*   Scalability: Storage and bandwidth loads are offloaded from the MFT server and distributed across a global network.

*   Confidentiality: End-to-end encryption guarantees that only intended parties can view the file contents.

*   Compliance: On-chain logs provide cryptographically verifiable proof of delivery, policy enforcement, and access, without exposing the file's contents.

From a system design perspective, this integration requires:

- IPFS and Filecoin clients (e.g., go-ipfs, web3.storage, nft.storage) embedded into the MFT pipeline.

- Smart contracts to manage CID metadata, credentials, and access workflows.

- Key management infrastructure (e.g., Vault, AWS KMS) to handle encryption, rotation, and policy-based decryption.

- Optional use of Chainlink Functions or oracles to bridge off-chain access logic with on-chain contracts.

15 Final Thoughts

As we conclude this deep exploration into the evolving world of Managed File Transfer (MFT), it is clear that the traditional boundaries of secure data exchange have expanded dramatically. What was once a utility-driven function confined to FTP scripts and scheduled batch jobs has now become a strategic pillar of enterprise data architecture, deeply intertwined with AI, cybersecurity, cloud-native design, edge computing, decentralized trust, and regulatory compliance.

The emergence of AI-powered MFT marks a transformative shift from reactive to proactive, from static pipelines to self-aware, policy-enforcing, and learning systems. AI models not only enhance the intelligence of transfer workflows but also enable contextual classification, dynamic risk scoring, behavioral anomaly detection, and even autonomous remediation, unlocking a new era of resilient and adaptive data movement. These capabilities are crucial in an age where data is the backbone of operational agility, and where the volume, velocity, and value of data exchanges continue to accelerate across every industry.

As enterprises decentralize their digital ecosystems through data mesh, data fabric, multi-cloud environments, edge devices, and blockchain networks MFT must also decentralize in intelligence and enforcement. It must operate at the edge, adapt to domain-specific policies, enforce zero-trust principles, and seamlessly interconnect with distributed data governance frameworks. The future of MFT lies not in replacing old systems, but in augmenting them with intelligence, modularity, and policy-driven adaptability turning data transfers into governed, observable, and business-aligned operations.

This book has aimed to bridge the gap between legacy paradigms and modern possibilities bringing together best practices, architectural insights, AI advancements, and real-world use cases to help architects, CISOs, DevOps engineers, and enterprise strategists prepare for what's next. But in reality, this is just the beginning.

The challenges ahead ranging from quantum-resilient encryption to global compliance harmonization demand innovation at the intersection of security, intelligence, and trust. And MFT, empowered by AI, is poised to be a foundational enabler of that trust in the digital economy.

As you return to your enterprise environments, I encourage you to look at MFT not just as an infrastructure requirement, but as a strategic asset, a platform to operationalize governance, accelerate collaboration, reduce risk, and future-proof your data ecosystem.

Let us shape the future of file transfer secure, intelligent, autonomous, and accountable.

15.1 Key takeaways

15.1.1. MFT Is No Longer Just a Transport Mechanism: It's a Strategic Data Governance Layer

Modern MFT platforms have evolved from simple file movement utilities into intelligent, policy-driven, and auditable data exchange frameworks. Organizations must now treat MFT as a critical layer of the enterprise data architecture, responsible not just for secure delivery, but also for data classification, risk enforcement, compliance auditing, and metadata management. Its integration with AI, DLP, and identity systems makes MFT a real-time decision-making component rather than a passive data mover.

15.1.2. AI Is the Game-Changer for Intelligent Content Inspection and Adaptive Enforcement

AI-driven enhancements enable MFT systems to automatically classify file content, detect sensitive information (PII, PHI, PCI, IP), and score risk levels based on context, behavior, and file metadata. By leveraging pre-trained NLP models (e.g., BERT, RoBERTa), named entity recognition (NER), and anomaly detection techniques (e.g., Isolation Forest, LSTM), MFT platforms become autonomous agents capable of triggering encryption, blocking unauthorized transfers, or routing files based on dynamic rules, all in real time. Model feedback loops and explainability layers ensure that these systems learn continuously and remain transparent for audits and compliance.

15.1.3. Modern MFT Architectures Must Be Cloud-Native, Scalable, and Modular

Scalability and deployment flexibility are key. MFT platforms must support containerized microservices, Kubernetes orchestration, API-driven extensibility, and multi-cloud or hybrid environments. Edge-based MFT agents (using Apache MiNiFi or K3s nodes) allow policy enforcement and content processing at the source, which is critical for low-latency, high-volume, or air-gapped environments. Integration with CI/CD pipelines and Infrastructure-as-Code (IaC) enables MFT to be version-controlled, testable, and rapidly deployable.

15.1.4. Policy-as-Code and Zero Trust Are Central to Secure MFT Design

The shift from implicit trust to zero-trust architectures requires MFT systems to integrate with Open Policy Agent (OPA) or Kyverno, enabling real-time, declarative access control based on user identity, content sensitivity, transfer context, and device posture. Secrets management through Vault, AWS KMS, or Azure Key Vault, combined with mutual TLS, secure boot, and runtime attestation, is vital for securing data at every layer of the transfer pipeline. Every decision from transfer initiation to file decryption must be policy-bound, logged, and verifiable.

15.1.5. Observability and Operational Intelligence Must Be Embedded

MFT systems must be fully observable exposing metrics (via Prometheus/Grafana) and logs (via ELK Stack) to operations, security, and compliance teams. AI-driven transfer analytics (e.g., transfer load forecasts, behavioral deviation alerts, classification error rates) feed into dashboards and SIEM platforms (e.g., Splunk, QRadar, Sentinel) to support continuous monitoring, SLA adherence, and incident triage. Observability is no longer optional; it is the foundation of trust and accountability.

15.1.6 Integration with Data Mesh, Data Fabric, and Edge Ecosystems Is Essential

As organizations decentralize data ownership (via Data Mesh) or virtualize access across silos (via Data Fabric), MFT must align with federated governance models, metadata registries, and domain-oriented data products. MFT becomes the mechanism by which data is shared across domains securely, versioned, schema-validated, and policy-enforced. At the edge, MFT nodes interact with IoT sensors and operational systems to enable autonomous, local data exchanges governed by global compliance rules.

15.1.7 Blockchain and Decentralization Introduce Immutable and Trustless MFT Models

Blockchain integration enables immutable audit trails, smart contract-driven policy enforcement, and decentralized access control for sensitive file exchanges especially in cross-border or multi-organizational settings. By combining MFT with DID/VC frameworks, IPFS/Filecoin/Arweave storage backends, and zero-knowledge proofs (ZKPs), future MFT systems will operate in trustless environments with cryptographically verifiable delivery, access, and compliance.

15.1.8 The Future of MFT Is Autonomous, AI-Augmented, and Policy-Aware

Ultimately, MFT is transforming into a self-learning, event-aware data delivery layer that can detect, decide, and act securely and at scale. From classifying medical records at the edge, to preventing IP leakage in real-time, to dynamically re-routing based on geopolitical policies, MFT will act as an autonomous data fabric enforcer. Backed by AI, enriched with policy-as-code, and secured by zero-trust architecture, the next-gen MFT stack will become indispensable for the data-driven enterprise of tomorrow.

15.2 Tips for Enterprises Looking to Modernize MFT

15.2.1. Begin with a Strategic MFT Assessment

Before modernizing your MFT landscape, conduct a comprehensive audit of your current file transfer workflows, tools, protocols, and endpoints. Identify:

- Legacy systems and custom scripts that lack visibility, encryption, or automation.

- High-risk transfer channels (e.g., FTP servers without TLS, unmonitored partner portals).

- Bottlenecks caused by manual approvals, static routing, or centralized intermediaries.

Develop a transfer inventory and data classification matrix: what kinds of files are moving, who owns them, how sensitive they are, and where they originate and terminate. This discovery phase provides the baseline for modernization, helping prioritize which flows should be automated, secured, or enhanced with AI.

15.2.2. Adopt a Modular, API-First MFT Platform

Legacy MFT solutions are often monolithic, hard-coded, and difficult to scale. Modern MFT platforms should be modular, extensible, and API-first offering:

- RESTful APIs and webhooks for dynamic integration with internal systems, cloud platforms, and external trading partners.

- Event-driven architecture (EDA) support to trigger transfers based on business rules or file arrival events.

- Pluggable components for classification, transformation, compression, encryption, and routing.

Look for solutions that support containerized deployment (Docker/Kubernetes) and can be integrated into your DevOps toolchain using Infrastructure as Code (IaC) and CI/CD pipelines. This ensures rapid deployment, rollback capability, and environment consistency across dev, test, and production environments.

15.2.3 Embed AI & ML for Dynamic Policy Enforcement and Automation

To move from reactive to proactive MFT operations, embed AI/ML engines at key stages:

- Pre-transfer content inspection using NLP-based classification (e.g., detecting PII, PHI, source code).

- Risk scoring based on file size, content sensitivity, destination, and historical behavior.

- Behavioral anomaly detection using unsupervised models (e.g., Isolation Forest, DBSCAN) to detect unusual patterns, such as an HR user suddenly transferring engineering files to an external IP.

Integrate AI outputs with your policy engine (e.g., Open Policy Agent) to automatically enforce routing decisions, quarantine files, require multi-level approvals, or trigger escalations to SOC teams. Enable feedback loops from human reviewers to retrain models and improve precision over time.

15.2.4 Design for Zero Trust and Policy-as-Code Enforcement

Modern security architecture demands zero-trust enforcement, especially when MFT is involved in moving high-value, sensitive, or regulated data. MFT systems must:

- Authenticate every connection, device, and user with mTLS, OAuth 2.0, or federated SSO (e.g., SAML, OIDC).

- Integrate with policy engines like OPA or Kyverno to enforce fine-grained access and routing decisions based on file tags, risk scores, user roles, device posture, and location.

- Use dynamic secrets management via Vault, AWS KMS, or Azure Key Vault for issuing short-lived encryption and authentication credentials.

Treat every file transfer as a transaction that must be evaluated against explicit trust criteria and logged for audit compliance.

15.2.5 Expand MFT to Edge, Cloud, and Multi-Tenant Environments

Today's file flows are no longer confined to data centers. MFT must operate:

- At the edge, close to data sources (e.g., in smart factories, hospital imaging systems, or logistics hubs) using lightweight agents like Apache MiNiFi or IoT-optimized MFT containers.

- In the cloud, with native integration to cloud storage services (S3, Azure Blob, GCS) and platform orchestration tools (Logic Apps, Lambda, Cloud Functions).

- In multi-tenant or federated environments, MFT must segment traffic, apply tenant-specific policies, and support cross-organization data exchange.

Design with hybrid orchestration in mind where local enforcement at the edge is synchronized with centralized monitoring, logging, and governance in the cloud.

15.2.6 Enable Observability, Auditing, and Predictive Intelligence

MFT modernization must go hand-in-hand with full-stack observability and predictive analytics:

- Expose real-time metrics (e.g., throughput, protocol usage, file classification outcomes) via Prometheus and visualize via Grafana dashboards.

- Capture logs, AI outputs, and policy decisions in the Elastic Stack (ELK), and stream them to SIEM systems like Splunk, Sentinel, or QRadar.

- Use historical transfer data to train forecasting models (LSTM, Prophet, ARIMA) for predicting usage peaks, partner downtime, or transfer delays.

This not only supports proactive capacity planning but also enables compliance teams to generate cryptographically verifiable audit reports with lineage and policy traceability.

15.2.7 Align MFT with Enterprise Data Strategy (Data Mesh, Fabric, Governance)

Ensure MFT modernization aligns with broader data architecture initiatives:

- Register MFT-processed files with enterprise data catalogs and governance platforms.

- Implement metadata tagging (classification, lineage, ownership) as part of the transfer process.

- Ensure MFT is integrated with data fabric architectures, serving as a governed ingress/egress layer that can enforce contracts, schema validation, and policy mapping across domains.

This positions MFT as a compliant and intelligent data delivery fabric, not an isolated utility.

15.2.8. Educate, Operationalize, and Iterate

Modernizing MFT isn't just a technology upgrade; it's a cultural and operational shift. Success depends on:

- Educating teams (DevOps, InfoSec, Data Governance) about the new capabilities, policies, and risks.

- Developing playbooks and runbooks for AI intervention, false positive handling, and escalation paths.

- Measuring success via KPIs: reduction in transfer delays, drop in policy violations, improved SLA adherence, and audit-readiness.

Treat modernization as an ongoing lifecycle, not a one-time project continually evolving as data volumes grow, compliance rules shift, and technologies advance.

Closing Words: The Future Flows Through Us

In a digital world that thrives on connectivity, velocity, and intelligence, data is not just a byproduct of business; it is the business. As this book has explored, the role of Managed File Transfer (MFT) has grown far beyond simply "moving files." It now sits at the critical junction of security, automation, governance, and AI, shaping how organizations exchange knowledge, operate across borders, and build trust in an era of increasing complexity.

We are standing at the convergence of transformative forces AI, edge computing, blockchain, data mesh, zero trust, and decentralized architectures and MFT must evolve to become a first-class participant in the enterprise intelligence ecosystem. Whether it's securing sensitive health records in real-time, orchestrating global supply chains, or enabling self-regulating data exchanges in smart cities, MFT is poised to become a core enabler of secure, policy-aware, and autonomous data flows.

But the journey doesn't end here. It is now up to technology leaders, architects, and innovators like you to take the next step: to rethink your data transfer strategy, to modernize your infrastructure with intelligence and automation, and to build MFT platforms that are as agile as your enterprise needs to be.

Let this book serve not just as a guide, but as a launchpad to ask the right questions, architect the right solutions, and lead your organization into the next generation of digital resilience. Because in the end, the future doesn't just flow through files; it flows through the visionaries who shape how those files move.

Thank you for being part of this journey. The future of MFT is in your hands.

www.ingramcontent.com/pod-product-compliance
Lightning Source LLC
LaVergne TN
LVHW060121070326
832902LV00019B/3077